The Official Guide to
Family Tree Maker 2010

The Official Guide to
Family Tree Maker® 2010

Tana L. Pedersen

ancestry publishing

Library of Congress Cataloging-in-Publication Data

Pedersen, Tana L., 1973-
  The official guide to Family tree maker 2010 / Tana L. Pedersen.
    p. cm.
  Includes bibliographical references and index.
  ISBN 978-1-59331-329-6 (alk. paper)
  1. Family tree maker. 2. Genealogy—Computer programs. 3. Genealogy—Data
processing. I. Title.
  CS14.P436 2009
  929'.10285—dc22

                                                              2009024765

Copyright © 2009
Ancestry.com Inc.
Published by
Ancestry Publishing, a division of Ancestry.com Inc.
360 West 4800 North
Provo, Utah 84604
All rights reserved.

10 9 8 7 6 5 4 3 2 1
ISBN-978-1-59331-329-6

Printed in the United States of America.

Contents

Contents

Contents

Contents

Contents

Contents

Acknowledgments

I would like to thank the many people who have been instrumental—both directly and indirectly—in the creation of this book.

First, to my son Braden. Thanks for being my biggest fan. To my parents, brothers and sister, and nieces and nephews who put up with endless stories about my latest genealogy discoveries, much appreciation for your love and support. I would also like to recognize Jenn Gardner Turner, Jette Olsen Standfield, and Karen Jones Olsen for their years of friendship and behind-the-scenes service.

A special thanks goes to the talented individuals at Ancestry Publishing whose guidance, suggestions, and kind words encourage me every day. Much appreciation to Matthew Rayback and Paul Rawlins for their critiques and edits and Rob Davis for the cover design.

In addition, I would like to thank Duff Wilson and Mark LeMonnier on the Family Tree Maker team for sharing their technical expertise.

Introduction

This guide is designed to help you learn Family Tree Maker 2010 quickly, leaving you more time to discover your family history. Even if you have never used a genealogy program before, you will find that the Family Tree Maker interface and options make it possible to keep track of even the most tangled of family trees.

This book is written with the novice computer user in mind. You will read about many of the useful features that the casual Family Tree Maker user never discovers, and you will be taken on a hands-on trip through the Family Tree Maker program. The many illustrations let you check your progress as you master each new feature or concept. Even if you are familiar with computers, though, you may have only recently been introduced to Family Tree Maker or simply want to know what great features you have not yet discovered in the program. This book offers you a step-by-step tour of the program and all that you can accomplish with it.

Before you begin entering your family's information, be sure to check out the "Getting Started" and "Exploring the Workspaces" chapters. These will give you the basic skills you need to navigate through Family Tree Maker and will make you familiar with the software's interface.

How the Guide Is Organized

As you read this book, you'll notice several features that provide you with useful information:

- **Tips** offer you timely hints about features and additional ways of performing tasks.

- **Notes** give you guidance on the best ways to complete tasks.

- **Sidebars** give you additional information on a variety of family history topics, such as maps and sources, that will enhance your ability to create a more professional family tree.

- A **glossary** explains terms you might not be familiar with, such as technical computer terms (icon, URL), Family Tree Maker terms (family group view, Fastfields), and genealogy terms (GEDCOM, Ahnentafel).

- **Appendixes** at the back of the book show you how to install the Family Tree Maker software, list keyboard shortcuts for some common tasks, and include information on source and chart templates.

If you still need help, a quick perusal of the Table of Contents should lead you right to the task you are trying to perform; if not, check the index in the back of the book.

Good luck, and have fun.

Chapter 1

Getting Started

Family Tree Maker makes it easy—and enjoyable—for almost anyone to discover their family history and gather it into one convenient location. And whether you're interested in printing family charts to share at a reunion, looking for a centralized location for storing your family photos and records, or setting out to collect every fact and story about your ancestors, Family Tree Maker is the program to help you do it all.

This chapter will give you the basic skills and knowledge you need to launch the application, navigate around the software, and create a family tree. Let's get started.

Starting Family Tree Maker

When you install Family Tree Maker, it creates two default shortcuts to the application that you can use to launch the program. You can use whichever method is easiest for you.

Double-click the **Family Tree Maker 2010** icon on your computer desktop or click **Start>All Programs>Family**

Tree Maker 2010>Family Tree Maker 2010. (For more information about installing Family Tree Maker, see appendix A, "Installing the Software.")

Closing Family Tree Maker

When you are finished working in your tree, you can close the program. Remember, there's no need to save your tree—Family Tree Maker automatically saves your changes as you make them. Click **File**>**Exit** or click the **Close** button (X) in the upper-right corner of the window.

Introduction to the Face of Family Tree Maker

To use any computer program effectively, the first step is to understand its unique interface and tools. Users who are familiar with Windows will immediately recognize many of the features available in Family Tree Maker. However, there are some toolbars, menus, and windows you'll want to learn how to use and navigate. Once you understand the software's basic structure, you can confidently begin building your tree.

Menus and Keyboard Shortcuts

Family Tree Maker menus work like any other Windows program. Simply click a menu name to display its options; then, click the option you want to use.

In this guide, menu options are shown in bold and each level is designated by a greater than sign (>). For example, if a step says "Click **Tools**>**Date Calculator**," you would click **Tools** on the menu bar, then click the **Date Calculator** menu option.

Some menu options have keyboard shortcuts. You can use these to access features and menu options without using the mouse. To learn how to use them and to see a list of commonly used shortcuts, see appendix B, "Keyboard Shortcuts."

Toolbars

The main toolbar in Family Tree Maker, located at the very top of the window, is designed to provide quick navigation to various workspaces—groupings of the most important features in the software (see figure 1-1).

*Click the **Plan** button to manage your trees.*

*Click the **Places** button to view maps of locations you've entered in your tree.*

*Click the **Sources** button to manage your sources and citations.*

*Click the **Web Search** button to search family history websites.*

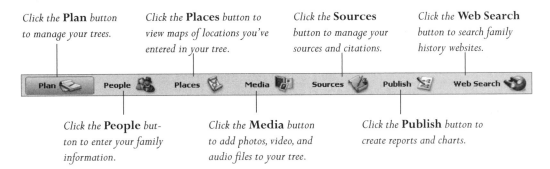

*Click the **People** button to enter your family information.*

*Click the **Media** button to add photos, video, and audio files to your tree.*

*Click the **Publish** button to create reports and charts.*

Figure 1-1. The main toolbar in Family Tree Maker

Family Tree Maker has other specialized toolbars that will be covered in later chapters.

Workspaces

The major features of Family Tree Maker are grouped into "workspaces." These workspaces are available by clicking the buttons on the main toolbar. For example, if you click the Media button on the main toolbar, the Media workspace opens, and you can view all the photographs, record images, and video and audio files you have in a tree.

Each workspace has a slightly different appearance and purpose, but generally, they all contain the same features, such as toolbars and tabs (see figure 1-2).

> Note: Each workspace will be covered in-depth in the following chapter, "Exploring the Workspaces."

The main toolbar gives you one-click access to every workspace.

Tabs let you go from a comprehensive view to a detailed view.

Some work areas can be resized. Place the cursor here and drag the panel to the size you like.

Menu bar

The back and forward buttons let you navigate to recently viewed workspaces.

Side panels can be "hidden" by clicking this arrow.

Figure 1-2. A Family Tree Maker workspace

Getting Help

Family Tree Maker has a convenient, built-in Help program. At any time, you can access Help for the current window you are viewing or search for specific topics in the Help program. In addition to the program help, you can access troubleshooting tips, read FAQs (Frequently Asked Questions), watch tutorials, and more at the official website for Family Tree Maker <www.familytreemaker.com>.

Using the Help Program in Family Tree Maker

1. Click **Help>Help for Family Tree Maker**. The Help Welcome window opens.

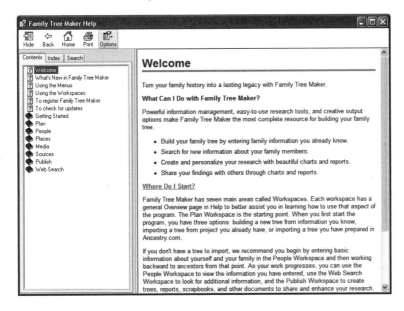

Use these three tabs on the window to view Help:

- **Contents tab**—displays a list of Help topics arranged like the table of contents of a book. You can double-click a book icon to see its contents. For books with subchapters, double-click on the subsequent icon (chapters) until you funnel down to individual Help topics.

- **Index tab**—works like the index in a book. Find the term you're interested in and double-click it to see the corresponding Help topic.

- **Search tab**—lets you search for keywords or phrases that may be contained in a Help topic, such as "source" or "printing."

> **Tip**
> To get help for the window you're currently accessing, press the **F1** key at the top of your keyboard.

Now that you've learned a few of the basic Family Tree Maker features, you're ready to create your first tree. Make sure you have some family information to enter or have a file, such as a GEDCOM or Ancestry.com tree, ready to use.

Creating Your First Tree

If this is your first time using Family Tree Maker on your computer, the program will open to the New Tree tab on the Plan workspace. Notice that the other buttons on the main toolbar are grayed out; these features will not be activated until you create your first tree.

Note: For detailed instructions on creating a tree, see chapter 11, "Working with Trees."

1. Open Family Tree Maker. If you need help, see "Starting Family Tree Maker" on page 1. You'll see the New Tree tab where you'll create your first tree.

2. Do one of these options:

- If you don't already have a genealogy file you want to use, you can create one by entering a few basic facts about your family; click **Enter what you know**. Enter your name and birth date and birthplace in the appropriate fields.

- If you have a genealogy file you'd like to use to start your tree, you can import it into Family Tree Maker; click **Import a tree from an existing file**. Click **Browse** to locate the file and then click **Open**.

- If you have a tree on Ancestry.com you'd like to use to start your tree, click **Download a tree from Ancestry**. Click **Download** next to the tree you want to download.

Then click **Import** to save the file as a new tree, or click **Merge** to merge the file with an existing tree.

If you choose to import the tree, you will be prompted to enter a name for the tree and save it; if you choose to merge the file with an existing tree, the Merge Wizard will open and guide you through merging the trees. A message tells you when the process is complete.

Naming a Tree

A typical name for the Reed family tree might be "Reed Family." Or, you can combine names and dates. If you are a Smith and your spouse is a Reed, you might call the tree "SmithReed." You are free to choose any name, but you may find it easier to keep it short and descriptive.

Choosing a Primary or "Home" Person

Each tree you create will have a primary person or "home" person. By default, the home person is the first person you entered in your tree. If you're creating a tree based on your family, the home person will most likely be you. However, the home person can be anyone in your tree. Having a home person makes it easy to navigate within your tree. Get lost in a maze of ancestors? Simply click the Go to Home Person button on the Index panel, and you'll know right where you are again.

Occasionally, you may want to switch the home person of your tree. For example, if you're working on a specific family line, you may want to make someone in that ancestral line the home person.

There are several ways to assign a new home person. Here are the two techniques you'll most likely use.

To change the home person on the Plan workspace

1. Click the **Plan** button on the main toolbar and then click the **Current Tree** tab. At the top of the window, you'll see the name of the home person.

2. Move the mouse over the words "Home Person" until a button appears.

ReedPedersen_2009 Tree			
Home Person...	Tana Lee Pedersen (1973 -)	People:	247
Current person:	Tana Lee Pedersen (1973 -)	Marriages:	39
Creation date:	5/11/2009 9:36 AM	File size:	1,914 KB
Last saved:	5/14/2009 10:07 AM		
Last backup:	6/25/2008 1:26 PM	More...	

3. Click **Home Person**. The Index of Individuals window opens.

```
Index of Individuals                                         [_][□][X]

Find: |                                    ◄ ►  🏠 📖 ▾

  Name                         Birth Date    Marr. Date    Death Date  ▲
  Bobbitt, John W.             09 Jun 1832   18 Oct 1852   13 Aug 1909 ▓
  Bobbitt, Lorine              04 Jun 1906                        1907 ▓
  Bobbitt, Mary Eliza          10 Apr 1886
  Bobbitt, Maurine             04 Jun 1906   18 Aug 1923   29 Mar 1992
  Bobbitt, Sarah Eleanor       Abt. 1863
  Bobbitt, Seymour             Abt. 1854
  Bobbitt, Twila Margaret      18 Jul 1899                 27 May 1991
  Bobbitt, Willis R.           Abt. 1861
  Bush, Rachel                 Oct 1833      Abt. 1866     15 Mar 1911
  Cothran, Claude M.
  Crossman, William B.
  Cullins, Clonnie
  Gedge, Anna                  05 Sep 1866                 09 Jun 1945
  Gedge, Emma                  30 Aug 1864                 11 Dec 1906
  Gedge, Flossie               Abt. 1904
  Gedge, Herbert Bush          10 Nov 1872   20 Nov 1895   08 Sep 1942
  Gedge, Leilan                12 Mar 1907                 02 Oct 2002  ▼

  People: 262                         OK      Cancel      Help

                        Spouse: Harold Arthur Reed
```

4. Click the name of the individual you want to be the home person and click **OK**. This individual becomes the new home person and remains the home person until you manually select a new one.

To change the home person on the People workspace

1. Click the **People** button on the main toolbar and then click the **Family** tab.

2. Find the person you want to be the home person in the pedigree view or Index panel.

> **Tip**
>
> To go to the home person, click the **Go to home person** button on the Index panel at any time.

3. Right-click the individual's name and click **Set As Home Person**.

This individual becomes the new home person and remains the home person until you manually select a new one.

Moving an Individual to the Primary or Root Position of a Tree

If you don't want to change the home person of your tree, you can still make an individual the focus of your tree by placing them in the "root position" temporarily. The individual in the root position is the central person that charts, reports, and workspaces are based on.

There are several ways to move an individual to the root position of a tree. Here are the three techniques you'll most likely use.

To change the root person using the pedigree view

1. Click the **People** button on the main toolbar; then click the **Family** tab.

2. Find the person you want to be the root person in the pedigree view.

3. Right-click the individual's name in the tree and click **Move to Root Position**.

   The individual becomes the person in the root position on the pedigree view.

To change the root person using the mini pedigree tree

1. Do one of these options:

   • On the mini pedigree tree, click once on the individual's name.

   • Click the mini pedigree tree's **Index of Individuals** button. Find the person you want and click **OK**.

Index of Individuals button

To change the root person using the Index panel

1. Click the **People** button on the main toolbar; then click the **Family** tab.

2. In the Index panel, click once on the name of the individual you want to be the root person. The individual becomes the person in the root position on the pedigree view.

Chapter 2

Exploring
the Workspaces

Family Tree Maker is organized so that you can quickly locate
and use all its important features, which are grouped together
in workspaces. In the "Getting Started" chapter you read a
brief introduction to the workspaces. This chapter will more
fully explore each of the seven workspaces you'll be using
as you create your family history trees—their appearance,
purpose, and unique features. To access a workspace, click its
corresponding button on the main toolbar. For example, click
the Publish button to go to the Publish workspace.

If you take a few minutes now to learn how each workspace
functions, you will soon discover how much easier it is to quickly
and efficiently enter your important information into a tree.

> Note: This chapter gives an overview of each
> workspace. Subsequent chapters will give in-
> depth instructions on how to use the features
> and options found on each workspace.

The Plan Workspace

The Plan workspace is the "control center" where you manage all of your family trees. It can be used as the starting point for new trees, or you can view statistics about the tree you're currently working on. The Plan workspace is divided into two tabs: the New Tree tab and the Current Tree tab.

The New Tree Tab

The New Tree tab (see figure 2-1) has three main sections: the Getting Started section, where you create new trees; Trees, which lists recently opened trees; and the Web Dashboard, which gives you access to your Ancestry.com account information and trees.

Choose one of these options to create a new tree.

The fields in this area change depending on how you are creating the tree.

A list of recently opened trees

The Web Dashboard

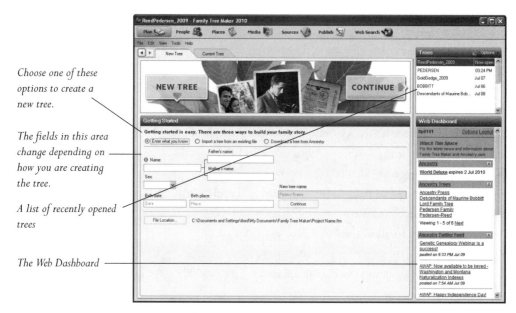

Figure 2-1. The New Tree tab

16

The Current Tree Tab

The Current Tree tab (see figure 2-2) has four main sections—two of which are the same as the New Tree tab: the Web Dashboard and Trees. The main display area of the workspace shows you the selected tree's statistics and a Research To-Do list. (You'll learn more about managing your trees in the "Working with Trees" chapter.)

Statistics about the tree you have open

A list of recently opened trees

The Web Dashboard

Research tasks for the tree you have open

Figure 2-2. The Current Tree tab

The Web Dashboard

The Web Dashboard gives you quick access to your Ancestry.com subscription; you can log in to your account, view your subscription expiration date, and display the Ancestry trees you've created.

To choose what information appears in the Dashboard, click the **Options** link.

> Note: The Web Dashboard is active only when your computer is connected to the Internet.

The People Workspace

The People workspace provides a comprehensive view of your tree file. You can see several generations of your family at once and easily navigate to each member of your family tree. In addition, the People workspace is where you will enter information about families and individuals into your tree.

The People workspace (see figure 2-3) is divided into two tabs: the Family tab and the Person tab.

Figure 2-3. The People workspace with the Family tab displayed

The Family Tab

The Family tab (see figure 2-3) is the easiest and most logical place for you to enter basic information about family members, and it contains four main sections. Because you will spend most of your time in Family Tree Maker using this tab, each section will be explained in detail.

The Pedigree View

The pedigree view (see figure 2-4) provides a comprehensive view of your family tree, allowing you to view two to five generations of your family at once and helping you navigate to members of your family tree. The primary or root person appears on the left side of the tree, and his or her ancestors branch out to the right.

*Click the **Enhanced nodes** checkbox to display portraits and life spans for individuals in the pedigree view; leave the checkbox blank to display only names in the view.*

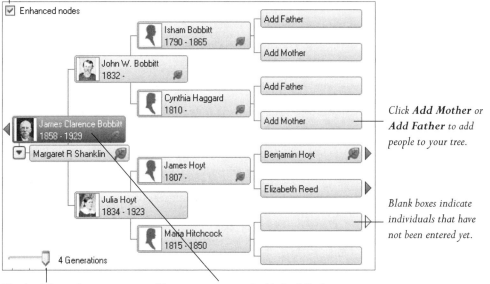

*Click **Add Mother** or **Add Father** to add people to your tree.*

Blank boxes indicate individuals that have not been entered yet.

Use the slider to change the number of generations displayed.

The primary person is highlighted. To change this person, see "Moving an Individual to the Primary or Root Position of a Tree" on page 11.

Figure 2-4. Pedigree view

To move to other generations in the pedigree view, use these navigational tools:

 Solid right-facing arrow. This arrow indicates that the family line has ancestors who are not being displayed in the current tree. You can resize the tree or click this arrow to view these additional generations.

 White right-facing arrows. This arrow indicates that no ancestors have been entered for the individual.

 Solid left-facing arrow. This arrow appears left of the current root individual and indicates that he or she has descendants. If he or she is a direct ancestor of the home person, clicking the arrow will display the next individual in the home person's direct line. Otherwise, it displays the first child listed in the family group view.

 Left arrow. When you move your mouse over an individual's name, Family Tree Maker displays this arrow and the person's birth and death information. Click this arrow to move the individual to the root position of the pedigree view.

 Down arrow. This arrow indicates that an individual has descendants, or children. Click this arrow to see a list of his or her children and then click on a name to place that child in the root position of the pedigree view.

Note: If the individual has more than one spouse in the tree, the drop-down list of descendants will display only the children of the individual's preferred marriage.

The Family Group View

The family group view, located under the pedigree view, focuses on a single-family unit—a couple and their children (see figure 2-5). In this view you can fill in basic information for the two primary individuals (for example, you can add children and additional spouses).

Click a "parent" button to display that family unit in the family group view.

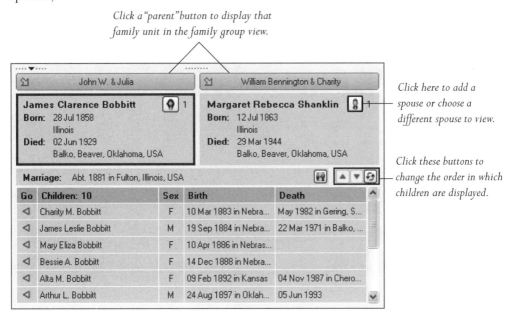

Click here to add a spouse or choose a different spouse to view.

Click these buttons to change the order in which children are displayed.

Figure 2-5. Family group view

The Editing Panel

The editing panel on the Family tab (see figure 2-6) is where you enter basic information about an individual, such as birth and death dates and places. You can customize this panel to display the facts you enter most often for your family. For example, if you have christening information for many individuals, you can display the Christening fact on the editing panel. To learn how to change the panel, see "Customizing the Family Tab Editing Panel" on page 406.

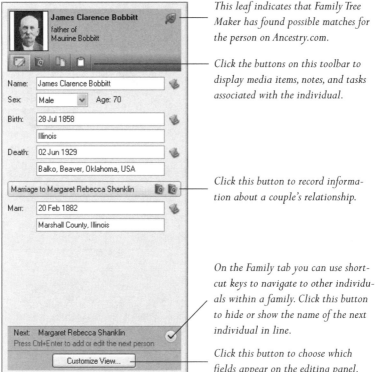

This leaf indicates that Family Tree Maker has found possible matches for the person on Ancestry.com.

Click the buttons on this toolbar to display media items, notes, and tasks associated with the individual.

Click this button to record information about a couple's relationship.

On the Family tab you can use shortcut keys to navigate to other individuals within a family. Click this button to hide or show the name of the next individual in line.

Click this button to choose which fields appear on the editing panel.

Figure 2-6. Editing panel

To use navigation keyboard shortcuts for data entry

When you're adding or editing information on the Family tab in the People workspace, you can move between individuals in the currently selected family group (father, mother, children) using keyboard shortcuts, which simplifies data entry.

1. Go to the **Family** tab on the People workspace. At the bottom of the editing panel, you'll see the name of the next individual who can be accessed using the keyboard shortcut.

2. Press **CTRL+Enter** to move to the next person in line (from father to mother to children). (You can also press **CTRL+SHIFT+Enter** to move from children to mother to father.)

    Note: When you reach the last family member in a group, you'll be prompted to add another child or spouse to the family, depending on who the last individual was.

The Index Panel

The Index panel (see figure 2-7) lists the individuals in your tree, giving you quick shortcuts to any person you want to work on.

The Show additional data button lets you display names and dates in the index.

*Click the **Go to home person** button to move the home person to the root position of the pedigree view.*

Choose a sort option from the drop-down list.

Index: 247

Sort: Family, Given Name

Find:

(Hoyt), John Hait
(Shanklin), Permelia A.
Bell, Abigail
Bennington, Sarah
Bennington, Sarah
Bobbitt, Alta M.
Bobbitt, Arthur L.
Bobbitt, Bessie A.
Bobbitt, Charity M.
Bobbitt, Cornelia
Bobbitt, Eugene A.
Bobbitt, Fern Edna
Bobbitt, Francis M.
Bobbitt, Isham
Bobbitt, James Clarence
Bobbitt, James Leslie
Bobbitt, Jessie
Bobbitt, John W.
Bobbitt, Lorine
Bobbitt, Mary Eliza
Bobbitt, Maurine
Bobbitt, Sarah Eleanor
Bobbitt, Seymour
Bobbitt, Twila Margaret
Bobbitt, Willis R.
Bush, Rachel
Cothran, Claude M.
Crossman, William B.
Cullins, Clonnie
Gedge, Anna

The house icon indicates that this individual is the home person.

Filter...   Apply filter

Index

Bookmarks

History

Click this button to choose which individuals appear in the index.

Click this button to display individuals you have added bookmarks for.

Click this button to display the last 200 individuals you have edited.

Figure 2-7. Index panel

By default, the People workspace displays the index of individuals, which contains every person in your tree. You can display birth, marriage, and death dates for each individual using the **Show additional data** button.

In addition to viewing all the people in your tree, you can click the **Bookmarks** button to see a list of individuals you have specifically bookmarked, or you can click the **History** button to see the individuals you have most recently edited in your tree.

Use the scroll bar to move up and down the list to find an individual, or type a name in the Find field to jump to a particular person. You can also filter the list to show a subset of individuals, which can be useful if your tree is very large and you want to focus on a particular line (see the next task, "Using the Filter Individuals Window").

Using the Filter Individuals Window

The Index panel shows the names of every person in your tree. You can filter this list to show a subset of individuals. For example, if you are working on a certain family line, or entering information for only the females in your tree, you can limit which individuals are shown in the Index.

This task shows you how to choose which individuals appear in the Index panel. When completing other tasks in Family Tree Maker, such as merging two trees or selecting individuals for a report, you will follow this same series of steps to select a group of individuals in the Filter Individuals window.

1. Go to the **Family** tab on the People workspace.

2. Make sure all individuals in your tree are displayed by clicking the **Index** button at the bottom of the Index panel.

3. Click **Filter** at the bottom of the Index panel. The Filter Individuals window opens. The left side of the window lists all the individuals in your tree.

4. Use this chart to choose a specific group of people from your tree:

To do this	Do this
Choose individuals one at a time	Click the name of an individual in your tree and click **Include**.
	Note: You can click **Include All** to include everyone in your tree.
Choose a group of individuals	Click **Ancestors** to include all of the selected person's ancestors.
	Click **Descendants** to include all of the selected person's descendants.

5. Click **Filter In** or **Filter Out** to further specify which individuals are included in your list (e.g., all individuals born in a certain location). The Filter Individuals by Criteria window opens.

6. Do one of these options:

   - Click **Vital facts** to filter by name, gender, birth, marriage, or death.

   - Click **All facts** to filter by any fact in your tree, including custom facts you've created.

   - Click **Other** to filter by media, source, fact, or relationship information.

   The remaining fields will change depending on which type of facts you chose to filter by.

7. Complete these fields as necessary:

In this field	Do this
Search where	Choose the fact you want to use from the drop-down list (for example, choose "Emigration"). Then choose a requirement for the value from the drop-down list. You can choose from "Equals," "Does not equal," "Is before," "Is after," "Is blank," or "Is not blank." Note: If you have chosen "All facts," you can also choose whether to search in the Date, Place, or Description fields.
Value	Enter a date, name, or keyword that you want the selected fact to match. Note: Click **Match all values** if the date, name, or keyword has to match the fact exactly; click **Match any value** if the date, name, or keyword can match any of the words in the fact.
Secondary facts	When searching "All facts," click this checkbox if you want the search to include alternate facts.

8. Click **OK**.

9. When all the individuals you want appear in the "Individuals included in filter" list, click **OK**.

> **Tip**
> You can turn off the current filter in the Index panel by deselecting the **Apply filter** checkbox.

The Person Tab

The Person tab (see figure 2-8) lets you add additional facts, notes, sources, and media items for an individual; view relationships between family members; and view timelines. It is divided into three main sections: tabs that let you store notes, media items, and research tasks; the editing panel (which changes based on which fact is selected); and the main display area, where you view timelines, relationship charts, and additional facts about an individual.

*Click **Facts** to enter additional details about an individual's life.*

*Click **Timeline** to see a historical timeline for an individual.*

*Click **Relationships** to view the individual's immediate family and their relationships.*

Click these tabs to access tasks, media items, and notes associated with a specific individual.

Use the editing details panel to edit a fact.

Figure 2-8. The Person tab

The Places Workspace

The Places workspace (see figure 2-9) displays all the locations you've entered in your tree—and gives you the opportunity to view online maps of them, too. The Places workspace is divided into three main sections: the Places panel that shows every location you have entered in your tree; the display area that shows a map of the selected location; and the details panel that shows the individuals who are associated with the location.

Locations you have entered in your tree

The map display area—a red pushpin marks the selected location. Each time you choose a new location, the map will automatically recenter.

A question mark icon indicates that the location has not yet been recognized by Family Tree Maker. For information on resolving these errors, see page 166.

Individuals who have facts associated with the selected location

Figure 2-9. The Places workspace

The Media Workspace

The Media workspace acts as a storage space where you keep your multimedia items. The Media workspace is divided into two tabs: the Collection tab and the Detail tab.

The Media Collection Tab

The Media Collection tab (see figure 2-10) has three main sections: the Groups panel that lists the media items in the tree; the display area that shows thumbnails or smaller versions of the original images; and the editing panel, where you enter information about each media item.

Click here to view details about an item.

Click here to view an item's notes.

Click here to view an item's links.

Use the slider to make the thumbnail images larger or smaller.

Groups panel   *Display area*   *Editing panel*

Figure 2-10. The Media Collection tab

The Media Detail Tab

The Media Detail tab (see figure 2-11) has three main sections: the display area that shows an image of the media item; tabs that store notes for an item and let you link the item to individuals and sources; and the Media Detail editing panel, where you enter information about each item.

A mini navigation bar lets you quickly browse thumbnails of all your media items.

Use these buttons to change the display of an image in the workspace.

Links and Notes tabs   *Display area*   *Media Detail editing panel*

Figure 2-11. The Media Detail tab

The Sources Workspace

The Sources workspace (see figure 2-12) organizes all your sources and source citations. It has four main sections: the Source Groups panel that lets you sort your sources by people, titles, and repositories; the sources display area that shows the citations of the selected group; the tabs that show the individuals linked to a source and let you store related notes and media items; and the editing panel, where you can enter or update specific source citations.

Use the Source Citation Information panel to edit a source citation.

Source Groups panel   *Source citations that you have created.*   *Click these tabs to view media items, notes, and individuals associated with this source citation.*

Figure 2-12. The Sources workspace

The Publish Workspace

The Publish workspace offers a variety of tree charts and reports that you can view, print, and share. The Publish workspace is divided into two tabs: the Collection tab and the Detail tab.

The Publish Collection Tab

The Publish Collection tab (see figure 2-13) has three main sections: the Publication Types panel that shows the types of charts and reports that are available; the display area, which shows thumbnails of a selected group of charts or reports; and an explanation of each report.

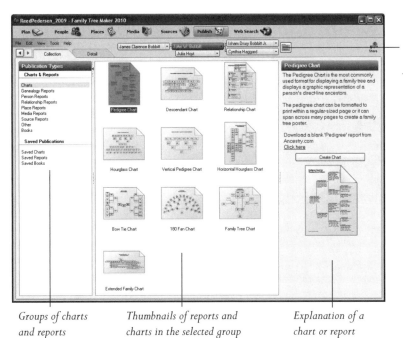

A mini pedigree tree lets you quickly navigate to others in your tree.

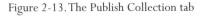

Groups of charts and reports   *Thumbnails of reports and charts in the selected group*   *Explanation of a chart or report*

Figure 2-13. The Publish Collection tab

The Publish Detail Tab

The Publish Detail tab (see figure 2-14) has two main sections: the display area, where you can preview a chart and any changes you've made to it; and the editing panel that lets you customize the chart by determining its content and format.

A mini pedigree tree lets you quickly navigate to others in your tree

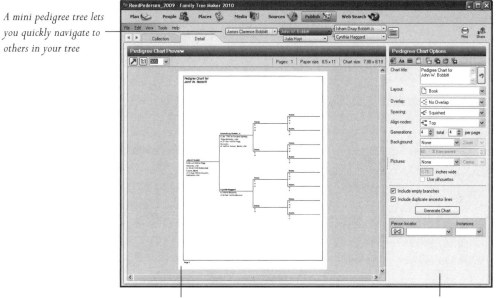

The chart or report preview area

The editing panel lets you customize the information that appears in a chart or report.

Figure 2-14. The Publish Detail tab

The Web Search Workspace

The Web Search workspace (see figure 2-15) lets you search online for your ancestors without leaving Family Tree Maker. And if you find results that match an individual in your tree, you can quickly merge the information into your file. The Web Search workspace is divided into three main sections: the Search Locations panel, which shows a "favorites" list of websites you like to visit; the browser, where you view websites; and tabs that let you add media items and notes and view events in your tree side-by-side with the information you've discovered.

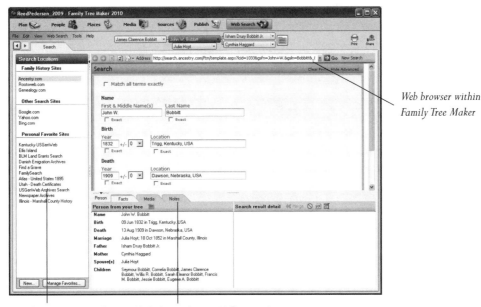

Web browser within Family Tree Maker

Search Locations panel   *Click these tabs to add facts, media items, and notes you've discovered online.*

Figure 2-15. The Web Search workspace

Changing the Layout of a Workspace

Each workspace has a default layout that shows all the features and options that are available in this area. Depending on what you're trying to do, you may want to display one area of a workspace more than the others. The flexible design of Family Tree Maker makes it easy to change the layout so it works for you. In this example, you'll learn how to rearrange the People workspace, but the process is the same for all workspaces.

1. Click the **People** button on the main toolbar to access the People workspace. Notice the four different sections of the workspace: the Index panel, the pedigree view, the family group view, and the editing panel.

    You can resize or hide each panel to make room for whatever task you're working on.

These arrows let you hide or show entire sections of the workspace.

These cursors let you resize the section to the size you want.

2. Click the small arrow to the right of the Index panel to hide the panel. The pedigree view and the family group view now stretch across the window.

3. Click the arrow again to display the panel.

4. Click the arrow above the family group view to hide the view. The pedigree view stretches to the bottom of the window.

5. Click the arrow beneath the pedigree view to display the family group view.

6. To resize the editing panel, move the mouse between the editing panel and the other views until you see the resize cursor (two arrows with a line between).

7. Drag the panel until it's the size you want.

8. To return the editing panel to its default size and location, place your cursor between the editing panel and the other views and double-click the mouse.

Chapter 3

Building Your Tree

Much of your time using Family Tree Maker will be spent entering the names, dates, and events that you have uncovered about your family. As you begin building your tree, the best strategy is to start with what you know—basic details about yourself, your spouse, your children, and your parents. As you continue, your focus will then turn to your ancestral lines, such as your grandparents and great-grandparents. Family Tree Maker makes it easy to create a tree and quickly add generations of family members.

When you've finished entering the basic birth, marriage, and death information for your family, you can expand your tree by adding additional details about their marriages, immigration stories, medical histories, and more. You can also add notes, sources, and images relating to these facts.

In This Chapter

- Entering Information About an Individual
- Adding More Details
- Adding Spouses
- Adding Children
- Adding Parents
- Adding an Unrelated Individual
- Changing Relationships
- Editing an Individual's Information
- Viewing Timelines
- Merging Individuals
- Deleting Individuals from a Tree

Entering Information About an Individual

For each individual in your tree, you'll begin by entering basic details about him or her, including birth and death dates. Then, as you discover new and noteworthy facts and stories, you can add this information to your tree.

Entering Basic Information

After you have entered an individual's name into your tree, you can add basic information about the person, including birth and death dates and places.

1. Go to the **Family** tab on the People workspace.

Entering Names in Family Tree Maker

Generally, when recording the name of a family member that you find in a source, you will enter the name exactly as it appears in the record or source you are viewing. However, when you are entering names in Family Tree Maker, there are some formatting practices that will keep your files organized and your names consistent:

- **Capitalize surnames.** You may choose to follow a common practice in genealogy—writing the entire last name for each individual in capital letters. This makes it easier to distinguish first and middle names from last names. For example, James Bobbitt would be written James BOBBITT. (If you choose to capitalize last names, you might want to make sure that the spell checker does not search for capitalized words. For more information, see "Spell Checking Preferences" on page 415.)

- **Use maiden names.** When entering names for females, be sure to enter the woman's maiden name (her last name before she was married), even if the record you have shows her married name. This practice helps you avoid confusing an individual with another person in your tree and makes it easier to trace her side of the family.

- **Use backslashes to indicate surnames that are more than one word or no surname.** You might encounter instances where the surname (last name) is not just a single word. This is especially true with European names. You will need to identify the surname in Family Tree Maker with backslashes (\). Otherwise, Family Tree Maker will read only the last word as the surname. Here are some examples:

  George \de la Vergne\   Peter \Van Der Voort\
  Pierre \Bourbeau dit Lacourse\   Teresa \Garcia Ramirez\

  You also need to use backslashes when entering a name for someone who does not have a last name, such as a person of Native American descent. For instance, your ancestor might have been known as Running Bear. You would enter the name as Running Bear\\. Without the backslashes, Family Tree Maker would read "Bear" as the individual's last name.

2. Click on an individual's name in the pedigree view. The individual's name and gender will be displayed in the editing panel. You'll enter a few basic facts here.

Note: You can choose which fields appear in the editing panel. For instructions, see "Customizing the Family Tab Editing Panel" on page 406.

Fastfields

Fastfields is a special feature that allows you to save time by not having to enter the same information over and over again. Location Fastfields remember the names of any location you've entered into a tree. This means that when you move the cursor into a location field and start typing the name of a town that you've previously entered into Family Tree Maker, Fastfields automatically tries to fill it in for you. Fastfields also works for name and source fields. For more information, see "Fastfields Preferences" on page 411.

3. Enter a birth date in the appropriate field.

   Note: The date will change to the standard format used by most genealogists: date, month, year. If you want, you can change the display order of dates. For instructions, see "Date Preferences" on page 416.

4. To enter information in the next field, click in the field or press the **Tab** key; then, enter the individual's birth location in the **Birth Place** field.

   Note: You may notice that some locations are automatically completed as you begin to type in a field. This is the Family Tree Maker feature called "Fastfields" at work. To use the suggested location, click it in the drop-down list. To ignore the suggestion, simply continue typing.

5. Enter a death date and location in the appropriate fields.

   Now that you've entered a few basic facts about an individual, you can add more details.

6. Do one of these options:

   - To add more facts about the individual, see "Adding a Fact" on page 47.

   - To add the individual's spouse to your tree, see "Adding a Spouse" on page 60.

   - To add the individual's children to your tree, see "Adding a Child to a Family" on page 66.

   - To add the individual's parents to your tree, see "Adding Parents" on page 70.

Entering Locations in Family Tree Maker

Recording locations consistently and completely is an important part of organizing your family history. Generally, when entering a place, you will record the location from the smallest to largest division. For example, in the United States, you would enter city or town, county, state, country (Haddam, Washington, Kansas, United States). For foreign locations, you would enter city or town, parish or district, province, country (Birmingham, West Midlands, England). You may choose to not enter a country for a location if it is the country in which you live and where most of your ancestors lived. If you do leave off country information, include this fact somewhere in your project.

You can abbreviate place names if you want. However, make sure you use the standard abbreviations that will be recognized by others who might want to look at your research. Also, be consistent; don't spell out some place names and abbreviate others.

Adding More Details

You can add details and facts about an individual that do not fit elsewhere in your tree (e.g., religion, education, hobbies).

Adding a Fact

In addition to events such as birth and death, you can add many facts you've learned about an individual. Some examples include christenings, burials, employment, and occupations.

1. Go to the **Person** tab on the People workspace.

2. Make sure the individual you want to enter a fact for is displayed.

3. Click the **Facts** button. The Individual and Shared Facts section opens.

Tip

The Add fact button drop-down list lets you quickly add the birth, marriage, and death facts. If you have customized the editing panel on the Family tab to display additional facts, these will also appear in the drop-down list.

4. To add a fact, click the **Add fact** (+) button in the Individual and Shared Facts toolbar. The Add Fact window opens.

Facts	Type
Graduation	Individual
Height	Individual
Immigration	Individual
Marriage	Shared
Marriage Bann	Shared
Marriage Contract	Shared
Marriage License	Shared
Marriage Settlement	Shared
Medical Condition	Individual
Military Serial Number	Individual
Military Service	Individual
Mission (LDS)	Individual
Name	Individual
Namesake	Individual
Nationality	Individual
Naturalization	Individual
Occupation	Individual

OK Cancel Help New...

Note: If the type of fact you want to add is not included in the software, you can create your own. For instructions, see "Creating a Custom Fact" on page 400.

5. Choose a fact from the list and click **OK**. The new fact will appear in the Individual and Shared Facts section.

6. In the editing panel, complete the **Date**, **Place**, and **Description** fields as necessary.

Tip

You can use the Date Calculator to help you determine the date or age of an individual at a certain event. For more information, see "Date Calculator" on page 384.

Military Service: ✔ Options ▼
1917
France
Worked as a motorcycle courier

Note: You can add a source citation to this fact. Highlight the fact. On the Sources tab in the editing panel, click the Add Source Citation button. See chapter 4 for more information about adding source citations.

Commonly Used Facts

After you've entered the basic facts for an individual, you'll probably want to enter more details. Here's a chart of some commonly used facts that you might enter for an individual:

Fact Name	Purpose
Address	Addresses can be useful for recording the contact information of living relatives or for recording the area where an ancestor was known to have lived.
Also Known As	If an individual was known by a nickname rather than his or her given name, you'll want to record this additional name in order to distinguish the individual from others in your tree.
Cause of Death	Knowing your family's health history may help you prevent and treat illnesses that run in family lines. You can record an individual's cause of death or use the Cause of Death Notes tab to enter any details you feel are important about the individual's medical history, from long-term illness to simple things such as "suffers from allergies." Note: You can also enter information in height, weight, and medical condition facts.
Christening	Birth records are not always available for individuals in your tree; therefore, christening records become useful because they may be the earliest available information you can find for an ancestor.
Emigration/ Immigration	Emigration and immigration records are the first step in finding your ancestors in their homeland. Use these fields to record dates, ports of departure and arrival, and even ship names.
Physical Description	Although not necessarily beneficial to your research, a physical description of an ancestor can be a fascinating addition to any family history.
Title	If an individual has a title, such as Captain, as part of his or her name, you'll want to record this information in order to distinguish the individual from others in your tree.

Entering Name Suffixes in Family Tree Maker

Do not enter name suffixes such as "Jr." or "III" in the Title fact. Titles entered in that fact will be printed in front of the individual's name on reports (e.g., III George Hunt instead of George Hunt III, or Jr. George Hunt instead of George Hunt Jr.). If your ancestor was a Jr. or a Sr., enter the suffix in the Name fact at the end of the name without a comma (e.g., George Hunt Jr.). Family Tree Maker automatically recognizes name suffixes, so no comma is necessary.

Adding Alternate Facts

You may have conflicting information about the same life event (e.g., two different birth dates). Multiple facts for the same event are referred to as "alternate facts" in Family Tree Maker. You should record facts *and* alternate facts in your tree. This is especially valuable if you are unsure which fact is correct. Creating an alternate fact is the same process as adding another fact, and both facts will appear side-by-side in the Individual and Shared Facts section. When you have two facts for an item, one fact will be "preferred," meaning it will be included in charts and reports, and one fact will not.

In this example, the death fact has one preferred fact and one alternate fact.

Preferred fact

Alternate fact

Choosing a Preferred Fact

If you enter multiple facts for the same event, you will have to choose a preferred fact. Typically, this is the fact that you believe to be most accurate or complete. Once you mark a fact as preferred, it will be the default fact displayed in the various views, charts, and reports.

1. Go to the **Person** tab on the People workspace.

2. Make sure the individual with the alternative facts is displayed.

3. Click the **Facts** button. The Individual and Shared Facts section opens.

4. Click the alternate fact that you want to make the preferred fact.

5. In the editing panel, click the **Options** button and choose **Preferred** from the drop-down list.

> **Tip**
>
> You can mark a fact as preferred by right-clicking the fact and choosing **Set As Preferred** from the drop-down list.

The Preferred column in the Individual and Shared Facts section now shows the fact as preferred.

Making a Fact Private

You may have entered facts about an individual that you do not want to share with other family members or researchers. If you make a fact "private," you can choose whether or not you want to include the information in reports or when you export your tree.

Tip
You can mark a fact as private by right-clicking the fact and choosing **Mark Private** from the drop-down list.

1. Go to the **Person** tab on the People workspace.

2. Make sure the individual with the fact you want to mark as private is displayed.

3. Click the **Facts** button and then click the fact that you want to make private.

4. In the editing panel, click the **Options** button and choose **Mark as Private** from the drop-down list.

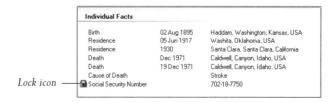

The lock icon appears next to the fact in the Individual and Shared Facts section.

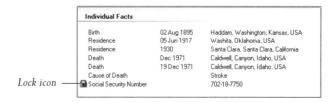

Lock icon

Adding Notes

You may have family stories, legends, or research resources that you want to refer to occasionally. Family Tree Maker lets you enter this detailed information in "notes"—up to 1 MB of space, or about 200 printed pages, per note.

Entering a Personal Note

Personal notes might be as simple as a physical description of an individual or as lengthy as a transcript of an interview with your grandmother.

1. Go to the **Person** tab on the People workspace.

2. Make sure the individual you want to enter a note for is displayed.

3. Click the **Notes** tab.

4. Click the **Person note** button in the Notes toolbar.

Person note button —

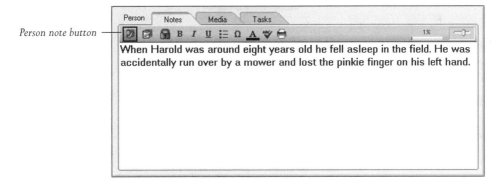

5. Enter the text you want to include for the individual.

   Note: You should *not* record source information on the Notes tab; if you do, the information won't be included in reports.

> **Tip**
>
> If you are entering notes from another document on your computer, you can usually "copy and paste" so you don't have to retype existing text. For instance, you could copy text from a Word document and then paste it into the Notes tab.

Tip

You can create a report of all the research notes you've entered in your tree. For instructions, see "Research Note Report" on page 246.

Entering a Research Note

Many times when you find a record or learn a new fact about someone in your tree, you will discover clues that can help you learn more about your family. You can create research notes to remind you of the next steps you want to take.

1. Go to the **Person** tab on the People workspace.

2. Make sure the individual you want to enter a note for is displayed.

3. Click the **Notes** tab.

4. Click the **Research note** button in the Notes toolbar.

Research note button ——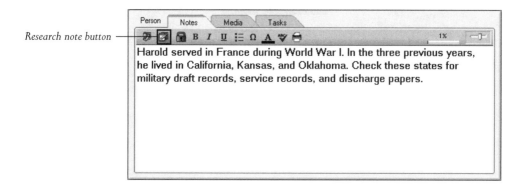

5. Enter the text you want to include for the individual.

    Note: You should *not* record source information on the Notes tab; if you do, the information won't be included in reports.

Tip

You can print an individual note by clicking the **Print note** button on the Notes toolbar.

Changing a Note's Display Size

You can resize your notes to make the text larger and easier to read or make the text smaller to fit more words on the tab. When you resize a note, it changes the display only; it does not affect permanent settings or the print size of a note.

1. After entering a note, drag the slider on the right side of the notes toolbar to make the text larger or smaller.

Slider

Formatting a Note's Text

1. After entering a note, you can use the formatting buttons on the toolbar to change the text.

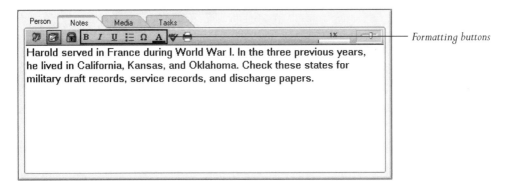

Formatting buttons

2. Use this chart to help you format the text:

To do this	Do this
Make text bold	Highlight the text and click the **Bold** button.
Make text italicized	Highlight the text and click the **Italic** button.
Underline text	Highlight the text and click the **Underline** button.
Make a bulleted list	Highlight the text and click the **Bullets** button.
Add a diacritic (such as accent marks)	Place the cursor where you want to enter the character and click the **Symbols** button. Choose the character you want to enter and click **Insert**.
Change the text color	Highlight the text and click the **Color** button. Choose the color you want and click **OK**.

Making a Note Private

You may have information about an individual that you do not want to share with other family members or researchers. If you make a note "private," you can choose whether or not you want to include it in reports or when you export your tree.

1. After entering a note, click the **Mark as private** button. You can tell the note has been marked as private because the lock icon has a yellow box around it.

Mark as private button ——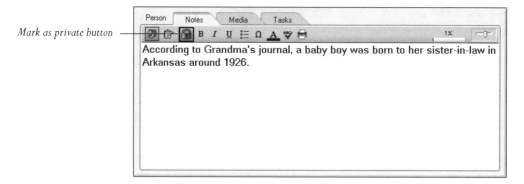

Adding Media Items for an Individual

You can add photos, images, sound files, videos, scanned documents, and more to an individual. For example, if you have a baby photo of your grandfather or a photo of his military uniform, you'll want to add it to his Media tab. You can also assign a specific photo to an individual that will be used all on charts and reports.

> Note: For more information on adding media items to a tree, see chapter 5, "Organizing Your Media Items."

Adding a Media Item

1. Go to the **Person** tab on the People workspace.

2. Make sure the individual you want to add a media item for is displayed.

3. Click the **Media** tab at the bottom of the window. The tab shows thumbnails of any media items you've linked to this individual.

Tip

You can change the order in which media items appear on an individual's Media tab. For instructions, see "Arranging an Individual's Media Items" on page 140.

4. Click the **New** button on the **Media** tab. The Select Media Item window opens.

5. Use the **Look in** drop-down list to find the folder where the image is located. When you find the correct folder, double-click the folder to open it.

6. Click the image you want to add to your tree. The image will appear in the Preview box.

7. Click **Open**. A message asks whether you want to link the file to your tree or create a copy of the file.

8. Click **Copy this file** to create an additional copy of the file in a Family Tree Maker media folder, or click **Link to this file** to leave the file where it is on your computer.

9. Click the checkbox for the category you want this item to belong to; you can select multiple categories. (For more information about categories, see "Creating Media Categories" on page 141.)

10. Click **OK**. The item is added to the individual's Media tab.

Note: When you add a picture or other media item to Family Tree Maker, the original file is not moved from its location on your computer.

Assigning a Portrait to an Individual

You can decide which image will appear as the default photograph for an individual in the People workspace and in reports and charts.

1. Click the **People** button on the main toolbar. Make sure the individual you want to add a portrait to is the focus of the Family tab or Person tab.

2. In the editing panel, right-click the silhouette image. If the photo you want is already in your tree, click **Link to Existing Picture**; if you need to add the image, click **Add New Picture**.

3. Do one of these options:

    •   If you are linking to an item, click the item and then click **OK**.

    •   If you are adding a new item, use the **Look in** drop-down list to find the folder where the image is located. Click on the image you want and then click **Open**.

    You will now see the photo next to the individual's name in the editing panel. (If you are using a new image, it will automatically be added to your tree; you can view it on the Media workspace.)

Adding Spouses

Family Tree Maker makes it easy to add spouses and enter information about marriages.

Adding a Spouse

1. Go to the **Family** tab on the People workspace.

2. Make sure the individual you want to add a spouse to is displayed.

3. Click **Add Spouse** in the pedigree view or the family group view.

Tip

You can also add a spouse using a menu option; choose **Person**> **Add Person**> **Add Spouse**.

4. Enter the spouse's name (first name, middle name, and last name). Don't forget to use maiden names for the females in your family.

5. Choose a gender from the drop-down list and click **OK**. The spouse becomes the focus of the pedigree view and editing panel.

   In the editing panel, you can enter a date and place for the marriage.

Entering Details About a Relationship

1. Go to the **Family** tab on the People workspace.

2. Make sure the couple whose marriage you want to add information about is the focus of the family group view.

3. In the editing panel, click the **Marriage to** button.

The Edit Relationship window opens.

4. Enter a marriage date and place in the appropriate fields. You can also click the Notes or Media tabs to include additional information about the relationship.

Adding Multiple Spouses

You may need to add more than one spouse for an individual—for example, if a widower or divorcée remarries.

1. Go to the **Family** tab on the People workspace.

2. Make sure the individual you want to add another spouse to is displayed.

3. In the family group view, click the **Spouse** icon next to the individual you want to add another spouse to. From the drop-down list, you have the choice of accessing the information for an existing spouse or adding a new spouse.

4. Choose **Add Spouse** from the drop-down list. The Add Spouse window opens.

Spouse button

5. Enter the spouse's name in the blank field and click **OK**. Family Tree Maker displays a new family group view, including the new spouse. After making any necessary edits to this alternate spouse, click the **Spouse** button again to go back to the original spouse.

Choosing a Preferred Spouse

If you enter more than one spouse for an individual, you need to indicate who is the preferred spouse. Usually this is the spouse whose children are in your direct line. Once you make someone the preferred spouse, he or she will be the default spouse displayed in the family group view, pedigree view, and charts and reports.

1. Go to the **Family** tab on the People workspace.

2. Make sure the individual with multiple spouses is the focus of the pedigree view and the family group view.

> **Tip**
> To determine the order in which spouses are listed, click **Person>Set Spouse Order**.

3. Click the **Person** tab and then click the **Relationships** button. You should see two names listed under the Spouses heading.

4. In the **Spouses** list, click the name of the individual you want to make the preferred spouse.

Relationships				Facts	Timeline	Relationships	
Name	Birth	Death	Relation				Preferred
Mother							
Sarah Thompson	1827	25 Sep 1860	Mother - Natural				Preferred
Spouses							
Louisa Fanny Newman	Abt. 1865		Spouse - Ongoing				Preferred
Mary Willis	Abt. 1853	25 Apr 1904	Spouse - None				
Children							
Henry Joseph Gold	27 Mar 1872		Son - Natural				
Cyrus William Gold	28 Mar 1876	22 Nov 1956	Son - Natural				
Thomas Gold	25 Aug 1878		Son - Natural				
Mary Elizabeth Gold	10 Sep 1880		Daughter - Natural				
Abraham John Gold	16 Oct 1882	14 May 1906	Son - Natural				
Alma Nephi Gold	18 Nov 1884		Son - Natural				
Lehi Moroni Gold	11 Dec 1886		Son - Natural				
Helaman Mosiah Gold	01 Jul 1889		Son - Natural				
Elmina Rachel Gold	31 Dec 1892		Daughter - Natural				
Sarah Hannah Gold	03 Dec 1873	05 Nov 1963	Daughter - Natural				

5. In the editing panel, click the **Preferred spouse** checkbox.

Switching Between Multiple Spouses

You can view the information and children of only one spouse at a time, so you may need to switch between multiple spouses when you want to work with a specific family. You will also need to change spouses if you want to add information about that particular marriage.

1. Go to the **Family** tab on the People workspace.

2. Make sure the individual with multiple spouses is the focus of the pedigree view and the family group view.

3. In the family group view, click the **Spouse** button next to the individual. From the drop-down list, choose the other spouse.

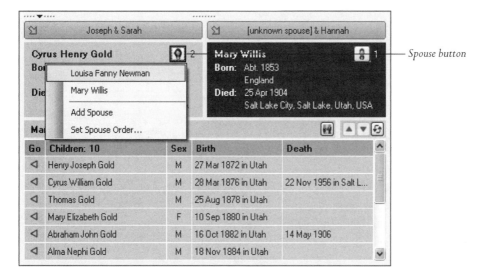

Spouse button

The family group view now displays the individual and the alternate spouse you have selected. After making any necessary edits to this alternate spouse, click the **Spouse** button again to select the preferred spouse.

Adding Children

You can add children to an individual at any time. Or if you add a child to a family and later discover you've entered them with the wrong parents, you can link the child to the correct family.

Adding a Child to a Family

1. Go to the **Family** tab on the People workspace.

2. Make sure the couple whose family you want to add children to is the focus of the pedigree view and the family group view.

3. Click **Add Child** in the family group view.

4. Enter the child's name (first name, middle name, and last name).

> Note: When entering a child's name, Family Tree Maker will assume that the child has the same surname as the father and add his surname automatically. You can ignore the suggested last name by typing over the surname.

5. Choose a gender from the drop-down list and click **OK**. The child becomes the focus of the editing panel but not the pedigree view.

Note: If you enter more children than will fit in the family group view, a scroll bar will appear and you can navigate to any children not visible on the window. You can also see the total number of children currently entered for a family in the family group view under the Children heading.

Sorting Children in the Family Group View

You can order the children in a family in any way you'd like. Perhaps you're working on a particular individual and you want him or her to be at the top of the list while you're working on him or her. Or perhaps you always want your direct ancestor to be displayed at the top of the list.

1. Go to the **Family** tab on the People workspace.

2. Make sure the family whose children you want to sort is the focus of the family group view.

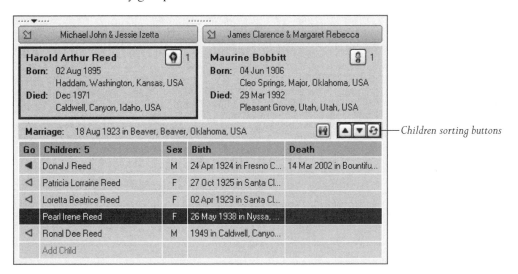

Children sorting buttons

3. Do one of these options:

  - To change the display order of a specific child, click the individual's name in the family group view; then, click the up or down arrow buttons.

  - To sort the children by birth date, click the **Sort children by birth** button.

Detaching a Child from the Wrong Parents

If you have attached a child to the wrong parents, you can easily detach the child from the family without deleting the child from your family tree.

1. Go to the **Family** tab on the People workspace.

2. Make sure the family you want to detach a child from is the focus of the family group view. Then, click the child's name in the family group view.

3. Click **Person>Attach/Detach Person>Detach Selected Person**. The Detach window opens.

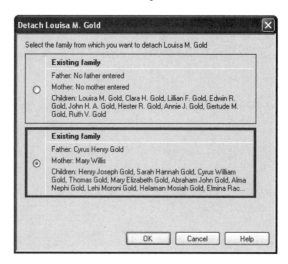

4. If necessary, choose which family you want to detach the individual from and click **OK**.

The child is no longer connected to this family but remains in your tree. To access the individual at a later time, you'll need to locate him or her in the Index panel.

Attaching a Child to a Father and Mother

You might discover you have entered an individual and his or her parents into your tree, but you did not know they were related when you entered them. You can still link them together.

1. Go to the **Family** tab on the People workspace.

2. Make sure the individual you want to attach to his or her parents is the focus of the pedigree view and the family group view. If the child isn't in the direct line of the home person, you might need to select the individual in the Index panel.

3. Click **Person>Attach/Detach Person>Attach Mother/Father**. The Select the Mother/Father to Attach window opens.

Select The father To Attach				
Find:				
Name	**Birth Date**	**Marr. Date**	**Death Date**	
Gold, Abraham John	16 Oct 1882		14 May 1906	
Gold, Alma Nephi	18 Nov 1884			
Gold, Annie J.	Abt. 1896			
Gold, Clara H.	Abt. 1901			
Gold, Cyrus Henry	Abt. 1848		30 Mar 1930	
Gold, Cyrus William	28 Mar 1876		22 Nov 1956	
Gold, Edwin R.	Abt. 1906			
Gold, Elmina Rachel	31 Dec 1892			
Gold, Gertude M.	Abt. 1894			
Gold, Helaman Mosiah	01 Jul 1889			
Gold, Henry Joseph	27 Mar 1872			
Gold, Hester R.	Abt. 1898			
Gold, John H. A.	Abt. 1909			
Gold, Joseph		27 Jan 1845		
Gold, Lehi Moroni	11 Dec 1886			
Gold, Lillian F.	Abt. 1903			
Gold, Louisa M.	Abt. 1892			
Gold, Mary Elizabeth	10 Sep 1880			
Gold, Ruth V.	Abt. 1893			
People: 245		OK	Cancel	Help

4. Choose the father or mother from the list and click **OK**. If the father or mother has multiple spouses, you'll need to choose which family the child belongs to.

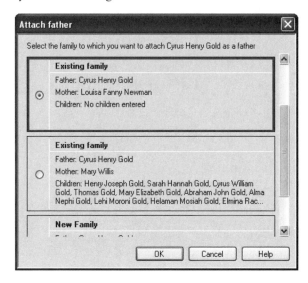

5. Choose the family to attach the individual to and click **OK**.

Adding Parents

In addition to letting you enter information about your immediate family, you can add multiple generations of a family—grandparents, great-grandparents, aunts and uncles, and so on.

1. Go to the **Family** tab on the People workspace.

2. Make sure the individual you want to add a father or mother to is the focus of the pedigree view and the family group view.

3. Click **Add Father** or **Add Mother** in the pedigree view or click **Add Parents** in the family group view.

4. Enter the parent's name (first name, middle name, and last name). Don't forget to use maiden names for the females in your family.

5. Choose a gender from the drop-down list and click **OK**. The parent becomes the focus of the pedigree view and editing panel.

Adding an Unrelated Individual

During your family research, you might discover a person that you think is related to your family, but you have no proof. You will still want to add this person to your tree so you can keep track of his or her information. Family Tree Maker lets you add individuals without having to link them to other family members in your tree. If you find out that they are part of your family, you can easily link them in.

1. Click the **People** button on the main toolbar.

2. Click **Person>Add Person>Add Unrelated Person**. The Add Unrelated Person window opens.

3. Enter the person's name (first name, middle name, and last name).

4. Choose a gender from the drop-down list and click **OK**. The new individual becomes the focus of the pedigree view and editing panel.

Changing Relationships

As you continue your research, you might discover you were mistaken on a marriage you entered or on a parent-child relationship. This is likely to occur when you come across multiple generations of individuals with the same name (for instance, you may have confused John Smith with his grandson, also named John Smith). Family Tree Maker lets you clarify and change relationships as necessary.

Choosing a Relationship Between Parents and a Child

You can indicate a child's relationship to each of his or her parents (e.g., natural, adopted, foster).

1. Go to the **Family** tab on the People workspace.

2. Make sure the individual (child) whose relationship you need to change is the focus of the pedigree view.

3. Click the **Person** tab and then click the **Relationships** button.

4. Click the father or mother's name.

5. In the editing panel, choose a relationship from the **Relationship** drop-down list.

Choosing a Type of Relationship for a Couple

You can choose what type of relationship a couple in your tree has with each other (e.g., partner, friend, spouse).

1. Go to the **Family** tab on the People workspace.

2. Make sure the couple whose relationship you need to change is the focus of the family group view.

3. Click the **Person** tab and then click the **Relationships** button.

Relationships				Facts	Timeline	Relationships	
Name	Birth	Death	Relation				Preferred
Siblings							
Luzilla May Reed	1886	13 Apr 1940	Sister				
Lela M. Reed	11 Sep 1887	Dec 1968	Sister				
George M. Reed	27 Sep 1889	01 Jan 1966	Brother				
Florence L. Reed	09 Dec 1891		Sister				
Edwin Ernest Reed	03 Dec 1893	Sep 1974	Brother				
Cora Evelyn Reed	31 Mar 1901	25 Jul 1982	Sister				
Spouse							
Maurine Bobbitt	04 Jun 1906	29 Mar 1992	Spouse - None				Preferred
Children							
Donal J Reed	24 Apr 1924	14 Mar 2002	Son - Natural				

4. Click the spouse's name.

5. In the editing panel, choose a relationship from the **Relationship** drop-down list.

Choosing a Status for a Couple's Relationship

The status of a couple's relationship will default to "Ongoing." If necessary, you can change this status. For example, if a couple gets a divorce, you can record this with their relationship status.

1. Go to the **Family** tab on the People workspace.

2. Make sure the couple whose relationship status you need to change is the focus of the family group view.

3. Click the **Person** tab and then click the **Relationships** button.

Relationships					Facts	Timeline	Relationships		
Name	Birth	Death	Relation					Preferred	
Siblings									
Luzilla May Reed	1886	13 Apr 1940	Sister						
Lela M. Reed	11 Sep 1887	Dec 1968	Sister						
George M. Reed	27 Sep 1889	01 Jan 1966	Brother						
Florence L. Reed	09 Dec 1891		Sister						
Edwin Ernest Reed	03 Dec 1893	Sep 1974	Brother						
Cora Evelyn Reed	31 Mar 1901	25 Jul 1982	Sister						
Spouse									
Maurine Bobbitt	04 Jun 1906	29 Mar 1992	Spouse - None					Preferred	
Children									
Donal J Reed	24 Apr 1924	14 Mar 2002	Son - Natural						

4. Click the spouse's name.

5. In the editing panel, choose a status from the **Status** drop-down list.

Tip

The Current Tree tab on the Plan workspace shows which individual you edited last.

Editing an Individual's Information

When you first begin entering information in your tree, you'll probably spend most of your time in the People workspace—entering facts, sourcing events, and even adding photos and scanned records. As you find additional details or want to clarify information you've already entered, you can quickly edit an individual's information without interrupting the task you're currently working on.

1. Do one of these options:

   • In the Places, Media, or Sources workspace, right-click the individual's name in the Index panel and choose **Edit Person**.

   • In the Publish workspace, right-click the individual's name in the mini pedigree tree and choose **Edit Person**. You can also double-click the individual's name in a chart or report.

   The Edit Person window opens.

2. Do one of these options:

   - To add or edit facts for the individual, click the **Facts** tab. (For more information about what you can do on this tab, see "Adding More Details" on page 47.)

   - To add research or person notes about an individual, click the **Notes** tab. (For more information about what you can do on this tab, see "Adding Notes" on page 53.)

   - To add, edit, or delete a media item for an individual, click the **Media** tab. (For more information about what you can do on this tab, see "Adding Media Items for an Individual" on page 57.)

3. When you have finished editing an individual's information, click **OK**.

Viewing Timelines

Timelines can be a great tool to put the life of your ancestor in context—historical and otherwise. Family Tree Maker lets you view three timeline variations: events in an individual's life; events in an individual's life and important events in his or her immediate family (such as birth, marriage, and death); events in an individual's life and historical events.

Viewing an Individual's Timeline

You can view a timeline of all the events you've entered for an individual. Each life event is represented by a horizontal bar showing its date and location and the person's age at the time.

1. Go to the **Person** tab on the People workspace.

Tip
You can also create a printable timeline. For instructions, see "Timeline Report" on page 254.

2. Make sure the individual whose timeline you want to view is the focus of the tree.

3. Click the **Timeline** button.

Including Family Events in a Timeline

You can view an individual's life events shown side-by-side in a timeline with the births, marriages, and deaths of immediate family members.

1. To display the individual's life along with family events, click the down arrow next to the **Timeline** button and select **Show Family Events**.

Events in an individual's life are indicated by green markers, and events in his or her family's life are indicated by pink markers.

Timeline				Facts	Timeline	Relationships	
Year / Age	Event		Date / Place			Description	
1895	Birth		02 Aug 1895 Haddam, Washington, Kansas, USA				
1896	Birth		1896 Kansas				
1906 10	Birth (Spouse) Maurine Bobbitt		04 Jun 1906 Cleo Springs, Major, Oklahoma, USA				
1910 14	Census		1910 Elk City, Washita, Oklahoma, USA				
1917 21	Residence		05 Jun 1917 Washita, Oklahoma, USA				
1923 28	Marriage Maurine Bobbitt		18 Aug 1923 Beaver, Beaver, Oklahoma, USA				
1924 28	Birth (Son) Donal J Reed		24 Apr 1924 Fresno County, California, USA				
1925 30	Birth (Daughter) Patricia Lorraine Reed		27 Oct 1925 Santa Clara, California				
1929 33	Birth (Daughter) Loretta Beatrice Reed		02 Apr 1929 Santa Clara County, California, USA				
1930 34	Residence		1930 Santa Clara, Santa Clara, California				

2. To return to a timeline of just the individual's life, click the same arrow and deselect **Show Family Events**.

Including Historical Events in a Timeline

You can view an individual's life events in the context of significant historical events.

1. To display the individual's life along with historical events, click the down arrow next to the **Timeline** button and select **Show Historical Events**.

   Events in an individual's life are indicated by green markers, and historical events are indicated by yellow markers.

2. To return to a timeline of just the individual's life, click the same arrow and deselect **Show Historical Events**.

> **Tip**
> You can include both family events and historical events in an individual's timeline. Simply select both options from the drop-down list.

Merging Individuals

After months and years of gathering names and dates, eventually your family tree may become a bit disorderly. You might discover that the Flossie in your tree is actually the Florence you also have in your tree—not two distinct individuals. If you have two individuals you've entered in your tree who are the same person, you will want to merge them (instead of deleting one) so that you don't lose any information you've entered.

If you know which two individuals are duplicates, you can quickly merge them together. However, you may have people lurking in your tree who have duplicates, but you just don't realize it. Luckily Family Tree Maker has a tool that can quickly assess your family tree and show you individuals who could possibly match each other.

> Note: Before you merge individuals in your tree, you might want to make a backup of your original tree. For instructions, see "Backing Up a File" on page 377.

Finding Duplicate Individuals

After adding a lot of new information to your project or merging a family member's tree with yours, it's a good idea to check your project to see if you have any duplicate individuals.

1. Click **Edit>Find Duplicate People**. The Find Duplicate People window opens.

    In the first two columns you'll see the individuals who might be duplicates. Click a column header to sort the list alphabetically. In the third column you'll see a match score—the higher the number the more likely the individuals are a match; a 1,000 means the individuals are almost exact matches.

2. If you want to merge a pair of individuals (or just compare the two), click their row in the window and click **Compare/ Merge**. The Individual Merge window opens. For instructions on how to complete the merge, see the next task, "Merging Duplicate Individuals."

Merging Duplicate Individuals

At some point, you may realize two individuals you've entered in your tree are actually the same person. You can merge these two individuals and retain all facts and dates associated with each person.

1. Go to the **Family** tab on the People workspace.

2. Make sure the individual you want to keep as the primary individual in the merge is the focus of the pedigree view and the family group view.

3. Click **Person>Merge Two Specific Individuals**. The Index of Individuals window opens.

4. Find the duplicate individual in the list. You can use the scroll bar to move up and down the list, or type a name (last name first) in the **Find** field.

5. Click **OK**. The Individual Merge window opens.

6. In the Person 1 and Person 2 columns, choose how you want the individuals to be merged:

- **Make preferred.** Merge the information as the "preferred" fact for the individual.

- **Make alternate.** Merge the information as an alternate fact for the individual.

- Click **Discard this fact** to *not* merge the information into your tree. You may choose to discard some facts for a person, although it is usually a good idea to include all facts in case they turn out to be relevant. Click the **Keep sources** checkbox to merge the source information for the discarded fact.

The Merged Result column shows how the information will be merged together.

7. Click **OK** to complete the merge.

Deleting Individuals from a Tree

If you find that you have mistakenly added an individual to your tree who isn't related to you, you can delete the individual and his or her information from your tree. Or if you receive a file from a family member that contains a branch you aren't related to, you can delete that family line from your tree as a group.

> Warning: Deleting individuals from a tree is permanent. You have one chance to restore the deleted person after removing them by using the Undo feature in the Edit menu *immediately* after the deletion. You should create a backup of your tree before deleting anyone. (For instructions, see "Backing Up Files" on page 377.)

Deleting an Individual

> **Tip**
>
> You cannot remove an individual from your tree by deleting his or her name in the Name field or by detaching him or her from other family members. You must delete the individual.

1. Go to the **Family** tab on the People workspace.

2. Make sure the individual you want to delete from your tree is the focus of the pedigree view and the family group view.

3. Click **Person>Delete Person**. A message asks you to confirm that you want to delete the individual. Click **Yes**.

    All notes, tasks, and media links associated with the person will be permanently deleted.

Deleting a Group of Individuals

To delete a group of individuals, you first need to display them in a tree chart. Because this feature works on every chart, you can choose the chart that best displays the individuals you want to remove from your tree. However, the Extended Family chart can display every individual in your tree and is generally the best chart to use.

1. Go to the **Collection** tab on the Publish workspace.

2. Click the name of the individual whom you want to be the focus of the chart in the mini-navigation pedigree tree or click the **Index of Individuals** button and choose a person.

3. Double-click the chart that will best display the group of people you want to delete. Don't worry if individuals you don't want to delete appear in the chart; you can use the selection tools to further refine your choices.

4. To select specific individuals or groups to delete, right-click an individual's name in the chart. A drop-down list lets you choose specific groups to include (e.g., ancestors, descendants, individuals of the same generation). For more information on selecting groups of individuals, select **Help>Help for Family Tree Maker**.

> **Tip**
>
> You can also select specific individuals in a chart by pressing the CTRL key and clicking on each individual you want to delete.

5. After you have selected the group of individuals you want to delete, right-click one of the highlighted boxes and select **Delete from File>Selected Persons** from the drop-down list.

Chapter 4

Documenting Sources

Documenting sources—recording where you discovered a fact about your family—is one of the most important aspects of your research. If you find your father's birthplace on his World War I draft card, you'll want to include this information in your tree when you record his birth date and place. If you discover your great-grandfather's will that lists the names of all his children, you'll want to create a source for this document.

Sources are valuable for many reasons. When you cite a source, you are proving to others which records you based your facts on; if you eventually share your research with your family or other researchers, your family history will be judged for accuracy based on your sources. And if your sources are detailed and correct, others will be able to follow your research footsteps. In addition, sources help you keep organized—you can keep track of records that you've already found so you don't waste time revisiting old sources.

In This Chapter

- Understanding Sources and Source Citations
- Sources
- Source Citations
- Finding a Source Citation

Understanding Sources and Source Citations

Family Tree Maker lets you create both sources and source citations. Here's an explanation of each:

- A source contains unchanging facts about an object, for example, the author, title, and publication information for a book. Creating sources saves you time and helps you avoid typing in the same information multiple times. Each source can be used for multiple source citations.

- Source citations are individual details for a fact such as the page number of a book you have entered as a source.

To help you understand how sources and source citations work together, let's look at an example from the 1930 United States Federal Census. First, you would create a source for the census that would include information like this:

- A title—1930 United States Federal Census

- Where you located the source—www.ancestry.com

- Publishing details—Ancestry.com. 1930 United States Federal Census [database on-line]. Provo, UT, USA: Original data: United States of America, Bureau of the Census. Fifteenth Census of the United States, 1930. Washington, D.C.: National Archives and Records Administration, 1930.

(If your source were a book, you would include the author and call number; each type of source will have slightly different information.)

As you can see, this basic information about the 1930 census won't change regardless of who you find in the records. However, because you'll find different families and individuals in different locations throughout the census, the census fact for each person will need its own source citation. A source citation for an individual you found in the 1930 census might include this information:

- Source—1930 United States Federal Census

- Citation text—Harold Reed household, Santa Clara Township, Santa Clara County, California. Enumeration district 43-10. Supervisor's district 10. Sheet number 14A.

A source citation for a different individual might include information like this:

- Source—1930 United States Federal Census

- Citation text—Michael Reed household, Kokomo Township, Beaver County, Oklahoma. Enumeration district 26. Supervisor's district 234. Sheet number 5B.

Both individuals can be found in the 1930 census (the source), but the source citation for each individual has changed because the individuals were located in different places in the source.

How Complete Is Your Tree?

Regardless of how many generations you've added to your tree or how attractive your pedigree charts are, your family history won't be as valuable unless the information you've gathered is recorded accurately. Here are a few questions you might ask to discover if your tree is as complete as it can be.

- Are the names of people and locations spelled the same way every time?
- Do your media items contain descriptions and dates?
- Is each fact documented and sourced?
- Do you have duplicate individuals in your tree?
- Have you checked for transposed or inaccurate dates?
- Have you looked for spelling errors?

Sources

Each time you add information to your tree, you'll want to create a source that describes where you found the information. If you find your grandparents' marriage date in the family Bible, you should create a source for that Bible. If you find the image of a death record for your great-aunt in an online database, you should create a source for that database. You need to create only one source for each item; you can use the source for as many source citations as necessary.

Family Tree Maker lets you enter sources in two ways: using templates or a basic source format. Source templates are useful because you don't have to guess which details need to be entered. Choose the type of source you're creating (for example, for an obituary), and Family Tree Maker displays the relevant fields. Templates ensure that your sources are consistent and that you capture the most important elements of a source. If you don't want to use source templates (for example, because you prefer to use your own system of citation or you can't find a template that matches the item you're sourcing), you can create a source by simply completing the standard fields (such as author, title, and publisher) in the basic source format.

Adding a Source to a Fact

You will most likely add a source as you create a source citation for a fact or event you have entered in your tree. Although you can add facts in various ways, this section focuses on how to add a source while entering facts on the Family tab and the Person tab in the People workspace.

> Note: You can create a source at any time by clicking Edit>Manage Sources.

Adding a Source from the Family Tab

1. Go to the **Family** tab on the People workspace.

2. In the editing panel, click the **New source citation** button to the right of the field for which you want to add a source. Then choose **Add New Source Citation** from the drop-down list.

— *New source citation button*

> **Tip**
> The source citation button doesn't appear until you click in the field or move the mouse over the field.

The Add Source Citation window opens. Continue with "Creating a Source from a Template" on page 93 or "Creating a Source Using the Basic Format" on page 99.

Adding a Source from the Person Tab

1. Go to the **Person** tab on the People workspace.

2. In the Individual and Shared Facts section, highlight the fact for which you want to add a source.

3. In the editing panel, click the **New** button on the **Sources** tab. Then choose **Add New Source Citation** from the drop-down list.

The Add Source Citation window opens. Continue with "Creating a Source from a Template" on page 93 or "Creating a Source Using the Basic Format" on page 99.

Using Source Templates

Family Tree Maker includes more than 170 source templates to help you source everything from homemade samplers and online databases to vital records. The source templates are based on the QuickCheck models used in Elizabeth Shown Mills's book *Evidence Explained*—the premier reference for citing genealogy sources. To see a list of the source templates included in Family Tree Maker, see appendix D, "Source Templates."

> Note: You do not have to create sources using these templates. You can also enter your own data in the standard fields Family Tree Maker has always provided. For instructions, see "Creating a Source Using the Basic Format" on page 99.

Creating a Source from a Template

Using a source template is simple. To determine which template you should use for a specific record, you can enter keywords and choose from a list of suggestions, or you can view a list of all the available templates and choose the one that fits best.

1. Access the Add Source Citation window. For help, see "Adding a Source from the Family Tab" on page 91 or "Adding a Source from the Person Tab" on page 92.

2. Click **New** on the Add Source Citation window. The Add Source
   window opens.

3. To choose a template, do one of these options:

   • To search for a template, enter a keyword in the **Source
     template** field. To narrow the list, enter multiple keywords.
     For example, "property" brings up eleven results, while
     "property grant" brings up one result. Click a template from
     the drop-down list that appears. Skip to step 8.

   • To choose a template from a categorized list, click **More**.
     The Select Source Template window opens. Continue with
     step 4.

   Note: If you want to use the basic source format,
   simply leave the Source template field blank.

4. In **Source group**, choose the group that most closely matches the item you're sourcing. The categories list changes to reflect the selected source group.

5. Choose the appropriate category from the **Category** drop-down list. The templates list changes to reflect the selected source group and category.

6. Choose a template from the **Template** drop-down list. A description of the template is displayed beneath its title.

7. Click **OK** to return to the Add Source window; the fields that appear now reflect the template you've chosen.

8. Complete these fields as necessary and click **OK**. A chart of some commonly used source elements appears in the next section.

Commonly Used Source Elements

After you've chosen a source template, you can complete information about the specific elements for that template. Here's a chart of a few commonly used elements that you might enter for a source:

Source Element	What to Record
Author	The full name of the author exactly as it appears in the source.
Call number	Enter the call number that is assigned to the source at the repository where you found the item. It could be a microfilm number, a Dewey decimal system number, or some other numbering system unique to a particular library or archive.
Collection	The name of a specific collection.
Comments	Enter any comments about the source and the information found in it. This information will not print on your reports; it is for your personal reference. You might include a description of the item or even information about its legibility.
Database title	The title of an online database.
Date	The copyright date (usually only a year), date of creation, or date the information was accessed.
Publisher	The name of the publishing company.
Source repository	Choose a repository from the drop-down list. For more information on repositories, see "Adding a Repository for a Source" on page 100.
Title	The title of the source exactly as it appears in the source.
URL	The website's URL (Uniform Resource Locator). Because URLs or Web addresses can be long and difficult to transcribe accurately, you might want to copy and paste the URL directly from your Web browser into your source.
Website title	The title of the website.

Transferring an Existing Source to a Source Template

If you have created a source using the basic format and now want to use a standardized template, you don't have to re-create the source; you can map the fields in your original source to fields in a template, and the contents will transfer over automatically.

1. Click the **Sources** button on the main toolbar.

2. In **Source Groups**, double-click the source you want to transfer to a template. The Edit Source window opens.

3. To find the template you want to use, enter keywords in the **Source template** field or click **Change** to select a template from a categorized list. The Change Source Type window opens.

4. Do one of these options:

   • Click **Existing template** to view the field names from the original source. The drop-down lists contain the template fields you can map to.

   • Click **New template** to view the field names from the template. The drop-down lists contain the original source fields you can map to the new template.

Change Source Type

Map fields using

⦿ Existing template   ○ New template

For each field in the existing source template, choose the field to be used in the new source template.

Newspaper Article - Online Archive (by Newspaper Name)

Title	Newspaper name
Author	Item format
Publisher name	Discard data
Publisher location	City
Publish date	Year
Call number	Discard data
Comments	Discard data

OK   Cancel   Help

5. For each field, do one of these options:

   • Choose **Discard data** from the drop-down list to leave the field blank.

   • Choose a field to move the contents to.

6. Click **OK** to return to the Edit Source window. The contents of the original source appear now in the template's fields.

   Note: If your original source includes a source repository but the template does not use the Source repository field, your repository information will be discarded. You might want to add the repository information to the Comments field in the template.

Creating a Source Using the Basic Format

If you don't want to use source templates, you can create a source by simply completing the standard fields (such as author, title, and publisher) using the basic source format.

1. Access the Add Source Citation window. For help, see "Adding a Source from the Family Tab" on page 91 or "Adding a Source from the Person Tab" on page 92.

2. Click **New** on the Add Source Citation window. The Add Source window opens.

3. Complete these fields on the **Source** tab:

In this field	Do this
Title of source	Enter a title for the source.
Author	Enter the author or originator's name.

In this field	Do this
Publisher name	Enter the name of the publishing company.
Publisher location	Enter the place of publication (for example, London, England).
Publish date	Enter the copyright date for the source (usually only a year).
Source repository	If you want to, choose a repository from the drop-down list. For more information about repositories, see the next task, "Adding a Repository for a Source."
Call number	Enter a call number, if one exists. (The call number is the number assigned to the source at the repository where you found the item. It could be a microfilm number, a Dewey Decimal system number, or some other numbering system unique to a particular library or archive.)
Comments	Enter any comments about the source and the information found in it. This information will not print on your reports; it is for your personal reference.

4. To include a media item as part of the source (for example, a photo of a book), continue with "Attaching a Media Item to a Source" on page 103.

5. Click **OK**. You can now add a source citation for the fact.

Adding a Repository for a Source

A repository is the location where an original source exists. This could be a library, archive, county courthouse, or cousin's home, for example. If you have information about a source's repository, you can include this information for a source.

Note: You can also create a repository when you are creating a source or source citation.

1. Click **Edit>Manage Repositories**. The Repositories window opens.

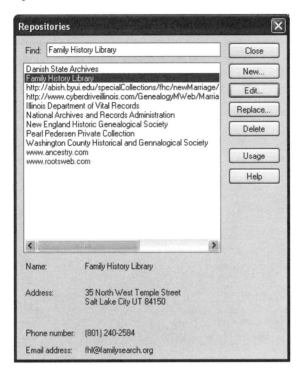

Tip

You can edit a repository in the Sources workspace by double-clicking its name.

2. Click **New**. The Add Repository window opens.

3. Enter the name, address, and phone number for the location. You can also add an e-mail address, if one exists.

4. Click **OK**.

5. Click **Close**.

Viewing the Use of a Repository

You can view the sources that are associated with a specific source repository.

1. Click **Edit>Manage Repositories**. The Repositories window opens.

2. Click a repository in the list. You can use the scroll bar to move up and down the list.

3. Click **Usage**. The Repository Usage window shows you a repository and the sources it is linked to.

4. Click **Close**.

Attaching a Media Item to a Source

If you have an image or recording of a source, you can link it to a source.

> Note: If you link the source to a media item that isn't already in your tree, the item will be added to the tree's Media workspace.

1. Access a source. For help, see "Adding a Source to a Fact" on page 90.

2. Click the **Media** tab on the Source window.

3. Click **Attach New Media**. The Select Media Item window opens. Locate the media item and click **Open**.

A message asks whether you want to link the file to your tree or create a copy of the file.

4. Click **Copy this file** to create an additional copy of the file in a Family Tree Maker media folder, or click **Link to this file** to leave the file where it is on your computer.

5. Click a checkbox for the category you want this item to belong to; you can select multiple categories. (For more information about categories, see "Creating Media Categories" on page 141.)

6. Click **OK**. The item is added to the source and copied to the Media workspace.

Merging Sources

If you have accidentally created multiple sources for the same document, book, or record, you can merge these sources without losing any information.

1. Click **Edit>Manage Sources**. The Sources window opens.

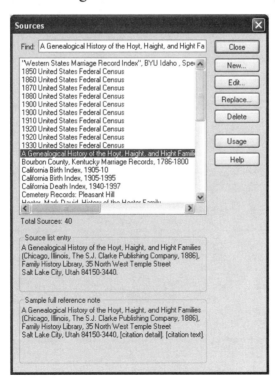

2. In the list of sources, click the source that you want to *replace*. You can use the scroll bar to move up and down the list.

   Note: If you want to see which facts are associated with the source before you replace it, click the Usage button.

3. Click **Replace**. The Replace Sources window opens.

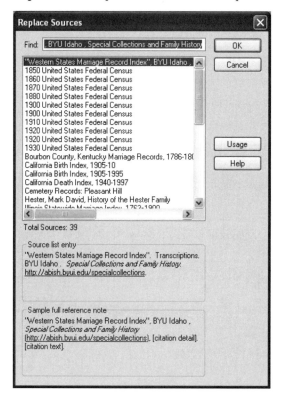

4. In the list of sources, click the source that you want to *keep*.

5. Click **OK**. A message asks if you want to replace the source.

6. Click **Yes**. All facts associated with the first source will now be associated with the source you chose to keep.

7. Click **Close**.

Viewing the Use of a Source

You can view the individuals and facts that are associated with a specific source.

1. Click **Edit**>**Manage Sources**. The Sources window opens.

2. Click a source in the list. You can use the scroll bar to move up and down the list.

3. Click **Usage**. The Source Usage window shows you the source and the individuals and facts it is linked to.

> **Tip**
>
> You can also print a report that shows the usage of every source in your tree. For more information, see "Source Usage Report" on page 278.

4. Click **Close**.

Source Citations

When possible, you should cite the source of every name, event, or fact that you enter in your tree. Family Tree Maker lets you create source citations in a variety of ways. As you cite each fact you'll need to decide which method is most effective in that situation. If you're adding a source that you've never used before in your tree, you will want to add a new source citation as well. If you have already created a source citation for an item like a specific census record, you won't need to create a new citation; simply link everyone in the household to the same citation. But what if you have already created a source citation for a specific county history and your ancestors are mentioned on two different pages? Instead of creating a new source citation that duplicates the original or linking the two different facts to the same citation, you can copy the original source citation, change the cited page number, and instantly have two citations.

Examples of Source Citations

Here are some examples of source citations for common records you might encounter in your research:

Federal Census Record

Harold Reed household, 1930 U.S. census, Santa Clara Township, Santa Clara County, California, enumeration district 26, supervisor's district 3, dwelling 64, family 73; National Archives micropublication T9, roll 320.

Marriage Certificate

Reed-Bobbitt marriage, 18 August 1923, County Clerk's Office, Beaver, Oklahoma.

Newspaper Obituary

Cora Reed obituary, *The Greenleaf Journal*, Washington County, Kansas, 5 March 1881, page 3.

Photograph

Harold and Edwin Reed portrait, original, inscribed on back, "Harold and Edwin 1902-03." Photograph is 4 1/4" x 6 1/2."

You can create more than one source citation for the same fact. For example, you might find an immigration date for your great-grandmother on a naturalization record and a census record. You can add source citations for both records, which allows you to compare conflicting information and keep track of the sources you've already searched.

Adding a New Source Citation

Every time you add a fact to your tree, you should take a minute to document where you discovered the information, whether it's a book in a library, a record you located online, or a photograph you discovered in an old trunk. When you create a new source citation, you'll link it to the appropriate source and then add any additional identifying information such as page number, volume number, or explanatory text.

1. Access the Add Source Citation window. For help, see "Adding a Source from the Family Tab" on page 91 or "Adding a Source from the Person Tab" on page 92.

2. Complete these fields on the **Source** tab:

In this field	Do this
Source title	Choose a source from the drop-down list. (For help, see "Sources" on page 90.)
Citation detail	Enter specific details about where you found the information, such as the page or volume number or website address.
Citation text	Enter any additional information. For example, you might enter a quote from a book or add a paraphrased summary of the source text.
Include citation text in reference note	Click this checkbox to include text in the Citation text field in printed reference notes. If this text is just for your own information, make sure the checkbox is not selected. (The source title and citation detail are automatically included in printed reference notes.)

You can also format the citation text, include a media item, or add a personal note as part of a source citation. For instructions, see "Formatting a Source Citation" on page 115, "Attaching a Media Item to a Source Citation" on page 115, and "Adding a Note to a Source Citation" on page 117.

3. Click **OK**.

In the Individual and Shared Facts section, you'll notice that the sources column now contains a number, indicating that you have one source cited for the fact.

The sources column is indicated by a scroll icon.

Linking a Fact to an Existing Source Citation

If you have already created a citation for a specific source, such as a death certificate, you don't have to create a new source citation for each fact or individual that is included in this source; you can use the existing citation. For example, if you find information about your grandparents in your aunt's death certificate (such as their names and birthplaces), you don't have to create a new source citation for the death certificate again; you can simply link to the citation you already created.

1. Go to the **Person** tab on the People workspace.

2. Make sure the individual you have entered a fact for is displayed.

3. Click the **Facts** button. The Individual and Shared Facts section opens.

4. Click the fact you want to add a source citation to in the Individual and Shared Facts section.

5. On the **Sources** tab in the editing panel, click the **New** button and choose **Use Existing Source Citation** from the drop-down list.

The Find Source Citation window opens.

6. Click the citation you want to link to from the list.

7. Click **Link to Citation**. The citation information now appears on the Sources tab.

Copying and Updating a Source Citation

If you have a source citation in your tree that is similar to one you need to create, you don't need to create a brand new citation. Simply copy the source citation, change the relevant details, such as the page or volume number, and paste it to a fact. For example, if you find several of your family members in the same city directory for Cleveland, Ohio, you can create a source citation for the first family and then copy, paste, and update the source citation for every other family that shows up in the same directory.

1. Go to the **Person** tab on the People workspace.

2. Make sure the individual you have entered a fact for is displayed.

3. Click the **Facts** button. The Individual and Shared Facts section opens.

4. In the Individual and Shared Facts section, click the fact that has the source citation you want to copy.

5. On the **Sources** tab in the editing panel, right-click the source citation you want to copy and choose **Copy** from the drop-down list.

6. Access the **Person** tab for the individual you want to copy the source citation to.

7. In the Individual and Shared Facts section, click the fact that you want to add the source citation to.

8. In the editing panel, click the **New** button on the **Sources** tab and choose **Paste Duplicate Source Citation** from the drop-down list.

9. In the **Sources** tab, double-click the source citation you just added. The Edit Source Citation window opens.

10. Update the source citation as necessary and click **OK**.

Formatting a Source Citation

You can use a few basic formatting options to change how a source citation will look in footnotes and reports.

1. Click the **Reference Note** tab in a source citation. The citation details and citation text you have entered for the source citation are displayed.

2. To italicize text, highlight the appropriate text and click the **Italics** button. To underline text, highlight the appropriate text and click the **Underline** button.

3. Click **OK**.

Attaching a Media Item to a Source Citation

If you have an image or recording of a source, you can link it to a source citation. For example, you might have a scan of a marriage certificate or census record that you want to include in your tree.

> Note: If you link the source to a media item that isn't already in your tree, the item will be added to the tree's Media workspace.

1. Click the **Media** tab in a source citation.

2. Click **Attach New Media**. The Select Media Item window opens. Locate the media item and click **Open**.

3. Click **OK**.

Adding a Note to a Source Citation

You can use the Notes tab to include any additional information you have about a source that you weren't able to include elsewhere. For example, you can enter a note about how you discovered a source or where the source is located.

1. Click the **Notes** tab in a source citation.

2. Enter a note. The notes are automatically saved.

3. Click **OK**.

    Note: For information about formatting notes in Family Tree Maker, see "Formatting a Note's Text" on page 55.

Rating a Source Citation

Family Tree Maker lets you rate the reliability of sources. You can rate each source citation to note both the legibility of the source as well as its potential accuracy (i.e., primary source, secondary source, family legend, etc.).

1. Click the **Sources** button on the main toolbar.

2. Find the source citation you want to rate and click it in the Source Citations list.

3. Click the **Links** tab.

4. If the source citation has more than one individual linked to it, click the person's name on the Links tab.

Sorting Out Sources: Original and Derivative

As you analyze the quality of your sources, you'll want to determine whether they're original or derivative.

- Original sources are just what the name implies—original records (or digital copies of originals) of passenger lists; birth, marriage, and death certificates; censuses, land records, and more.
- Derivative sources are records that have been extracted, transcribed, or translated from the original. For example, a marriage certificate is an original record, but an online index that transcribes the names and dates on the record is a derivative source.

5. Click the **Rate the source** icon (a yellow star). The Rate Source window opens.

Note: You can click the gray (X) button or the Reset button to clear the current rating.

Sorting Out Sources: Primary and Secondary

As you're gathering records for your family, you'll find two types of sources: primary and secondary.

- Primary sources are documents that were created at the time of the event (or soon after) by someone who had direct knowledge of the event. Examples include birth and death certificates, photographs, diaries, letters, and contemporary newspapers.

- Secondary sources are published works that were created sometime after an event by someone who might not have been personally aware of the event. For example, you might find your grandfather's birthplace listed on a birth certificate (a primary source for birth information) and in a census record (a secondary source for birth information). While both sources are valuable, the primary source (birth certificate) is a more reliable source.

Be aware that records can contain both primary and secondary information. For example, a marriage certificate would be a primary source for a marriage date but a secondary source for a bride's birth date or birthplace.

6. Use this chart to change the source's rating:

To do this	Do this
Rate the source yourself	In the **Quality score** field, click the number of stars you want to assign the source. The more stars you choose, the higher the quality of the source. Note: In the Ratings column, self-rated stars appear in blue.
Use a standardized rating system	Click the **Use standardized ratings** checkbox. Choose how to rate the source: • **Source.** Choose whether the source is an original document or a transcription or translation of the original. • **Clarity.** Choose the legibility of the source. • **Information.** Choose whether this information comes from primary or secondary sources. • **Evidence.** Choose whether the source states a fact or requires additional evidence. Note: In the Ratings column, standardized stars appear in gold.

7. If necessary, you can add additional comments about your ratings in the **Justification** field.

8. Click **OK**. You will see the rating you chose for the source on the Links tab.

    Note: You can also see the rating in the People workspace. Click the Person tab; then select the sourced fact in the Individual and Shared Facts section. The rating appears on the Sources tab in the editing panel.

Linking a Source Citation to an Individual

Several individuals in your family tree might have the same citation information for a fact. For example, an entire family usually appears on the same census record page. Instead of entering the information (enumeration district, dwelling number, etc.) manually for each person, you can link all the citation information and relevant images and notes to as many people as you'd like.

1. Click the **Sources** button on the main toolbar.

2. Find the source citation you want to link to an individual and click it in the Source Citations list.

3. Click the **Links** tab.

4. Click the **New** button. The Link To window opens.

Tip

To unlink an individual from a source, click the person's name on the Links tab. Then click the **Unlink** icon (a broken link).

5. In the **Name** column, click the name of the individual you want to link the source to.

6. In the **Facts** column, click the fact you want to link the source citation to.

7. Click **OK**.

Merging Source Citations

If you have accidentally created multiple source citations for the same page of a book or the same household in a census, you can merge these source citations without losing any links to individuals or media items you've connected them to.

1. Click the **Sources** button on the main toolbar.

2. Find the source citation you want to replace and click it in the Source Citations list.

3. Click **Source>Replace Source Citation**. The Find Source Citation window opens.

4. In the list of source citations, click the citation that you want to keep.

5. Click **OK**. A message asks if you want to replace the source citation.

6. Click **Yes**. All individuals and media items associated with the first source citation will now be associated with the remaining citation.

Finding a Source Citation

You can quickly locate specific source citations using some helpful Family Tree Maker features.

Sorting All Source Citations

1. Click the **Sources** button on the main toolbar.

2. In **Source Groups**, choose one of these sorting methods from the **List by** drop-down list:

   - **All source citations.** This is the default sort. Every source citation in your tree is displayed in alphabetical order.

   - **Source title.** Citations are sorted according to the sources they are linked to.

   - **Repository.** Citations are sorted according to the repositories they are linked to.

   - **Person.** Citations are grouped by the individual they are linked to. (Because source citations may be linked to many individuals, each source can appear multiple times.)

3. Click a source, repository, or individual from the list. (A scroll icon appears next to each group that contains sources.)

   The Sources workspace displays every source citation that matches the sort.

Note: Family Tree Maker remembers the last sort you have chosen. For example, if you leave the Sources workspace to add a media item, when you come back to the Sources workspace your sort settings will not have changed.

Searching for a Specific Source Citation

1. Click the **Sources** button on the main toolbar.

2. In **Source Groups**, choose a sorting method from the **List by** drop-down list:

3. Enter the appropriate source name or keyword in the **Find** field.

   As you begin typing, you'll notice the highlight moves closer and closer to the appropriate source in the Source Groups panel.

> **Tip**
> You can also view your most recently accessed sources by clicking the **History** button in the Source Groups panel.

Chapter 5

Organizing Your Media Items

As you gather names, dates, and facts, you'll realize that these tell only part of your family's story. In order to really bring your ancestors to life, you'll want to illustrate your family history with photographs, important documents, and video and sound clips.

Family Tree Maker helps you organize your multimedia items all in one central location. You can link media items to specific individuals; record important notes and information about the items; use the images in selected trees, reports, and charts; and more.

In addition to enhancing printed trees, you can add images of the source records you've found. For example, you can include an image of a rare document, such as a land grant that is not available to the public. By scanning this document and keeping it in your family tree, you are preserving a copy of the original, making this resource available to others you share your research with, and storing a visual record of a source.

In This Chapter

- Adding Media Items to Your Tree
- Linking Media Items
- Arranging an Individual's Media Items
- Creating Media Categories
- Creating a Slide Show
- Finding a Media Item

Adding Media Items to Your Tree

You can add photos, images, sound files, videos, scanned documents, and much more to a tree. You can add items that are already on your computer or you can scan items directly into Family Tree Maker.

Note: For more information on adding media items for an individual, see chapter 3, "Building Your Tree."

Adding a Media Item from Your Computer

1. Go to the **Collection** tab on the Media workspace. The tab displays thumbnails of the media items you've added to your tree.

2. Click the **Add media** button in the toolbar above the editing panel.

Add media button ——

What Media Items Can I Add to My Tree?

Photographs are usually the first thing that comes to mind when we want to illustrate our family history. But don't limit yourself; many personal objects can be scanned or photographed. Here are some ideas of items you might want to include:

- Important records, such as birth and marriage certificates, censuses, passports, diplomas, obituaries, and Bibles.
- Photographs of heirlooms or items with sentimental value, such as jewelry, medals, trophies, artwork, quilts, christening outfits, and furniture.
- Images of ancestral houses and hometowns, businesses, maps, cemeteries, and headstones.
- Family documents, such as letters, funeral books, diaries, Christmas cards, awards, and newspaper and magazine articles.
- Sound clips of favorite songs, bedtime stories, and oral history interviews.

3. Choose **Add New Media** from the drop-down list. The Select Media Item window opens.

4. Use the **Look in** drop-down list to find the folder where the image is located. When you find the correct folder, double-click the folder to open it.

Tip

You can select multiple items by holding down the CTRL key and clicking on each image you want.

5. Click the image you want to add to your tree. The image will appear in the Preview box.

6. Click **Open**. A message asks whether you want to link the file to your tree or create a copy of the file.

Copy To Media Folder ☒

⦿ Copy this file to the media folder
for this tree and link to it there
○ Link to this file where it is
(without copying it)

Categories:
☐ Couple
☐ Documents
☑ Group Portrait
☐ Other
☐ Photos

[OK]
[Cancel]
[Help]
[Edit...]

☐ Always use this selection without prompting me

Tip

You might want to add copies of your media items to the Media folder so that all your heritage photos and other media items are gathered into one central location on your computer. This makes them easier to find and easier to back up in a group.

7. Click **Copy this file** to create an additional copy of the file in a Family Tree Maker media folder, or click **Link to this file** to leave the file where it is on your computer.

8. Click the checkbox for the category you want this item to belong to; you can select multiple categories. (For more information about categories, see "Creating Media Categories" on page 141.)

9. Click **OK**. The item is added to the Media workspace.

Note: When you add a picture or other media item to Family Tree Maker, the original file is not moved from its location on your computer.

Scanning an Image into Your Tree

If you have images you'd like to include in your tree that aren't already on your computer's hard drive, you don't have to scan the items to your computer and then manually add them into your tree; you can scan them directly into your tree.

When you scan an image, you can choose the resolution in which the item will be saved. The higher the resolution, or DPI (dots per inch), the sharper your image will look—and the larger the file size that will be created. If you plan on viewing your images online or sharing them via e-mail, you'll want to scan images at 72 to 150 DPI; if you want to print images in charts and reports, you'll want to use 200 to 300 DPI.

1. Make sure your scanner is connected to your computer and turned on.

2. Go to the Media workspace.

3. Click **Media>Scan Media**. Family Tree Maker connects to your scanner.

4. Choose any necessary scanner settings and click **Scan**. The image is added to the Media workspace.

Tip

To delete a media item, right-click the item in the Media workspace and choose **Delete Media** from the drop-down list.

Entering Information About a Media Item

You can enter captions, dates, and descriptions for the media items you have in your tree.

1. Go to the **Collection** tab on the Media workspace.

2. Double-click the media item you want to edit, or click the image and then click the **Detail** tab.

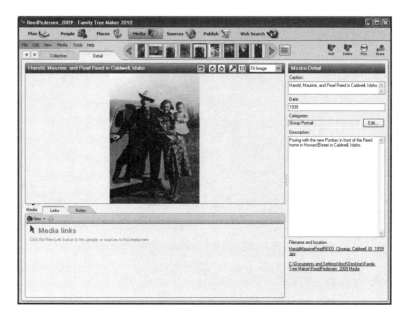

3. In the Media Detail editing panel, complete these fields as necessary:

In this field	Do this
Caption	Enter a brief title for the item. You can add more detailed information in the Description field.
Date	Enter a date of origin for the item.

In this field	Do this
Categories	Click **Edit**. Mark the checkbox for the category you want this item to belong to; you can select multiple categories. Click **OK**. (For more information about categories, see "Creating Media Categories" on page 141.)
Description	Enter a description of the item: for photos you may want to enter the names of the individuals or information about the location depicted; for heirlooms you may want to explain what the item is and its significance to your family.

Note: The "Filename and location" field shows the file name of the media item and where it is located on your computer. You can click the location link to open the folder in which the media item resides.

Changing a Media Item's File Name

Family Tree Maker lets you change a media item's actual file name on your hard drive—from within the software. This can be useful if you've imported a tree and its media files have been copied to your computer with generic names; you can use Family Tree Maker to make their file names more identifiable.

1. Go to the **Collection** tab on the Media workspace.

2. Do one of these options:

    • Right-click a media item and choose **Rename Media File** from the drop-down list.

    • Click a media item and choose **Media>Rename Media File**.

    The Rename Media File window opens.

3. Enter the new name for the file and click **OK**.

Viewing or Editing a Media Item

When you're viewing a media item, you can change the display of the image by rotating the image or zooming in and out on the image. You can also open the original file in a photo-editing program if you need to update it.

1. Go to the **Collection** tab on the Media workspace.

2. Double-click the media item you want to change the display for, or click the image, then click the **Detail** tab. The media item appears in the display area.

Image toolbar buttons

3. Use this chart to change the item's display:

To do this	Do this
Open the image in photo-editing software	Click the **Open file** button in the image toolbar. The image will open in the default program you use to edit images.
Rotate the image	Click the **Rotate right** button in the image toolbar to move the image in a clockwise direction; click the **Rotate left** button in the image toolbar to move the image in a counterclockwise direction.

To do this	Do this
Change the display size	Click the **Size to fit** button in the image toolbar to display the entire image in the current window; click the **Actual size** button in the image toolbar to show the actual size of the image.
Zoom in and out on the image	Choose a zoom setting from the drop-down list in the image toolbar.

Entering a Note About a Media Item

If you have additional information that won't fit in a media item's description, you can enter it in the item's notes. For example, a photo of your grandmother in her graduation robes may include notes about when and where she received her college education and what her degree was for.

1. Go to the **Collection** tab on the Media workspace.

2. Double-click the media item you want to add a note to, or click the image and then click the **Detail** tab.

3. Click the **Notes** tab at the bottom of the window.

4. Click "Enter media notes here." A cursor appears.

5. Enter a note. The notes are automatically saved as you type.

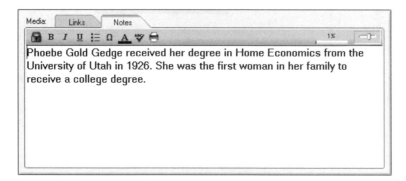

Note: For more information about using notes in Family Tree Maker, see "Adding Notes" on page 53.

Linking Media Items

You may have a family photo that includes several individuals in your tree. You don't have to add the picture to each individual; simply add it once to the Media workspace and then link it to the necessary individuals. You can also link media items to sources. Do you have a scanned image of your grandson's birth certificate? Add the image to your tree and quickly link it to the source you've created for this fact.

Linking a Media Item to an Individual

Not only can you link media items to specific individuals, but you can link these items to specific facts as well. For example, if you have a photograph or drawing of the ship on which your grandparents immigrated to America, you can link the picture to your grandparents and the fact about their immigration.

1. Go to the **Collection** tab on the Media workspace.

2. Double-click the media item you want to link to a person, or click the image and then click the **Detail** tab.

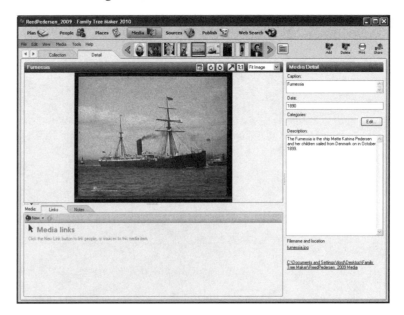

3. Click the **Links** tab at the bottom of the window.

4. Click the **New** button and choose **Link to Person** from the drop-down list. The Add Media Link window opens.

5. In the **Name** column, click the name of the individual you want to link the item to.

6. Do one of these options:

   - To link the item to the person, click **Link to person only**.

   - To link the item to a specific fact (such as birth or marriage), click **Link to person's fact**. Then, click the fact in the list below.

7. Click **OK**.

> **Tip**
> You can also link an item to a person on the Collection tab. Right-click the item and choose **Link to Person** from the drop-down list.

Linking a Media Item to a Source

You can link any type of media item to a relevant source. For example, if you find your grandfather's World War I draft registration card, you can save the image to your hard drive and link it to the source citation for his military service.

1. Go to the **Collection** tab on the Media workspace.

2. Double-click the media item you want to link to a source, or click the image and then click the **Detail** tab.

3. Click the **Links** tab at the bottom of the window.

4. Click the **New** button and choose **Link to Source Citation** from the drop-down list. The Find Source Citation window opens.

5. Choose one of these options from the **View by** drop-down list:

    • Choose **All source citations** to view every citation in your tree.

    • Choose **Source title** to group the source citations by their sources.

    • Choose **Repository** to group source citations by the location (such as a courthouse) they are found in.

    • Choose **Person** to view source citations for each individual in your tree.

    As you choose different source options from the drop-down list, you'll notice that the corresponding groups are displayed below.

6. Click the appropriate source or individual.

7. In the Source citations section, click the citation you want the media item to be linked to.

8. Click **Link to Citation**.

Arranging an Individual's Media Items

When you add media items for an individual, they are arranged in alphabetical order by default. If you want, you can change the order in which they appear on the Media tab. For example, you may want to display the pictures by date or age.

1. Go to the **Person** tab on the People workspace.

2. Make sure the individual you want to arrange media items for is displayed.

3. Click the **Media** tab at the bottom of the window. The tab shows thumbnails of any media items you've linked to this individual.

Move media buttons —

4. Click the item you want to move. In the Media toolbar, use the **Move Media Forward** and **Move Media Backwards** buttons to rearrange the media items. The items will remain in the sort you've chosen.

5. To return the media items to their default alphabetical sort, click the **Auto Sort Media** button in the Media toolbar.

Creating Media Categories

As you add each media item to your tree, you can assign it to categories. These categories make your media items easier to search for, sort, and view. You can use the default categories as they are, modify them, or create your own. If you decide to create your own categories, you want might want to set up a system before you add your media items. For example, you may want to have event categories (e.g., Weddings, Birthdays, Travel) or categories based on item types (e.g., Photos—Portraits, Movies—Holidays).

1. Go to the **Collection** tab on the Media workspace.

2. In the editing panel, click the **Edit** button. The Categories window opens.

3. Do one of these options:

   - To create a new category, click **Add**.

   - To edit a category, click the category name, then click **Edit**.

   The Add or Edit Category Name window opens.

4. Enter a name or edit the current name for the category.

5. Click **OK**.

6. When you finish adding and editing your categories, click **OK**.

Creating a Slide Show

You can create a slide show of pictures you've included in your tree—and even include a soundtrack. You can view your completed slide shows using *Windows Media Player*.

1. Click the **Media** button on the main toolbar.

2. Click **Media>Create Slide Show**. The slide show window opens.

Tip

You can also create a slide show for a specific individual by clicking the **Create slide show** button on the individual's Media tab.

3. Complete these fields as necessary:

In this field	Do this
Title	Enter a name for the slide show. (This will be the item's file name on your computer also.)
Images to include	If you want to include pictures from a specific category, choose the category name from the drop-down list. Click the **Include relationship media** checkbox to include images linked to relationships; click the **Include fact media** checkbox to include images linked to facts.
Image caption	Choose how you want captions displayed in the slide show: • **None.** No captions will be displayed. • **Use Captions Only.** If a caption has been entered for an image it will be displayed. • **Use Filenames Only.** File names will be displayed. • **Use Captions or Filenames.** If a caption has been entered for an image it will be displayed; if no caption has been entered, an image's filename will be displayed. Click the **Font** button to choose a font style, size, and color for captions and file names used in the slide show.
Movie size	Choose the display size of the slide show from the drop-down list. Note: The larger the movie, the more memory required.
Movie quality	Choose the display quality of the slide show from the drop-down list. Note: The better quality the movie, the more memory required.
Transition delay	Choose the number of seconds an image is displayed.
Sound track	If you would like to add music to the slide show, click the **Browse** button and locate the audio file you'd like to use. You can use any MP3 or Windows Media Audio (.wma) file.

4. Click **Next**. A window opens, displaying all the images you've chosen. You can change the order in which images appear or delete images you don't want.

5. Click **Next**. A preview window opens.

6. Do one of these options:

   - To save the slide show to your tree, click **Add slide show to the media collection**.

   - To view the finished slide show in *Windows Media Player*, click **Launch slide show in Windows Media Player**.

7. Click **Finish**. A message asks whether you want to save the file to your tree or save the file to another location.

Save To Media Folder
⊙ Save this file to the media folder for this tree and link to it there   [OK]
○ Save the slide show file in another location   [Cancel]   [Help]
Categories:
☑ None   [Edit...]
☐ Audio
☐ Census Records
☐ Documents
☐ Other
☐ Always use this selection without prompting me

8. Click **Save this file to the media folder** to save the slide show to the Family Tree Maker media folder, or click **Save the slide show in another location** to choose a location.

9. Click the checkbox for the category you want this item to belong to; you can select multiple categories. (For more information about categories, see "Creating Media Categories" on page 141.)

10. Click **OK**. The item is added to the Media workspace.

Finding a Media Item

Eventually, you may have so many media items stored in your tree that you have difficulty finding a particular item. You can quickly locate specific items using some helpful features.

Sorting All Media Items

1. Go to the **Collection** tab on the Media workspace.

2. In **Groups**, choose one of these sorting methods from the **List by** drop-down list:

    •   **All media.** This is the default sort. Every photo, record image, video, and audio file in your tree is displayed in alphabetical order.

    •   **Media category.** Items will be sorted according to the category you assigned them. (Because items can be assigned to more than one category, they can appear in multiple sorts.)

    •   **Source title.** Items are sorted according to the sources they are linked to. (Because items may be linked to more than one source, they can appear in multiple sorts.)

    •   **Person.** Items are sorted according to the individuals they are linked to. (Because items may be linked to many individuals, they can appear multiple times.)

3. Click a category, source, or individual from the list. (A photo icon appears next to each group that contains media items.)

   The Media workspace displays every item that matches the sort.

   Note: Family Tree Maker remembers the last sort you have chosen. For example, if you leave the Media workspace to view a map, when you come back to the Media workspace your sort settings will not have changed.

Searching for a Specific Media Item

1. Go to the **Collection** tab on the Media workspace.

2. In **Groups**, choose a sorting method from the **List by** drop-down list.

3. Enter the appropriate name or keyword in the **Find** field.

    As you begin typing, you'll notice the highlight moves closer and closer to the appropriate media item in the Groups panel.

> **Tip**
>
> You can also view your most recently accessed media items by clicking the **History** button in the Groups panel.

Chapter 6

Placing Your Family on the Map

As you gather the names and dates of important events in your ancestors' lives, you'll also record the locations where these events took place—the homes, towns and cities, states, and countries that shaped their daily lives.

Often, these locations exist only as names in a report or on a pedigree chart. Family Tree Maker brings these ancestral homelands to life by letting you virtually visit each place in your tree. For example, you can see satellite images and maps of the town in Denmark where your grandfather was born, the apartment house in Chicago where your great-grandparents lived, or even the lake where you went swimming with your cousins every summer.

Family Tree Maker gives you the chance to become familiar with lands that you may never be able to visit in real life. See where your family lived, follow their immigration path, or watch their progress as they move from city to city, sometimes across the country.

In This Chapter

- Viewing a Map
- Viewing Facts Associated with a Location
- Viewing Locations Associated with People
- Printing a Map
- Standardizing Locations
- Changing a Location's Name
- Entering GPS Coordinates for a Location
- Entering a Display Name for a Location

Microsoft® Bing™ Maps

Family Tree Maker has partnered with Microsoft *Bing Maps* to give you access to some of the most exciting technology available today. *Bing Maps* takes you beyond typical road maps by combining them with special satellite and aerial imagery to let you experience the world as it looks today.

As you visit different locations, you'll notice that the level of detail that you can see for each town, region, or country varies. In some areas you can zoom in close enough to see cars, rooftops, and street intersections; in other areas your view will disappear when you get within a mile of the location. Fortunately, *Bing Maps* is updated regularly and regions that may not have many images now will in the future. The most detailed views are of the United States, the United Kingdom, Canada, and Australia.

And if you're worried about how these satellite images may affect your privacy, you'll be glad to know that these images are not "live." In addition, you may be able to see details of houses, roads, and trees, but the images are of a low enough resolution that you can't read signs or identify people.

Note: This feature is subject to change without notice.

Each time you enter a place name for a fact or event, Family Tree Maker adds this location to a "master list" of locations. To view this master list, simply go to the Places workspace. You can then view maps and satellite images of a location, identify individuals in your tree who are associated with certain locations, and more.

It is also a good idea to regularly check this list and make sure that you're entering location names consistently throughout your tree; if necessary, you can quickly edit a location in the Places workspace. (For more information on the Places workspace, see page 29).

Viewing a Map

The interactive online maps in Family Tree Maker are easy to navigate using a few simple tools. You can zoom in and out on the map, change the type of map you're viewing, and more.

Note: You must be connected to the Internet to use the online mapping feature.

1. Click the **Places** button on the main toolbar.

2. To access a map, click a location in the **Places** panel.

    Immediately, a road map (the default view) will appear in the display area, the specified location centered on the map and marked with a red pushpin. In the top, left-hand corner of the map you'll notice the Map Tools. These tools remain on the map regardless of which view you're looking at.

Tip

You can hide the Map Tools by clicking the arrow button on the far right side of the toolbar.

To change the type of map you're viewing, simply click the appropriate view in the Map Tools.

3. Click **Aerial** to view a satellite image of the location.

4. In the aerial view, you can click **Labels** to switch between the aerial view and a combination of the road view and the aerial view.

5. Click **Road** to display the street map again.

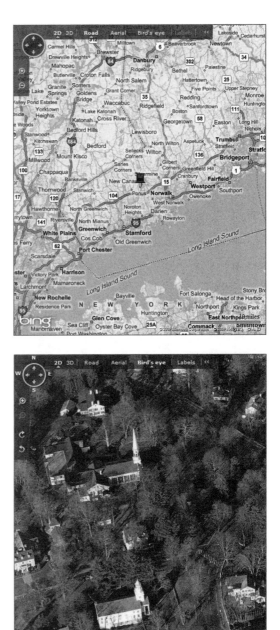

6. To see a street-level view of the location, click **Bird's eye**. Click the points of the compass on the Map Tools to change the direction you are viewing.

Note: At this time, the bird's-eye view is available only for parts of the United States and United Kingdom.

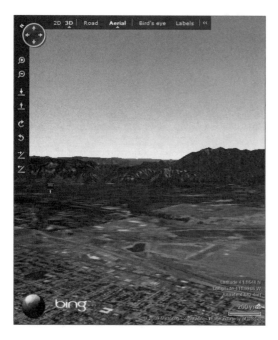

7. Click **3D** to change the map from two dimensions to three. You can use the 3-D mode in the road and aerial views. (The first time you click the 3D button, you will be prompted to download additional plug-in software from Microsoft. You can't view 3-D maps without this software.)

To rotate the image, press the **CTRL** key on your keyboard and hold down the left mouse button as you move the mouse around. Maneuvering in 3-D can be tricky, so it might take some practice before you're able to view the map exactly as you'd like.

Note: You can also change the 3-D view by clicking the Rotate camera and Tilt buttons.

Tip

You can also use the arrow keys on your keyboard to move the map.

Moving Around a Map

If the part of the map that you want to see isn't available in the current view, you can quickly view any adjacent parts of the map by "dragging" it. Move the cursor over the map. When the cursor shape changes to a hand, click and hold down either mouse key. Now drag the map wherever you need.

Zooming In and Out on a Map

You can use the plus and minus buttons on the Map Tools to zoom in and out on the displayed map.

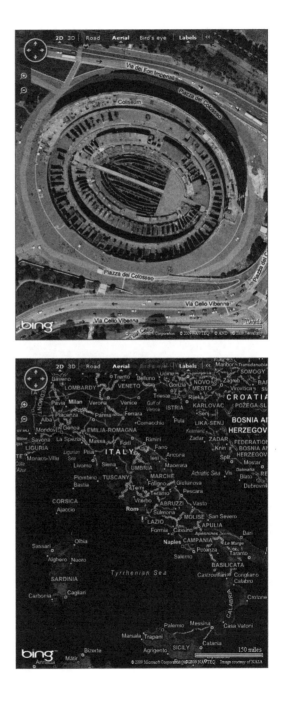

1. Click the plus sign (+) button to magnify the map one level at a time; click the button and hold the mouse button down to rapidly zoom in on the map.

2. Click the minus sign (-) button to minimize the map one level at a time; click the button and hold the mouse button down to rapidly zoom out on the map.

    Note: If you try to view an area where satellite imagery is not available, the map will change to a white screen.

Finding Places of Interest

In addition to viewing event locations you've added to your project, Family Tree Maker lets you search for nearby places of interest such as libraries, cemeteries, and churches. If you're planning a genealogy research trip, you can use Family Tree Maker to view all the cemeteries and churches in your ancestor's hometown. You can also type in other attractions and sites you want to search for—try entering "hotels", "parks", or even "gas station".

1. Click the **Places** button on the main toolbar.

2. If you have already entered the location in your project, click its name in the Places panel; otherwise, enter the location's name in the blank field above the map (the one on the right).

3. Choose a location type (such as cemeteries) from the drop-down list and click **Go**. (You can also type in your own search term in the drop-down list.) Blue pushpins will appear for each location that matches your search.

4. Move the mouse over each pushpin to see a name and address for the location (if available).

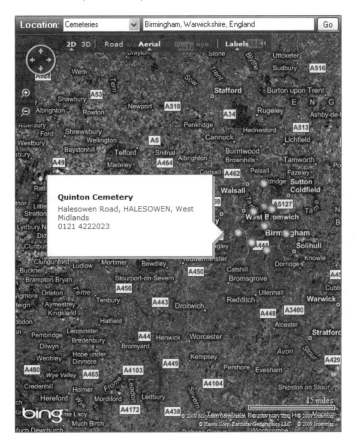

Viewing Facts Associated with a Location

When you enter a fact for an individual, you have the option to also enter the location where the event occurred. Family Tree Maker lets you easily view all the events that took place at a certain location—and view the people who are associated with each event.

1. Click the **Places** button on the main toolbar.

2. Click a location in the **Places** panel.

Individuals associated with the location

In the panel on the right side of the window, you'll now see the name of the location and underneath it, a list of names. The individuals in the list all have life events associated with the location.

3. Do one of these options:

- If you want to see the event that occurred at this location for a specific individual, click the plus sign (+) next to the individual's name.

- If you want to see the events that occurred at this location for all the individuals, click the **Expand all items** button on the toolbar and choose **Expand all**. (Click the **Collapse all items** button to close all the events.)

- If you want location events to always appear in the panel, click the **Expand all items** button on the toolbar and choose **Expand All on Load**.

Tip

You can print a report about the events and people associated with a location. For more information, see "Place Usage Report" on page 266.

Expand button

Collapse button

Note: You can click the Go To button to access the highlighted event or individual in the People workspace.

Viewing Locations Associated with People

Maps can be one of the most useful family history resources you'll use when tracing an ancestor. Family Tree Maker lets you see at a glance all the locations that are connected with a specific individual or family. You can view locations important to an individual, track migration patterns, and maybe discover where to locate more records. You can even print these maps to take with you on research trips or to share with others.

Viewing Locations for an Individual

1. Click the **Places** button on the main toolbar.

2. In the **Places** panel, choose "Person" from the **List by** drop-down list.

3. Click the name of the individual whose locations you want to see.

   A labeled aerial map will appear in the display area; the location associated with the individual's birth is indicated by a green marker, and the individual's death is indicated by a red marker.

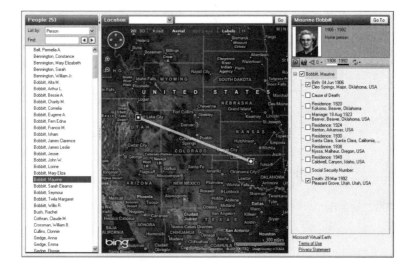

To the right of the map is a list of every fact—and its location—you've entered for an individual.

4. Click the checkbox next to a fact to include the location of that event on the map.

5. Move the mouse over each marker to see the location's name and the fact associated with it.

Viewing Locations for a Family

1. Click the **Places** button on the main toolbar.

2. In the **Places** panel, choose "Person" from the **List by** drop-down list and click the name of an individual.

3. To view the locations associated with the individual's immediate family (parents, siblings, spouse, and children), click the **Include immediate family** button in the mapping toolbar.

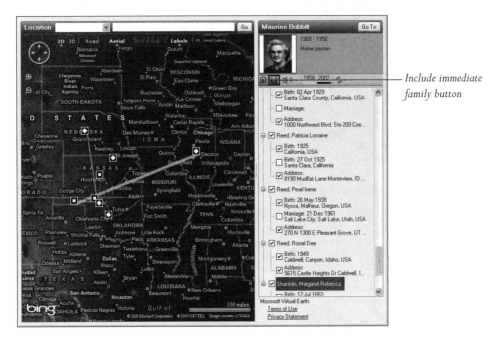

Include immediate family button

4. Click an individual's name to the right of the map to highlight his or her life events on the map.

The migration path for the individual is indicated by a thick line.

5. To view the locations associated with an individual's ancestors (up
    to four generations), click the **Ancestor generations** button in
    the mapping toolbar and choose the number of generations you
    want to display from the drop-down list.

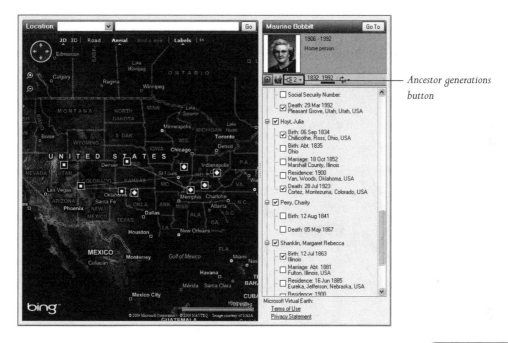

Ancestor generations button

A labeled aerial map will appear in the display area; birth locations are indicated by green markers, and death locations are
indicated by red markers; the migration path for each individual
is indicated by a colored line.

> **Tip**
>
> You can change the
> color of a migration
> path by clicking the
> line color buttons
> in the mapping
> toolbar.

Printing a Map

Family Tree Maker lets you print maps directly from the software, whether it's an aerial shot of your ancestor's farm or the migration path your great-grandfather took across the country.

Note: You can print two- and three-dimensional maps, but not bird's-eye views.

1. On the Places workspace, access the map you want to print. The map will print as it is shown in the display window (without the map tools). You may want to resize the workspace to display more of the map.

2. In the map toolbar, click the **Print** button and choose **Print Map** from the drop-down list. The Print window opens.

   Just like printing from any other application, you can choose a printer, select the number of copies to print, and more.

3. Click **OK**.

Maps and Family History

While maps are often sought for their visual appeal, they also can offer clues to locating records and information about your family. Using a variety of geographic resources, you can follow your ancestors' lives as they move from city to city, state to state, and sometimes country to country. Maps can also help you learn where local record repositories, courthouses, and cemeteries are located.

Here are some examples of different types of resources you might want to locate:

- **Atlases.** Contain groups of maps for states, cities, and more.
- **Gazetteers or geographical dictionaries.** In addition to place names, these include information about various land features such as mountains, lakes, and rivers, and sometimes even cemeteries.
- **Road maps.** Show roads, highways, railroads, cities, and more.
- **Topographical maps.** Show land features, including hills, mountains, and bodies of water.
- **Political maps.** Show boundaries for states, counties, cities.

You will want to locate maps that show the land as it existed when your ancestors lived there. Because state, county, and city boundaries change over time, the more historically accurate the map is, the more useful it will be.

Standardizing Locations

Family Tree Maker contains a locations database of more than 3 million place names. When you import a GEDCOM or other genealogy file, or you manually enter a location name into your tree, Family Tree Maker automatically checks each place name against its database, looking for misspellings and missing data, such as missing counties. If any errors are found, or if the place does not match any locations in the Family Tree Maker database, a question mark icon appears next to the location's name in the Places workspace.

To keep your Family Tree Maker tree accurate *and* to make sure locations are recorded the same way every time they're entered,

Tip

If you want to keep a location name "as is" and keep it from being identified as an error, click the name in the **Places** panel and choose **Place>Ignore Place Warning**.

you'll want to examine each "unidentified" location and make any necessary changes. In some cases, you'll want to leave the name exactly as it is. For example, if the town or city no longer exists, or the county boundaries have changed over the years, you'll want to keep the location's name as you found it in the record. You can identify locations one at a time or as a group.

Note: For information on the best practices for entering places, see "Entering Locations in Family Tree Maker " on page 46.

Checking a Single Location Against the Database

If you see a question mark icon next to a place name in your tree, you can try to identify the location in the Family Tree Maker database.

1. Click the **Places** button on the main toolbar.

2. Click an unidentified location in the **Places** panel (one with a question mark icon next to it). In the panel on the right side of the window, you'll see the location's name and any people and events associated with it.

3. Click the question mark icon next to the place name in the editing panel. The Resolve Place Name window opens; the "Suggested place names" section lists the locations that most closely match the location in your tree.

4. Do one of these options:

- If you find a location that matches the location in your tree, click its name in the "Suggested place names" section and then click **Replace**.

- If you do not find a location that matches the location in your tree, click **Ignore**.

Whether you choose to accept or ignore the suggested name change, the location has been "identified," and the question mark next to the location's name will disappear.

Tip
You can also enter a new location and click the **Search** button to have Family Tree Maker search its location database again.

Checking Multiple Locations Against the Database

If you've imported a new tree or merged another person's tree into your own, you'll likely have many place names that don't match the other locations in your tree. Instead of updating each location one at a time, you can resolve many issues at one time.

1. Click **Tools>Resolve All Place Names**.

2. If you want to back up your file before you update your locations, click **Yes**. The Backup window opens. Change any options as necessary and click **OK**.

   The Resolve All Place Names window opens. Each location that Family Tree Maker doesn't recognize is listed—along with a suggested replacement location.

3. For each location listed, complete these fields:

In this field	Do this
Unrecognized Place Name	Click this checkbox if you want to keep the place name as it is currently listed.
Suggested Place Name	Click this checkbox if you want to change the current location's name to the suggested name.
Desc.	Click this checkbox if you want Family Tree Maker to move this place name from a fact's Place field to its Description field.
Ignore	Click this checkbox if you want the unrecognized place name to be considered "recognized." The place name will not be considered an error in the future.
Other	If the suggested place name is incorrect, or you want to see other choices that might match the current place name, click **Other**. The Resolve Place Name window opens. Search for the location, or scroll through the suggested names. If you find the name you're looking for, click the name. Then click **Replace** to use the selected name.

4. When you've chosen an option for each location, click **OK**.

Changing a Location's Name

Family Tree Maker helps you standardize your place names by matching each entry against a location database. However, you may have locations in your tree that are non-standard—ones where you've entered addresses or descriptions, or places that don't match the Family Tree Maker database. If you discover that you've entered one of these locations incorrectly or just need to update a place name, Family Tree Maker lets you update every occurrence of the place in one step. For example, if you've included the name of a cemetery in a location, you can update the place so that the cemetery name is part of the description and only the city is the place name.

> Note: You can change a location's name in the Places workspace or in the People workspace. If you change the name in the People workspace, you can choose whether you want all instances of the location to be changed or only that specific instance. When you change the name in the Places workspace, every instance of the name will be changed.

1. Click the **Places** button on the main toolbar.

2. Double-click the location's name in the **Places** panel, or click the location's name and click **Place>Change Place Name**. The Change Place Name window opens. At the top of the window, you'll see how many facts are linked to this location.

3. In the **New place name** field, enter the updated name for the location.

Because the name is being changed in the Places workspace, all instances of this location will be changed to the new place name entered.

4. If you want, you can click the **Add description text** checkbox and enter a description for the location. This might be information you're taking out of the original location name—like an address.

5. When you've finished updating the name, click **OK**.

Entering GPS Coordinates for a Location

Although the online mapping feature is able to recognize millions of locations, there are times when it won't be able to identify the exact location of a place you've entered. Perhaps your relatives are buried in a rural cemetery that doesn't appear on the map. Or perhaps census records show that your family lived in a township that no longer exists. You can set the exact position for the location using GPS (Global Positioning System) coordinates.

1. Click the **Places** button on the main toolbar.

2. In the **Places** panel, click the name of the location to which you want to add GPS coordinates.

3. Place your cursor in the **Location** field and then click the **Location calculator** button that appears.

Location calculator button

GPS (Global Positioning System) Coordinates

GPS receivers can display a location's coordinates in a variety of formats. Although Family Tree Maker uses the Decimal Degrees (DD) format, it contains a Location Calculator that will convert other latitude and longitude coordinates to the default format. This example shows what the coordinates for Trafalgar Square in London, England, look like in the formats used by Family Tree Maker.

- Degrees:Minutes:Seconds (DMS)—51° 30' 28" N, 0° 7' 41" W
- Degrees:Decimal Minutes (DM)—51° 30.468' N, 0° 7.686' W
- Decimal Degrees (DD)—51.507778, -0.128056

The Location Calculator window opens. You can enter the coordinates in degrees:minutes:seconds, degrees:decimal minutes, or decimal degrees.

4. Enter the coordinates for the location and click **OK**.

Entering a Display Name for a Location

Recording locations in a complete and consistent manner is an important part of creating a quality family history. Unfortunately, those long location names can become unwieldy and clutter your reports and charts. Family Tree Maker lets you enter your own shortened or abbreviated display names that can be used for charts and reports. For example, instead of a birthplace being listed as Heidelberg, Baden-Württemberg, Germany, you can enter Heidelberg, Germany, as the display name.

1. Click the **Places** button on the main toolbar.

2. In the **Places** panel, choose "Place" from the **List by** drop-down list.

3. Click the name of the location you want to change.

4. In the **Short** field enter a display name.

Chapter 7

Creating Trees and Charts

After spending time gathering, compiling, and entering your family's history, it's time to reward yourself, show off your hard work, and bring your family history to life. Family Tree Maker offers a wide variety of family tree charts to help you. Add your own personal touch by customizing the charts with attractive backgrounds, colors, photos, fonts, and more. These charts help you quickly view the relationships between family members and are also a fun way to share your discoveries— hang a framed family tree in your home, print out multiple copies to share at a family reunion, or e-mail customized charts to distant relatives.

As you begin creating your own charts, you might want to experiment with various formatting options, print out the different versions, and see what you like best.

Pedigree Charts

The pedigree chart is the standard tool of genealogists. It shows the direct ancestors of one individual—parents, grandparents, great-grandparents, and so on.

Standard Pedigree Charts

In the standard pedigree chart, the primary individual is shown at the left of the tree, with ancestors branching off to the right—paternal ancestors on top and maternal ancestors on the bottom.

> **Tip**
> Too much information may make a chart almost unreadable. Either add less information or consider creating multiple charts.

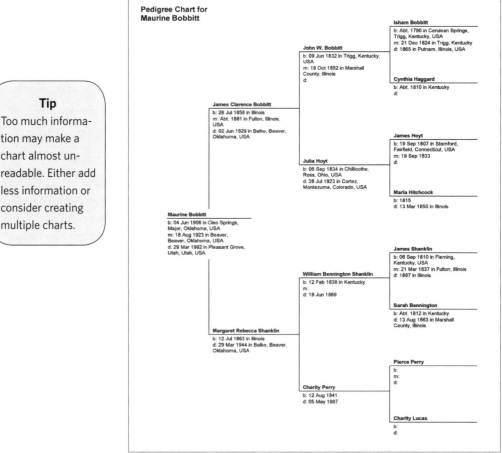

Figure 7-1. A standard pedigree chart with the default settings

The Official Guide to Family Tree Maker 2010

The chart in figure 7-1 is the default pedigree chart in Family Tree Maker. In figure 7-2, the chart has been enhanced using one of the custom templates that comes with Family Tree Maker.

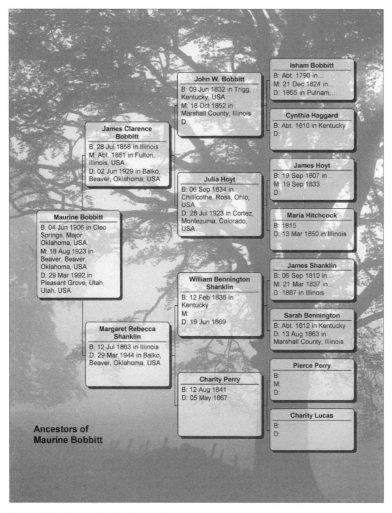

Figure 7-2. A standard pedigree chart using a custom template

Figure 7-3 shows another customized pedigree chart. In this example, the chart is horizontal and includes box borders, a page border, and thumbnail images.

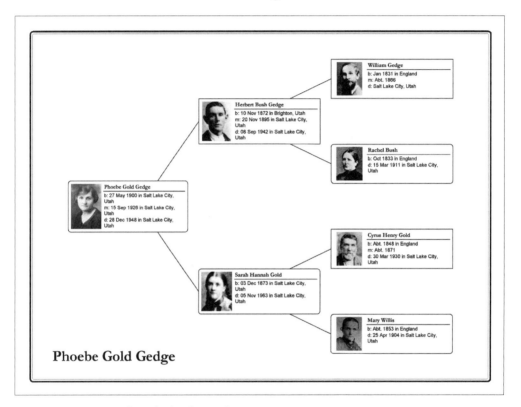

Figure 7-3. A customized standard pedigree chart

Note: All charts are based on the last individual you were viewing in your tree. To change the primary individual in the chart, click a different individual's name in the mini pedigree tree above the chart or click the Index of Individuals button and choose the person you want.

Creating a Standard Pedigree Chart

1. Go to the **Collection** tab on the Publish workspace.

2. In **Publication Types**, click **Charts**.

3. Double-click **Pedigree Chart**, or select its icon and then click the **Detail** tab.

4. Do one of these options:

   • To choose your own formatting options, see "Customizing a Chart" on page 208.

   • To apply a template to the chart, see "Using a Custom Template" on page 225.

5. If you have people in your tree who have intermarried (for example, cousins who married), click the **Include duplicate ancestor lines** checkbox to have these individuals appear in every instance where they occur in your tree.

6. Click **Generate Chart**.

Vertical Pedigree Charts

In the vertical pedigree chart, the primary individual is shown at the bottom of the page, with his or her ancestors branching above the individual—paternal ancestors on the left and maternal ancestors on the right.

The chart in figure 7-4 is the default vertical pedigree chart in Family Tree Maker. In figure 7-5, the chart has been customized with a new title, different fonts, additional dates and places, thumbnail

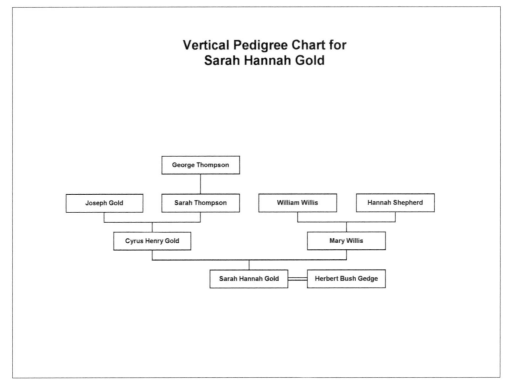

Figure 7-4. A vertical pedigree chart with the default settings

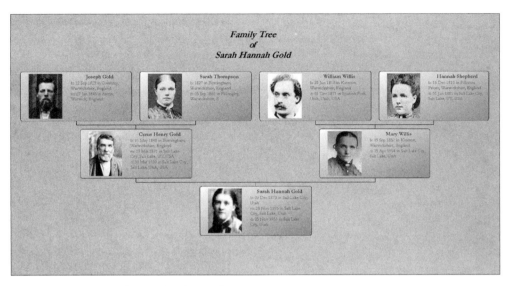

Figure 7-5. A customized vertical pedigree chart

photos, and a background image (one of several) that comes with
Family Tree Maker.

> Note: All charts are based on the last individual you
> were viewing in your tree. To change the primary
> individual in the chart, click a different individual's
> name in the mini pedigree tree above the chart or
> click the Index of Individuals button and choose
> the person you want.

Creating a Vertical Pedigree Chart

1. Go to the **Collection** tab on the Publish workspace.

2. In **Publication Types**, click **Charts**.

3. Double-click **Vertical Pedigree Chart**, or select its icon and then click the **Detail** tab.

4. Do one of these options:

- To choose your own formatting options, see "Customizing a Chart" on page 208.

- To apply a template to the chart, see "Using a Custom Template" on page 225.

5. Click **Generate Chart**.

Descendant Charts

The descendant chart shows the direct descendants of an individual—children, grandchildren, great-grandchildren, and so on. The primary individual is shown at the top of the chart, with descendants underneath in horizontal rows.

The chart in figure 7-6 shows a default descendant chart. The customized descendant chart in figure 7-7 uses a family photograph that has been uploaded to Family Tree Maker as the background image, and the box borders and fonts have been changed.

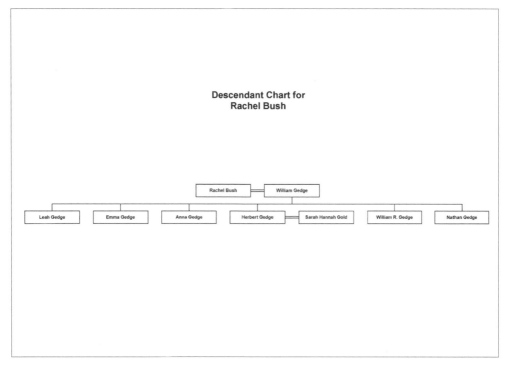

Figure 7-6. A descendant chart with the default settings

Figure 7-7. A customized descendant chart

Note: All charts are based on the last individual you were viewing in your tree. To change the primary individual in the chart, click a different individual's name in the mini pedigree tree above the chart or click the Index of Individuals button and choose the person you want.

Creating a Descendant Chart

1. Go to the **Collection** tab on the Publish workspace.

2. In **Publication Types**, click **Charts**.

3. Double-click **Descendant Chart**, or select its icon and then click the **Detail** tab.

4. Do one of these options:

   - To choose your own formatting options, see "Customizing a Chart" on page 208.

   - To apply a template to the chart, see "Using a Custom Template" on page 225.

5. Click **Generate Chart**.

Hourglass Charts

An hourglass chart shows both the ancestors and descendants of a specific individual. The individual appears in the middle of the chart, with ancestors branching off in a shape similar to an hourglass.

Note: Because of its shape and the number of individuals included, most hourglass charts will look best as posters. (To learn how to print a poster at a copy shop, see "Printing a Poster" on page 232.)

Standard Hourglass Charts

In the standard hourglass chart, the primary individual appears in the middle of the chart, with ancestors branching above and descendants extending below the person.

The chart in figure 7-8 shows the default hourglass chart in Family Tree Maker; it is laid out as a poster and uses landscape orientation. In figure 7-9, the default poster chart has been enhanced using one of the custom templates that comes with Family Tree Maker. Notice the white spaces running vertically and horizontally across the pages. These show the margins of a standard 8½" by 11" sheet of paper. If you want to print the tree at home, you can use these guides to tape the pages together.

You can also create standard hourglass charts that are useful for including in family history books. When you use the book layout, the chart is condensed into a series of individual family trees that appear on separate pages. The chart in figure 7-10 shows one page of a multi-page book-layout chart. Notice the numbered boxes above and to the right of the chart. When you are viewing the chart in Family Tree Maker, you can click one of these boxes to access that page of the chart. And when your chart is printed out, the numbered boxes help you navigate to related individuals found on other pages in the chart.

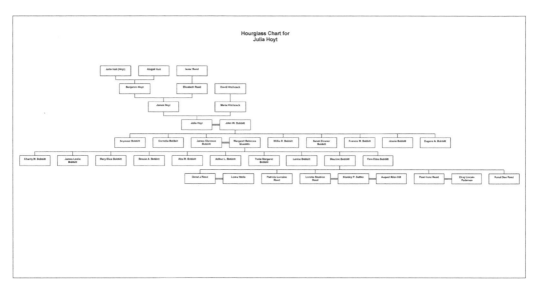

Figure 7-8. A default hourglass chart—three generations of ancestors and of descendants

Figure 7-9. A standard hourglass poster chart using a custom template

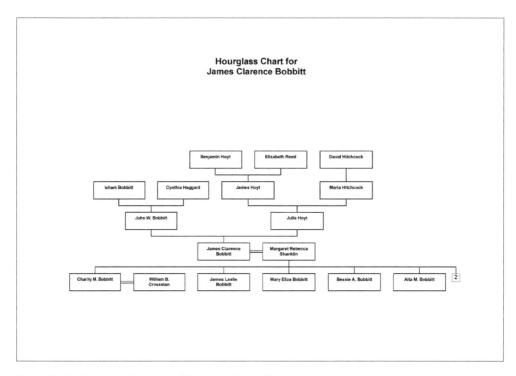

Figure 7-10. One page of a standard hourglass book chart

Note: All charts are based on the last individual you were viewing in your tree. To change the primary individual in the chart, click a different individual's name in the mini pedigree tree above the chart or click the Index of Individuals button and choose the person you want.

Creating a Standard Hourglass Chart

1. Go to the **Collection** tab on the Publish workspace.

2. In **Publication Types**, click **Charts**.

3. Double-click **Hourglass Chart**, or select its icon and then click the **Detail** tab.

4. Do one of these options:

    *   To choose your own formatting options, see "Customizing a Chart" on page 208.

    *   To apply a template to the chart, see "Using a Custom Template" on page 225.

5. Click **Generate Chart**.

Horizontal Hourglass Charts

In the horizontal hourglass chart, the primary individual appears in the middle of the chart with ancestors branching to the right and descendants extending to the left of the person. The chart in figure 7-11 shows the default horizontal hourglass chart. The customized chart in figure 7-12 uses a map as the background image, thumbnail images have been added, and siblings and spouses have been removed.

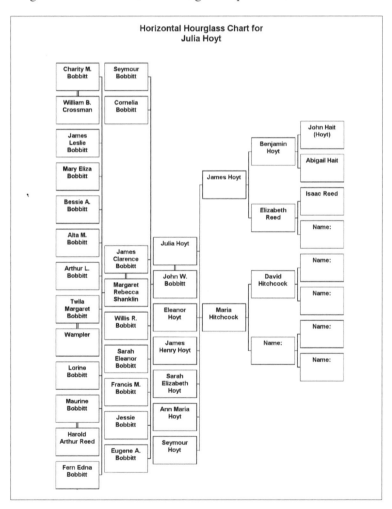

Figure 7-11. A default horizontal hourglass chart

Figure 7-12. A customized horizontal hourglass chart

Note: All charts are based on the last individual you
were viewing in your tree. To change the primary
individual in the chart, click a different individual's
name in the mini pedigree tree above the chart or
click the Index of Individuals button and choose
the person you want.

Creating a Horizontal Hourglass Chart

1. Go to the **Collection** tab on the Publish workspace.

2. In **Publication Types**, click **Charts**.

3. Double-click **Horizontal Hourglass Chart**, or select its icon and then click the **Detail** tab.

4. Do one of these options:

    •   To choose your own formatting options, see "Customizing a Chart" on page 208.

    •   To apply a template to the chart, see "Using a Custom Template" on page 225.

5. Click **Generate Chart**.

Bow Tie Charts

In the bow tie chart, the primary individual appears in the middle with paternal ancestors branching off to the left and maternal ancestors branching to the right.

> Note: Because of its shape and the number of individuals included, this chart is available only in poster layout. (To learn how to print a poster at a copy shop, see "Printing a Poster" on page 232.)

The chart in figure 7-13 shows the default bow tie chart in Family Tree Maker. In figure 7-14, the chart has been customized with larger boxes, a background image, and additional facts.

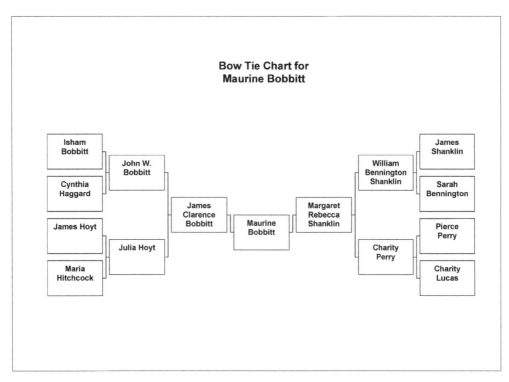

Figure 7-13. A default bow tie chart

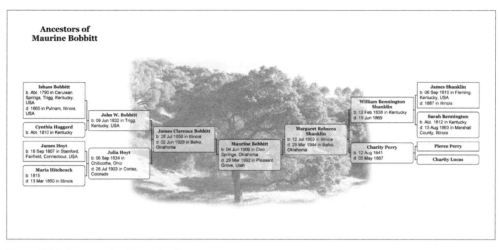

Figure 7-14. A customized bow tie chart

Note: All charts are based on the last individual you were viewing in your tree. To change the primary individual in the chart, click a different individual's name in the mini pedigree tree above the chart or click the Index of Individuals button and choose the person you want.

Creating a Bow Tie Chart

1. Go to the **Collection** tab on the Publish workspace.

2. In **Publication Types**, click **Charts**.

3. Double-click **Bow Tie Chart**, or select its icon and then click
    the **Detail** tab.

4. Do one of these options:

    •   To choose your own formatting options, see "Customizing a
        Chart" on page 208.

    •   To apply a template to the chart, see "Using a Custom Tem-
        plate" on page 225.

5. Click **Generate Chart**.

Fan Charts

The 180 fan chart shows the primary individual at the bottom of the chart with his or her ancestors arranged above in a semi-circle, one generation per level.

Note: Because of its shape and the number of individuals included, this chart is available only in poster layout. (To learn how to print a poster at a copy shop, see "Printing a Poster" on page 232.)

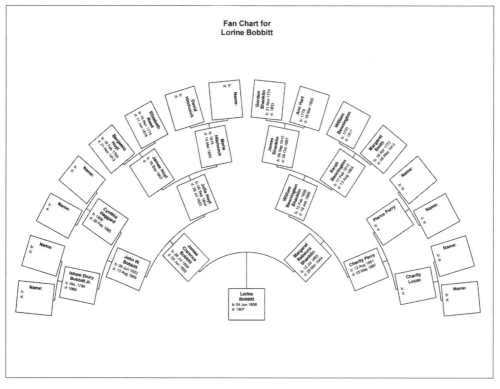

Figure 7-15. A default 180 fan chart

The chart in figure 7-15 shows the default fan chart. In figure 7-16, the chart has been enhanced using one of the custom templates that comes with Family Tree Maker. The chart spreads over four sheets, which have been combined into one poster-size chart.

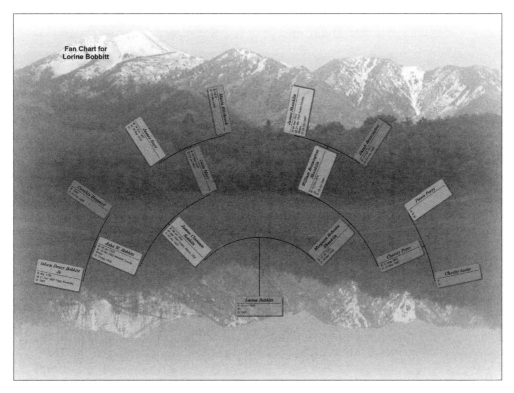

Figure 7-16. A custom 180 fan chart, stretched over four sheets of paper

Note: All charts are based on the last individual you were viewing in your tree. To change the primary individual in the chart, click a different individual's name in the mini pedigree tree above the chart or click the Index of Individuals button and choose the person you want.

Creating a Fan Chart

1. Go to the **Collection** tab on the Publish workspace.

2. In **Publication Types**, click **Charts**.

3. Double-click **180 Fan Chart**, or select its icon and then click the **Detail** tab.

4. Do one of these options:

- To choose your own formatting options, see "Customizing a Chart" on page 208.

- To apply a template to the chart, see "Using a Custom Template" on page 225.

5. Click **Generate Chart**.

Family Tree Charts

In the family tree chart, the primary individual appears at the bottom of the chart, with ancestors branching above him or her in a shape similar to a tree.

> Note: Because of its shape and the number of individuals included, this chart is available only in poster layout. (To learn how to print a poster at a copy shop, see "Printing a Poster" on page 232.)

The chart in figure 7-17 shows the default tree chart. In figure 7-18, the chart has been customized with thumbnails, a historical background photo, and new box borders and fonts.

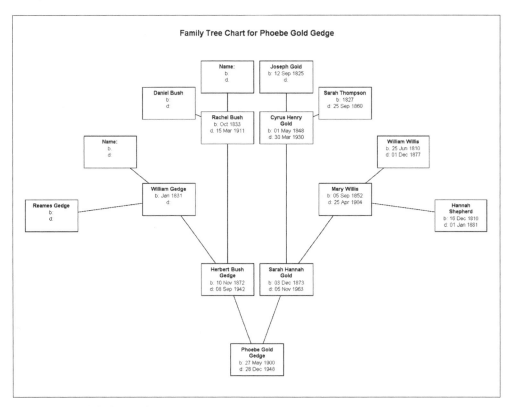

Figure 7-17. A default tree chart

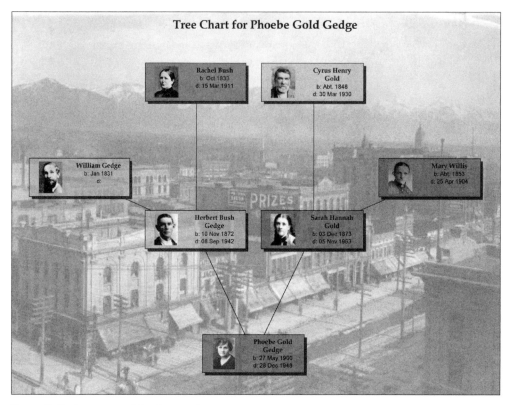

Figure 7-18. A customized family tree chart

Note: All charts are based on the last individual you were viewing in your tree. To change the primary individual in the chart, click a different individual's name in the mini pedigree tree above the chart or click the Index of Individuals button and choose the person you want.

Creating a Family Tree Chart

1. Go to the **Collection** tab on the Publish workspace.

2. In **Publication Types**, click **Charts**.

3. Double-click **Family Tree Chart**, or select its icon and then click the **Detail** tab.

4. Do one of these options:

    *   To choose your own formatting options, see "Customizing a Chart" on page 208.

    *   To apply a template to the chart, see "Using a Custom Template" on page 225.

5. Click **Generate Chart**.

Extended Family Charts

The extended family chart can display every individual you've entered in your tree or just the people you select. The chart is arranged so that each generation appears on a separate horizontal row: children, parents, and grandparents, etc.

> Note: Because of its shape and the number of individuals included, this chart is available only in poster layout. (To learn how to print a poster at a copy shop, see "Printing a Poster" on page 232.)

The chart in figure 7-19 shows part of a default extended family chart. In figure 7-20, the chart has been customized with new box borders and fonts and a template background image.

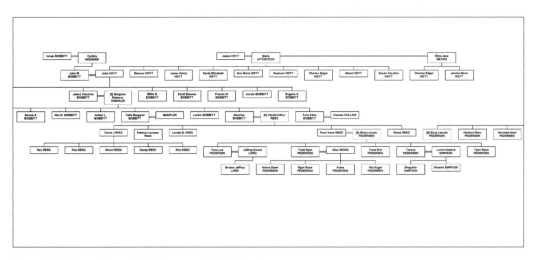

Figure 7-19. A section of a default extended family chart

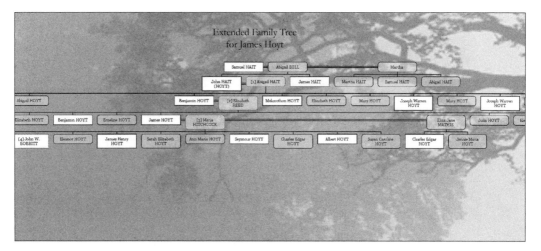

Figure 7-20. A section of a customized extended family chart

> Note: All charts are based on the last individual you
> were viewing in your tree. To change the primary
> individual in the chart, click a different individual's
> name in the mini pedigree tree above the chart or
> click the Index of Individuals button and choose
> the person you want.

Finding an Individual on a Chart

You can quickly find a specific individual on a chart using the Person Locator option located at the bottom of a chart's editing panel. To find an individual, choose his or her name from the **Person Locator** drop-down list. The chart will immediately re-center and the specific individual will be highlighted. If an individual appears in the chart more than once (for example, in families where cousins marry), you can view each occurrence using the **Instances** drop-down list. Although the Person Locator option works on all charts, it's especially useful on the extended family chart because the chart can display hundreds and even thousands of individuals.

Creating an Extended Family Chart

1. Go to the **Collection** tab on the Publish workspace.

2. In **Publication Types**, click **Charts**.

3. Double-click **Extended Family Chart**, or select its icon and then click the **Detail** tab.

4. Do one of these options:

   • To choose your own formatting options, see "Customizing a Chart" on page 208.

   • To apply a template to the chart, see "Using a Custom Template" on page 225.

5. Click the **Include all individuals** checkbox to display every person in your tree. Families or individuals who are not attached to the main tree will be displayed in separate trees at the bottom of the chart.

6. Click **Generate Chart**.

Relationship Charts

The relationship chart is a graphical representation of one person's relationship to another—including the relationship of each person in between. The common relative is shown at the top of the chart, with direct-line ancestors and descendants shown vertically beneath the individual.

Relationship: Maurine Bobbitt to Abigail Hait

Abigail Hait is the 3rd Great Grandmother of Maurine Bobbitt

3rd Great Grandmother

Abigail Hait
b: 09 Oct 1740

d: 27 Feb 1796

2nd Great Grandfather

Benjamin Hoyt
b: 19 Feb 1769

d: 21 Nov 1813

Great Grandfather

James Hoyt
b: 19 Sep 1807
  Stamford, Connecticut
d:

Grandmother

Julia Hoyt
b: 06 Sep 1834
  Chillicothe, Ross, Ohio, USA
d:

Father

James Clarence Bobbitt
b: 28 Jul 1858
  Illinois
d: 02 Jun 1929
  Balko, Beaver, Oklahoma

Self

Maurine Bobbitt
b: 04 Jun 1906
  Cleo Springs, Beaver, Oklahoma
d: 29 Mar 1992
  Pleasant Grove, Utah

Figure 7-21. A relationship chart with default settings

The chart in figure 7-21 shows a default relationship chart. In figure 7-22, the chart has been customized with different fonts, thumbnail images, a tiled background, and a defined footer.

Figure 7-22. A customized relationship chart

Note: All charts are based on the last individual you were viewing in your tree. To change the primary individual in the chart, click a different individual's name in the mini pedigree tree above the chart or click the Index of Individuals button and choose the person you want.

Creating a Relationship Chart

1. Go to the **Collection** tab on the Publish workspace.

2. In **Publication Types**, click **Charts**.

3. Double-click **Relationship Chart**, or select its icon and then click the **Detail** tab.

You can customize the chart by choosing various formatting options in the Relationship Chart Options editing panel.

4. Change the chart as necessary:

In this field	Do this
Chart title	Enter a new title for the chart.
Relation from	To choose the first person whose relationship you are calculating, click the index card icon next to the field. The Find Person window opens. Find the individual and click **OK**.
Relation to	To choose the second person whose relationship you are calculating, use the mini pedigree tree; click the person's name in the tree or the index card icon next to the tree to locate the person.
Background	Change the background image for the chart. For instructions, see "Adding a Background Image" on page 217.
Display relationship label for each node	Click this checkbox if you want each person in the tree to be labeled, showing how he or she is related to the primary individual.
Show thumbnail	Click this checkbox to include thumbnail images of the individuals on the chart.
Include civil/canon information	Click this checkbox to include canon and civil numbers in the report. (For more information on civil and canon numbers, see "Relationship Calculator" on page 382.)
Include preparer information	Click this checkbox to include your personal information on the chart.

Customizing a Chart

For many charts in Family Tree Maker, you can customize contents and format. For example, you can determine which individuals and facts are included in the chart and choose background images and text options.

Changing General Customization Options

There are a few customization options such as spacing and number of generations displayed that you can change for charts available in Family Tree Maker. This task explains how to change or modify these options.

Note: Not every option is available in every chart.

1. Access the chart you want to change. The editing panel displays the options you can change.

Pedigree Chart Options

Chart title:	Pedigree Chart for Julia Hoyt
Layout:	Book
Overlap:	Only Root Overlaps
Spacing:	Collapsed
Align nodes:	Center
Generations:	4 total 4 per page
Background:	None Zoom
	60 % transparent
Pictures:	None Center
	0.75 inches wide
	☐ Use silhouettes

2. Use this chart to help you customize a tree chart:

In this field	Do this
Chart title	Enter a new title for the chart.
Layout	Choose **Book** to display the chart in pages suitable for being placed into a book; if the chart flows onto multiple pages, each page includes references to the generations continued on other pages. Choose **Poster** to display the chart in pages that can be linked together to form a poster. Then click the **Advanced** button to customize the format. For instructions, see "Changing the Poster Layout" on page 222.
Overlap	Change the horizontal spacing of a chart. Choose **No Overlap** to display the boxes in equally spaced columns; choose **Columns Overlap** to display the chart in columns that overlap slightly; choose **Only Root Overlap** to display the chart with only the parents' column overlapping the primary individual's column; choose **Fishtail** to overlap all columns except for the last generation.

In this field	Do this
Spacing	Change the vertical spacing of a chart. Choose **Perfect** to display the rows with even spacing; choose **Collapsed** to display the rows closer together; choose **Squished** to display the rows with the minimum of space between them; choose **Custom** to use the settings created in the Advanced Layout mode. Note: You might choose to collapse or squish the columns if you have many people in your tree and you're trying to fit them all on one page.
Align nodes	Choose **Top** to connect individuals with lines drawn underneath their names; choose **Center** to connect individuals with lines drawn to the center of each person's information; choose **Bezier** to connect individuals with curved lines; choose **Straight** to connect individuals with straight lines.
Generations	Click the up and down arrows to choose the number of generations of ancestors and descendants you want to include in the chart.
Background	Change the background image for the chart. For instructions, see "Adding a Background Image" on page 217.
Pictures	Include photos of individuals in your tree in the chart. For instructions, see "Adding Family Photographs to a Chart" on page 214.
Center tree on page	Click this checkbox to display the tree in the center of the page. If you are putting the printed tree in a bound book, you will not want to center the tree, but leave space for a left margin.
Include empty branches	Click this checkbox to display empty boxes for individuals for whom you have entered no information.
Include siblings of primary individual	Click this checkbox to display the brothers and sisters of the individual.
Include spouses of primary individual	Click this checkbox to display the spouse(s) of the individual.
Boxes overlap page breaks	Click this checkbox if you don't want boxes that fall on a page break to be partially printed on both pieces of paper. Family Tree Maker will adjust the chart spacing so that no boxes are split over two pages.

Choosing Facts to Include in a Chart

When customizing a chart, you can often choose which items or facts you'd like to include. Keep in mind, the more facts you include, the more cluttered your tree will be.

1. Access the chart you want to change.

2. In the editing toolbar, click the **Items to include** button.

Items to include button

The Items to Include window opens. The default facts for the chart are in the Included facts list. You can add and delete facts for a chart and also change display options for each fact. For example, you can change the order in which a fact displays.

3. Choose one of these options:

- To delete a fact from a chart, click the fact in the Included facts list and click the red (**X**) button.

- To add a fact to the chart, click the blue (**+**) button. The Select Fact window opens. Choose a fact from the list and click **OK**.

4. In the Items to Include window, complete these fields as necessary:

In this section	Do this
Fact options	You may have multiple facts for the same event. Click **Include only preferred facts** to include only the facts designated as "preferred."
	Click **Include private facts** to include facts designated as "private."
	Click **Include blank facts** to include a fact field even if a fact has not been entered for an individual.
	If you have entered shortened place names for locations, click **Display user-defined short place name** to use these locations in the report.
Sources	Click **Include sources** to add a list of sources to the end of the chart.
Individual numbers	Click **Print individual number with name** to number individuals in the chart. Then enter the starting number for the first person.

5. To change the display options for a fact, click the fact in the Included facts list. Then click the **Options** button. The Options window opens.

Note: The options for each fact vary. For example, with births, marriages, and deaths, you can include dates and locations.

6. Change the options for the fact and click **OK**.

7. Click **OK**.

Including Source Information with a Chart

You can include source information with a family tree chart. Sources are not displayed in the actual tree; each sourced fact has a number next to it that corresponds to a list of sources found at the bottom of the chart (see figure 7-23).

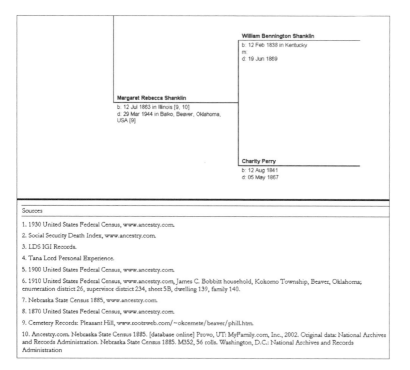

Figure 7-23. A pedigree chart that includes sources

1. Access the chart you want to change.

2. In the editing toolbar, click the **Items to include** button. The Items to Include window opens.

Items to include button —

Pedigree Chart Options

Chart title: Pedigree Chart for Julia Hoyt

3. Click the **Include sources** checkbox.

4. Click **OK**.

Adding Family Photographs to a Chart

You can personalize your charts and make them more appealing by adding photographs of individuals. In order to add a photograph to your chart, you must have already added the image to your tree and linked it to a specific individual. (For instructions, see "Assigning a Portrait to an Individual" on page 59.)

1. Access the chart you want to change.

2. In the **Pictures** field in the editing panel, choose an image type from the drop-down list:

   • Choose **Thumbnail** to use low-resolution thumbnail images.

   • Choose **Photo** to use the resolution of the actual assigned photo.

3. From the drop-down list, choose where the images will appear on the chart. If you want the image centered next to the person's information, click **Center**. If you want the image to be displayed at the top of the person's information, click **Top**.

4. If you want to change the size of the photo or thumbnail, enter a size in the **Inches wide** field.

   Note: The larger the image is, the less space will be available for facts.

5. Click **Use silhouettes** if you want to display a silhouette icon for those individuals who don't have photographs.

Changing the Header or Footer

You can define the headers and footers for each chart (the lines of text at the top and bottom of a chart).

1. Access the chart you want to change.

2. In the editing toolbar, click the **Header/Footer** button.

Header/Footer button ⎯⎯⎯⎯⎯⎯⎯⎯⎯⎯

Pedigree Chart Options

Chart title: Pedigree Chart for Julia Hoyt

The Header/Footer window opens.

Header/Footer

Chart note:

OK
Cancel
Help

☐ Draw box around footer
☐ Print "Created with Family Tree Maker" statement
☐ Include submitter info
☐ Include date of printing
☐ Include time of printing
☑ Include page/chart numbers   In footer

Starting number: 1

Starting number for continuation charts: 2

3. Complete these fields as necessary:

In this field	Do this
Chart note	Enter a note you want to appear in the footer.

In this field	Do this
Draw box around footer	Click this checkbox to have the footer enclosed in a box.
Print "Created with Family Tree Maker"	Click this checkbox to have this text added to the footer.
Include submitter info	If you have entered your name in "User Information," click this checkbox to have it appear in the chart's footer. (To enter your user information, see page 422.)
Include date of printing	Click this checkbox to include the current date in the footer.
Include time of printing	Click this checkbox to include the current time in the footer.
Include page/chart numbers	Click this checkbox to include page numbers in the chart. From the drop-down list, choose whether the number appears in the header or the footer. In the **Starting number** field, enter the number of the chart's first page; in the **Starting number for continuation charts**, enter the number of the second page of the chart.

4. Click **OK**.

Changing the Formatting of a Chart

You can change the text styles, borders, box formats, and background images for charts. (You can also change page setup options such as margins and page size. For instructions, see "Changing Printing Options" on page 230.)

Adding a Background Image

Family Tree Maker comes with several background templates—attractive images you can use as your chart's background. Or you can choose backgrounds from your own images stored on your computer or family pictures you've already added to your tree.

1. Access the chart you want to change.

2. In the **Background** field in the editing panel, choose an image from the drop-down list:

   - To choose a Family Tree Maker background template, click the image's name.

   - To choose an image you've already added to your tree, click **Select a media item**. The Find Media Item window opens. Choose an image and click **OK**.

   - To look for an item on your computer's hard drive, click **Browse for an image**. The Select Chart Background Image window opens. Choose an image and click **Open**.

3. Choose where the image will be displayed on the chart. If you want the image centered in the background, click **Center**. If you want the image stretched to fit the entire page, click **Stretch**. If you want a close-up of the image, click **Zoom**. If you want a series of the same image to fill the background, click **Tile**.

4. In the **Percent transparent** drop-down list, choose the intensity of the image. At 0 percent, the image will appear as it normally does, while a higher percentage will fade the image so the chart is easier to read.

Changing Fonts

You can change the appearance of the text in charts to make it more formal, more fun, or maybe just more readable.

1. Access the chart you want to change.

2. In the editing toolbar, click the **Fonts** button.

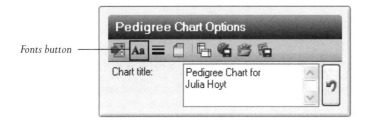

Fonts button

The Fonts window opens.

Fonts

Items to format:
- Names
- Facts
- Chart Title
- Chart Footer
- Reference notes
- Notes and sources
- Preparer Information

Font: Arial
Size: 8
Color: Black
Alignment: Left

☑ Bold ☐ Italic ☐ Underline

Sample

AaBbCcYyZz

OK   Cancel   Help

3. In the **Items to format** list, click the text element, such as the chart title, you would like to change.

4. Choose a font from the **Font** drop-down list. You can also change the size of the text, its style, color, and alignment. The Sample box shows how your text will appear in the chart.

5. Click **OK** to save your changes.

Adding Page Borders, Text Boxes, and Background Colors

You can personalize and enhance your charts by adding borders, background colors, and boxes.

1. Access the chart you want to change.

2. In the editing toolbar, click the **Box and line styles** button.

Box and line styles button

Pedigree Chart Options

Chart title: Pedigree Chart for Julia Hoyt

The Box, Border, and Line Options window opens.

3. Use this chart to change the boxes, border, and background:

To do this	Do this
Change the format of the boxes that enclose an individual's information	Click the type of box you want to format from the Boxes list. Then choose the border, fill, and shadow colors from the drop-down list. Click **Double line** if you want the box border to be two lines of color. Click **Rounded corners** if you want the boxes to have round corners. Click **All boxes same size** to make all boxes on the chart the same size. Click **Semi-transparent** to make the chart's background partially visible through the boxes. Click **Use gradient fill** to make the box's fill color go from light to dark.
Change the size of chart boxes	Enter the maximum width and height (in inches) for boxes in the poster layout. Note: You can change this default size. For instructions, see "Changing the Poster Layout" on page 222.

To do this	Do this
Change the page border of the chart	Choose the color of the border from the **Line** drop-down list.
	Choose the color of the background from the **Background** drop-down list. (Choose "None" if you do not want a color background.)
	Click **Double line** if you want the border to contain two lines of color.
	Click **Rounded corners** if you want the border lines to have round corners.
Change the lines that connect chart boxes	Choose the color of the pedigree lines and divider lines from the drop-down lists. Then choose the thickness of the lines.

4. Click **OK**.

Changing the Poster Layout

When you create some charts, you have the option to create them as a "poster." That way, you can print out each page of the chart and link them together to create a larger, poster-type chart.

1. Access the chart you want to change.

2. Choose **Poster** from the **Layout** drop-down list.

3. Click the **Advanced** button. The Advanced Layout window opens.

Notice the light gray lines running vertically and horizontally across the tree. These lines represent the margins of a standard 8½" by 11" sheet of paper. In this example, the chart is spread over six vertical sheets of paper. You can adjust the spacing of the poster to fit on the desired number of pages.

4. To change how the viewer displays the chart (not its actual print size), do one of these options:

- Click **Fit horizontally** to scale the chart to fit the window horizontally.

- Click **Fit vertically** to scale the chart to fit the window vertically.

- Click **Lock aspect** to keep the chart in proportion vertically and horizontally.

5. Drag the **Horizontal spacing** bar from side to side to change the amount of horizontal space between boxes.

6. Drag the **Vertical spacing** bar up and down to change the amount of vertical space between boxes.

This chart is now spread over four sheets of paper.

7. To change the position of the chart on the sheets of paper, do one of these options:

    •   Click **Reset** to change the chart back to its original settings.

    •   Click **Center** to center the chart on the current pages.

    •   Click **No Page Overlap** to prevent boxes and photos from printing partially on two different pieces of paper.

8. Click **OK**.

Using Chart Templates

Family Tree Maker comes with several templates you can use to quickly dress up your family tree charts with artwork, creative color schemes, formatted text boxes, and borders. And, you can also turn your own chart designs into templates.

Using a Custom Template

Maybe you want to create a beautiful pedigree chart to display on your wall, but you don't have an artistic bone in your body. Or maybe you just don't have any time. Family Tree Maker makes it easy to select an attractive template and instantly change the look of your chart. (To see an example of each custom chart template, see appendix C, "Custom Templates.")

You can apply these templates to any chart in Family Tree Maker. And if the results aren't exactly what you want, you can still add your own modifications.

1. Access the chart you want to apply a template to.

2. Click the **Use saved settings** button in the editing toolbar.

Use saved settings button

Tip

If you have applied a custom template to a chart and you don't want to use it anymore, you can quickly change back to the chart's default display. Click the **Use saved settings** button in the editing toolbar. Then choose **Default template** and click **OK**.

The Use Settings Template window opens.

3. Choose one of these options:

   • **Default template.** The chart will use the default settings.

   • **Preferred template.** The chart will use the template you have saved as "preferred." For instructions on creating a preferred template, see "Creating Your Own Template" on page 226.

   • **Custom template.** You can choose which Family Tree Maker custom template to use for the chart.

4. Click **OK**. If you have chosen to use a custom template, the Open window appears.

5. Choose a template from the list and click **Open**.

Creating Your Own Template

After you have customized a chart with your favorite fonts and colors and changed the spacing and layout to make everyone fit perfectly on the page, you don't want to lose your settings. You can save your modifications as a template, and you won't have to recreate your changes if you want to use them on another chart.

1. After you have modified the chart, click the **Save settings** button in the editing toolbar.

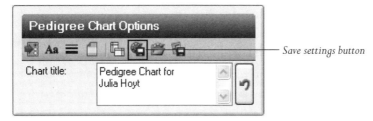

Save settings button

The Save Settings Template window opens.

2. Choose one of these options:

   • **Save as preferred template.** The preferred template can be applied in the Use Settings Template window without having to look through a list.

   • **Create new template.** The template will be added to the list of custom templates you can use for your charts.

3. Click **OK**.

Saving Charts

You can save charts you've created in two ways: within Family Tree Maker and as an exported file.

Saving a Chart in Family Tree Maker

After you've modified or customized a chart, you may want to save it. That way you can access the exact chart again without having to recreate it.

1. After you have modified the chart, click the **Save chart** button in the editing toolbar.

The Save Chart window opens.

Tip

To rename a chart you've saved, click the **Publish** button on the main toolbar. In **Publication Types**, click **Saved Charts**. Right-click the chart you want and click **Rename Item**.

2. Enter a name for the chart in the **Chart name** field. Be sure to use a name that will distinguish the chart from others. For example, don't use generic terms like "Descendant Chart" or "Pedigree Chart."

3. Click **Save**.

Saving a Chart as a File

You may want to save a chart to a file format that can be opened in software other than Family Tree Maker; for example, as an image or PDF. These files can be easily shared with others or posted on a website.

> Note: An Adobe PDF (Portable Document Format) is useful because PDFs keep the formatting you select. That way, if you print your chart or send it to a relative, the chart will look exactly as you see it on your monitor. You cannot make changes to a PDF within Family Tree Maker, and you need the Adobe *Reader* in order to view it. (Adobe *Reader* can be downloaded for free from the Adobe website.)

1. Access the chart you want to save.

2. Click the **Share** button in the toolbar above the editing panel.

3. From the drop-down list, choose one of these options:

   - **Export to PDF.** This option exports the chart to PDF in multiple pages.

   - **Export to One Page PDF.** This option exports the chart as one page (regardless of size). You might want to use this

> **Tip**
> To open a saved chart, click the **Publish** button on the main toolbar. In **Publication Types**, click **Saved Charts**. Then double-click the chart you want to open.

if you are having your charts printed at a copy store. (For instructions, see "Printing a Poster" on page 232.)

- **Export to Image.** This option lets you create an image of the chart as a bitmap, JPEG, or other image format.

Each format has its own export options you can choose from. After you choose a format type, you may be able to choose options such as page borders and text separators. Once you've made your selections, click **OK**. The Save As window opens.

4. Use the **Save in** drop-down list to find the location where you want to save the chart.

5. Enter a name for the chart in the **File name** field.

6. Click **Save**.

Printing Charts

When you are done creating and customizing a chart, you may want to print it out. Family Tree Maker makes it easy to choose setup options and print a report.

Changing Printing Options

Before you print a chart, you might want to change the margins, print orientation, or paper size. Changes you make to the print setup will apply only to the chart you're accessing.

1. Access the chart you want to change.

2. In the editing toolbar, click the **Page setup** button.

Page setup button

The Page Setup window opens.

3. Click the **Size** drop-down list to change the size of the paper if your printer is capable of printing larger sheets of paper. Otherwise, leave the selection at letter size, which is a standard 8 ½" x 11" sheet of paper.

4. If necessary, choose a paper type or paper tray from the **Source** drop-down list.

5. In the **Orientation** section, click **Portrait** if you want your document to print with the short edge of the paper at the bottom (the way a letter normally prints). This is the default setting. Click **Landscape** if you want your document to print with the long edge of the paper at the bottom.

6. In the **Margins** section, make any necessary changes to the margin size of your report. By default, each page prints with quarter-inch margins on all sides.

7. Click **OK**.

Printing a Chart

1.   Access the chart you want to print.

2.   Click the **Print** button in the toolbar above the editing panel.
     The Print window opens.

     Just like printing from any other application, you can choose a
     printer, select the number of copies, and choose a page range.

3.   Click **OK**.

Printing a Poster

Family Tree Maker lets you create many charts as posters. You
have the option of printing the pages off at home and taping them
together. Or, you can export your poster chart as a PDF and take it
to a copy shop to be printed on a single sheet of high-quality paper.

1.   Access the poster you want to print.

2.   Click the **Share** button in the toolbar above the editing panel.

3.   From the drop-down list, choose **Export to One Page PDF**.
     The PDF Export Options window opens.

PDF Export Options

Page range:	
☑ Compressed	
Don't embed these fonts:	
Images quality:	Highest
Application:	Family Tree Maker
Author:	Tana L. Pedersen
Keywords:	
Subject:	
Title:	Pedigree Chart

OK   Cancel

4. Change any options as necessary. Because this chart will be printed as a large poster, you will probably want to keep your image quality at the highest level possible.

5. Click **OK**.

   Your chart is now ready to upload to a flash drive, CD, or even a copy shop's website.

Sharing a Chart

Family Tree Maker lets you share charts with others—via e-mail—in a variety of formats.

> Note: You must be connected to the Internet and have e-mail access to use this feature.

1. Access the chart you want to e-mail.

2. Click the **Share** button in the toolbar above the editing panel.

3. From the drop-down list, choose **Send as PDF.** The PDF Export Options window opens.

4. Change the options as necessary and click **OK**. The Save As window opens.

5. Use the **Save in** drop-down list to find the location where you want to save the report.

6. Enter a name for the report in the **File name** field.

7. Click **Save**. Family Tree Maker opens a new e-mail (with the PDF attached) in your default e-mail program.

8. Send the e-mail as you would any other.

Chapter 8

Creating Reports

Family Tree Maker includes a number of reports to help you organize and understand all the information you have entered in your tree. Some reports, such as bibliographies and source usage, can help you keep track of your research. Other narrative reports, including relationship reports, are full of details and allow you to quickly see the connections between individuals in your tree. You can also create your own specialty reports and include only the information you're interested in.

Each report can be customized—options differ by report. You can change fonts, add background images, and more. The first part of this chapter explains each report and how individual reports can be changed. The next section of the chapter explains the customization options that can be used on all reports.

When you're finished, share these in-depth reports with interested family members or fellow researchers, or use the detailed information to plot out your next steps.

In This Chapter
- Genealogy Reports
- Person Reports
- Relationship Reports
- Place Usage Report
- Media Reports
- Source Reports
- Calendars
- Customizing a Report
- Saving Reports
- Printing Reports
- Sharing a Report

Genealogy Reports

Genealogy reports contain detailed information and facts about the individuals in your tree and are great for including in family history books or sharing with other researchers.

Ahnentafel Reports

The Ahnentafel (a German word meaning "ancestor table") is basically a numbered list of individuals. Its format is ancestor ordered,

---

Ahnentafel Report for Emma Gedge

Generation 1

1. **Emma Gedge** daughter of William Gedge and Rachel Bush was born on 30 Aug 1864 in Millcreek, Salt Lake, Utah. She died on 11 Dec 1906 in St George, Washington, Utah, USA.

Generation 2

2. **William Gedge**[1, 2] was born in Jan 1831 in England. He died in Salt Lake City, Salt Lake, Utah, USA.

    Notes for William Gedge:
    General Notes:
    Both parents born in England.

3. **Rachel Bush**[2, 3] was born in Oct 1833 in England. She died on 15 Mar 1911 in Salt Lake City, Salt Lake, Utah, USA[3].

    Notes for Rachel Bush:
    General Notes:
    Both parents born in England.

    William Gedge and Rachel Bush were married about 1866. They had the following children:

    + 1. i.   **Emma Gedge** was born on 30 Aug 1864 in Millcreek, Salt Lake, Utah. She died on 11 Dec 1906 in St George, Washington, Utah, USA.

    ii.   **Anna Gedge** was born on 05 Sep 1866 in Brighton, Salt Lake, Utah, USA. She died on 09 Jun 1945 in Salt Lake City, Salt Lake, Utah, USA.

    iii. **William Reames Gedge** was born on 30 Jun 1868 in Brighton, Salt Lake, Utah, USA. He died on 04 Jul 1964 in UT, USA.

    iv.   **Nathan Gedge** was born on 10 Feb 1871 in Utah.

    v.   **Herbert Bush Gedge**[2, 3, 4, 5, 6] was born on 10 Nov 1872 in Brighton, Salt Lake, Utah, USA. He married Sarah Hannah Gold on 20 Nov 1895 in Salt Lake City, Salt Lake, Utah, USA[7]. He died on 08 Sep 1942 in Salt Lake City, Salt Lake, Utah, USA[3].

Sources

1   1870 United States Federal Census, www.ancestry.com.
2   1880 United States Federal Census, www.ancestry.com, Hebert Gedge household, Brighton, Salt Lake, Utah; enumeration district 320, supervisor district 3, page 27, dwelling 64, family 73.
3   Utah Death Index, 1905-1951, www.ancestry.com.
4   1920 United States Federal Census, www.ancestry.com.
5   Utah Cemetery Inventory, www.ancestry.com.
6   Salt Lake City, Utah Cemetery Records, 1848-1992, www.ancestry.com.
7   Western States Marriage Records Index, http://abish.byui.edu/specialCollections/fhc/newMarriage/searchDetail.cfm?recordID=306649, Volume: F. Page: 361. Marriage ID: 306649
. GEDGE, Herbert (23) GOLD, Sarah H. (21).

Figure 8-1. Standard Ahnentafel

Ancestors of Emma Gedge

Generation 1

1. **Emma Gedge** was born on 30 Aug 1864 in Millcreek, Salt Lake, Utah. She was the daughter of 2. William Gedge and 3. Rachel Bush. She died 11 Dec 1906 in St George, Washington, Utah, USA.

Generation 2

2. **William Gedge**[1, 2] was born on Jan 1831 in England. He died in Salt Lake City, Salt Lake, Utah, USA. He married Rachel Bush on Abt. 1866.

   Notes for William Gedge:
   Both parents born in England.

3. **Rachel Bush**, born Oct 1833 in England, died 15 Mar 1911 in Salt Lake City, Salt Lake, Utah, USA[3], married Abt. 1866.

   Notes for Rachel Bush:
   Both parents born in England.

   Children of William Gedge and Rachel Bush are:

   + 1. i.   Emma Gedge, born 30 Aug 1864 in Millcreek, Salt Lake, Utah, died 11 Dec 1906 in St George, Washington, Utah, USA.

     ii. Anna Gedge, born 05 Sep 1866 in Brighton, Salt Lake, Utah, USA, died 09 Jun 1945 in Salt Lake City, Salt Lake, Utah, USA.

     iii. William Reames Gedge, born 30 Jun 1868 in Brighton, Salt Lake, Utah, USA, died 04 Jul 1964 in UT, USA.

     iv. Nathan Gedge, born 10 Feb 1871 in Utah.

     v.   Herbert Bush Gedge, born 10 Nov 1872 in Brighton, Salt Lake, Utah, USA[4, 5], died 08 Sep 1942 in Salt Lake City, Salt Lake, Utah, USA[3], married Sarah Hannah Gold 20 Nov 1895 in Salt Lake City, Salt Lake, Utah, USA[6].

Sources

1   1870 United States Federal Census, www.ancestry.com.
2   1880 United States Federal Census, www.ancestry.com, Hebert Gedge household, Brighton, Salt Lake, Utah; enumeration district 320, supervisor district 3, page 27, dwelling 64, family 73.
3   Utah Death Index, 1905-1951, www.ancestry.com.
4   Utah Cemetery Inventory, www.ancestry.com.
5   Salt Lake City, Utah Cemetery Records, 1848-1992, www.ancestry.com.
6   Western States Marriage Records Index,
    http://abish.byui.edu/specialCollections/fhc/newMarriage/searchDetail.cfm?recordID=306649,
    Volume: F. Page: 361. Marriage ID: 306649
    . GEDGE, Herbert (23) GOLD, Sarah H. (21).

Figure 8-2. Simple Ahnentafel

meaning that it starts with one individual and moves backward in time to that individual's ancestors. This format is used infrequently because it records two family lines in the same report.

Family Tree Maker gives you two different report options: the standard Ahnentafel (see figure 8-1) and the simple Ahnentafel (see figure 8-2). The main difference between the two is that the standard report is more descriptive and the simple report just includes names, dates, and facts.

Tip

All reports are based on the last individual you were viewing in your tree. To change the primary individual in the report, click his or her name in the mini pedigree tree above the report or click the Index of Individuals button and choose the person you want.

To read the report, you'll need to understand a bit about its numbering system. The Ahnentafel assigns the first individual the number 1. His or her father is number 2, and his or her mother is number 3. Men are always even numbers, and women are always odd numbers. You can easily determine who the father of an individual is by looking at his or her number—it is twice his or her own number. For example, if a man's number is four, his father's number is eight. The mother of an individual is twice the person's number plus one. So from the previous example, the mother of the individual would be nine.

1. Go to the **Collection** tab on the Publish workspace.

2. In **Publication Types**, click **Genealogy Reports**.

3. Double-click **Ahnentafel Report** or **Simple Ahnentafel Report**.

4. Change the report as necessary. For instructions, see "Customizing a Report" on page 282.

5. Click **Generate Report**.

Register Reports

The Register report is descendant ordered, meaning that it starts with one individual and moves forward in time through that individual's descendants. This is the format accepted by the New England Historic Genealogical Society, the oldest genealogical society in the United States, and can be used to prove your lineage.

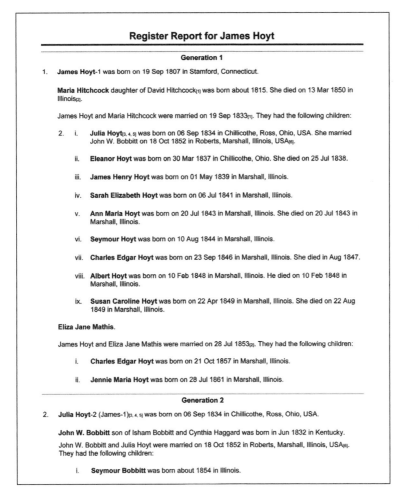

Figure 8-3. Standard Register

Family Tree Maker gives you two different Register report options: standard (see figure 8-3 on the previous page) and simple (see figure 8-4). The main difference between the two is that the standard report is more descriptive and the simple report just includes names, dates, and facts.

Descendants of James Hoyt

Generation 1

1. **James Hoyt**-1 was born on 19 Sep 1807 in Stamford, Connecticut. He married Maria Hitchcock on 19 Sep 1833[1], daughter of David Hitchcock. She was born about 1815[2]. She died on 13 Mar 1850 in Illinois[2]. He married Eliza Jane Mathis on 28 Jul 1853[2].

Children of James Hoyt and Maria Hitchcock are:

2.   i.   Julia Hoyt, B: 06 Sep 1834 in Chillicothe, Ross, Ohio, USA[3, 4, 5], M: 18 Oct 1852 in Roberts, Marshall, Illinois, USA[5].

    ii.   Eleanor Hoyt, B: 30 Mar 1837 in Chillicothe, Ohio, D: 25 Jul 1838.

    iii.   James Henry Hoyt, B: 01 May 1839 in Marshall, Illinois.

    iv.   Sarah Elizabeth Hoyt, B: 06 Jul 1841 in Marshall, Illinois.

    v.   Ann Maria Hoyt, B: 20 Jul 1843 in Marshall, Illinois, D: 20 Jul 1843 in Marshall, Illinois.

    vi.   Seymour Hoyt, B: 10 Aug 1844 in Marshall, Illinois.

    vii.   Charles Edgar Hoyt, B: 23 Sep 1846 in Marshall, Illinois, D: Aug 1847.

    viii.   Albert Hoyt, B: 10 Feb 1848 in Marshall, Illinois, D: 10 Feb 1848 in Marshall, Illinois.

    ix.   Susan Caroline Hoyt, B: 22 Apr 1849 in Marshall, Illinois, D: 22 Aug 1849 in Marshall, Illinois.

Children of James Hoyt and Eliza Jane Mathis are:

    i.   Charles Edgar Hoyt, B: 21 Oct 1857 in Marshall, Illinois.

    ii.   Jennie Maria Hoyt, B: 28 Jul 1861 in Marshall, Illinois.

Generation 2

2. **Julia Hoyt**-2(James-1)[3, 4, 6] was born on 06 Sep 1834 in Chillicothe, Ross, Ohio, USA[3, 4, 5]. She married John W. Bobbitt on 18 Oct 1852 in Roberts, Marshall, Illinois, USA[5], son of Isham Bobbitt and Cynthia Haggard. He was born in Jun 1832 in Kentucky[6].

Children of Julia Hoyt and John W. Bobbitt are:

    i.   Seymour Bobbitt, B: Abt. 1854 in Illinois.

    ii.   Cornelia Bobbitt, B: Abt. 1856 in Illinois.

3.   iii.   James Clarence Bobbitt, B: 28 Jul 1858 in Illinois[6, 7, 8], D: 02 Jun 1929 in Balko, Beaver, Oklahoma, USA[8], M: 20 Feb 1882 in Marshall County, Illinois[9].

Figure 8-4. Simple Register

1. Go to the **Collection** tab on the Publish workspace.

2. In **Publication Types**, click **Genealogy Reports**.

3. Double-click **Register Report** or **Simple Register Report**.

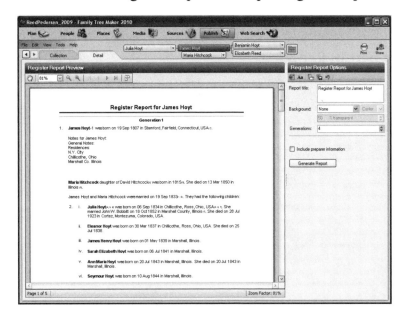

4. Change the report as necessary. For instructions, see "Customizing a Report" on page 282.

5. Click **Generate Report**.

Person Reports

Person reports focus on an individual in your tree. You can create a report of all the facts and sources you have recorded for a person, create a report of research notes or tasks in your Research To-Do list, or create a custom report.

Custom Report

Custom reports let you create reports with your own criteria. For example, you can create a custom report of birthplaces or causes of

Residents of Illinois		
Albert Hoyt		
	Birth:	10 Feb 1848 in Marshall, Illinois
	Death:	10 Feb 1848 in Marshall, Illinois
Ann Hoyt		
	Birth:	20 Jul 1843 in Marshall, Illinois
	Death:	20 Jul 1843 in Marshall, Illinois
Charles Hoyt		
	Birth:	23 Sep 1846 in Marshall, Illinois
	Death:	Aug 1847
Charles Hoyt		
	Birth:	21 Oct 1857 in Marshall, Illinois
Cora Hewitt		
	Birth:	Abt. 1865 in Illinois
Cornelia Bobbitt		
	Birth:	Abt. 1856 in Illinois
Edwin Hewitt		
	Birth:	1832 in New York, USA
	Marriage:	Abt. 1853 in Pennsylvania or Illinois
Eugene Bobbitt		
	Birth:	Jan 1877 in Illinois
Francis Bobbitt		
	Birth:	Abt. 1869 in Illinois
Isham Bobbitt		
	Birth:	Abt. 1790 in Cerulean Springs, Trigg, Kentucky, USA
	Marriage:	21 Dec 1824 in Trigg, Kentucky
	Death:	1865 in Putnam, Illinois, USA
James Bobbitt		
	Birth:	28 Jul 1858 in Illinois
	Marriage:	Abt. 1881 in Fulton, Illinois, USA
	Death:	02 Jun 1929 in Balko, Beaver, Oklahoma, USA
	Burial:	02 Jun 1929 in Balko, Beaver, Oklahoma, USA
James Hoyt		
	Birth:	01 May 1839 in Marshall, Illinois
James Shanklin		
	Birth:	06 Sep 1810 in Fleming, Kentucky, USA
	Marriage:	1827 in Fulton, Illinois, USA
	Marriage:	21 Mar 1837 in Fulton, Illinois
	Marriage:	Bet. 1861–1870
	Death:	1887 in Illinois
Jennie Hoyt		
	Birth:	28 Jul 1861 in Marshall, Illinois
John Bobbitt		
	Birth:	09 Jun 1832 in Trigg, Kentucky, USA
	Marriage:	18 Oct 1852 in Marshall County, Illinois
	Burial:	14 Aug 1909 in Dawson, Nebraska, USA

Figure 8-5. Custom report

death if you have recorded that information for several individuals in your tree. The Custom report defaults to a list of all individuals, birth dates, and death dates, so you can begin to customize it with all information intact.

The custom report in figure 8-5 has been modified to show only individuals who were born, married, died, or lived in Illinois. In addition to birth, marriage, and death facts, the report also includes census and residence information.

1. Go to the **Collection** tab on the Publish workspace.

2. In **Publication Types**, click **Person Reports**.

3. Double-click **Custom Report**, or select its icon and then click the **Detail** tab.

4. Use the editing panel to change the report. For instructions, see "Customizing a Report" on page 282.

5. Click **Generate Report**.

Individual Report

The Individual Report lists every fact and source you have recorded for a specific individual.

Individual Report for Cyrus Henry Gold

Individual Summary:	Cyrus Gold
Sex:	Male
Father:	Joseph Gold
Mother:	Sarah Thompson

Individual Facts:

Name:	Cyrus Gold
Birth:	01 May 1848 in Birmingham, Warwick, England [1]
Death:	27 Mar 1930 in Salt Lake City, Salt Lake, Utah, USA [2]

Shared Facts: Mary Willis

Marriage:	27 Mar 1871 in Salt Lake City, Salt Lake, Utah, USA [3]
Children:	Sarah Gold
	Cyrus Gold
	Thomas Gold
	Abraham Gold
	Alma Gold
	Lehi Gold
	Helaman Gold
	Elmina Gold
	Mary Gold
	Henry Gold

Shared Facts: Louisa Newman

Marriage:	08 Aug 1904 in Salt Lake City, Salt Lake, Utah, USA [4]
Children:	Earnest Gold
	Louisa Gold
	Ruth Gold
	Gertrude Gold
	Annie Gold
	Edwin Gold
	John Gold

Notes:

Person Notes:	[no notes]

Sources:

1 England, Register of Births, Cyrus Henry Gold.; General Register Office, Somerset House London.
2 Utah, State Board of Health, Death Certificates, Cyrus Henry Gold. File no. 599.
3 Desert Gedge Johnson, "Mary Willis- Wife of Cyrus Henry Gold"; Personal writings (; privately held by Tana L. Pedersen (copy)).
4 Salt Lake, Utah, Gold and Newman. Vol. P. Page 57. Marriage ID 354782.

1. Go to the **Collection** tab on the Publish workspace.

2. In **Publication Types**, click **Person Reports**.

3. Double-click **Individual Report**, or select its icon and then click the **Detail** tab.

4. Use the editing panel to change the report. For instructions, see "Customizing a Report" on page 282.

5. If you want the individual's facts to be listed in order of date, click the **Use chronological order for facts** checkbox.

6. If you have included an image of the individual in your tree, you can click the **Show individual thumbnail** checkbox to include the person's photo in the report.

7. Click **Generate Report**.

Research Note Report

The Research Note Report displays the research notes you've entered for individuals in your tree.

Note: For more information on research notes, see "Entering a Research Note" on page 54.

Research Note Report

Edwin HEWITT
Birth - Death: Abt. 1831 - ?
Research Note: Milton Hewitt moved to Kendall, Illinois, before Edwin did. Check for records in Kendall County.

Edwin was living with the Main family in Pennsylvania in 1850. Was he living with them in the 1840 census? When did he move to Pennsylvania and why?

Maria HITCHCOCK
Birth - Death: Abt. 1815 - 13 Mar 1850
Research Note: County histories show that Maria married James in New York City abt. 1837. Need to see if New York City kept marriage records back to that date. Census records also show she was born in New York state.

Oliver Cowdery PEDERSEN
Birth - Death: 26 Apr 1890 - 07 Feb 1976
Research Note: Oliver was in the Army stationed in Washington State when he was naturalized. Check for his papers there.

Mary WILLIS
Birth - Death: Abt. 1853 - 25 Apr 1904
Research Note: Mary Willis's mother, Hannah or Anna, was enumerated in the 1880 census in Salt Lake City with the Gold family. Further research needs to be done to see whether she was visiting her daughter at the time or had emigrated from England.

1. Go to the **Collection** tab on the Publish workspace.

2. In **Publication Types**, click **Person Reports**.

3. Double-click **Research Note Report**, or select its icon and then click the **Detail** tab.

4. Use the editing panel to change the report. For instructions, see "Customizing a Report" on page 282.

5. If you have marked some of your research notes as "private," you can click the **Show private research notes** checkbox to include them in the report.

6. Click **Generate Report**.

Task List

The Task List displays all the research tasks you've entered into your To-Do list. You can see each task's priority level, categories you've assigned it to, and creation and due dates. You can also choose to filter the report by tasks that have already been completed.

> Note: For more information on the To-Do list, see "Research To-Do List" on page 393.

Tip
You can also print a task list for a specific individual. For instructions, see "Creating a To-Do Task" on page 393.

Task List

☐ Locate Edwin Hewitt in the 1860 census.
Priority: High
Owner: General Task
Categories: Hewitts
Date Created: 5/21/2008
Date Due:

☐ Order a copy of Milton Hewitt's marriage record.
Priority: High
Owner: General Task
Categories: Hewitts, Marriage records
Date Created: 6/9/2008
Date Due: 6/13/2009

☐ Take photos at Fairview Pioneer Cemetery.
Priority: High
Owner: General Task
Categories: Photographs
Date Created: 6/9/2008
Date Due: 5/26/2009

☐ Find death records for William Bennington Shanklin in Missouri.
Priority: Medium
Owner: General Task
Categories: Death records, Shanklins
Date Created: 5/21/2008
Date Due:

☐ Scan the Bell Plain, Illinois, map.
Priority: Medium
Owner: General Task
Categories: Scan
Date Created: 6/9/2008
Date Due: 1/27/2009

☐ E-mail Aunt Chris about the Catherine Walborn photograph.
Priority: Low
Owner: General Task
Categories: Email, Photographs
Date Created: 6/9/2008
Date Due:

☐ Photocopy newspaper clipping of Cyrus and Mary's trip to America
Priority: Low
Owner: General Task
Categories: Scan
Date Created: 6/9/2008
Date Due:

1. Go to the **Collection** tab on the Publish workspace.

2. In **Publication Types**, click **Person Reports**.

3. Double-click **Task List**, or select its icon and then click the **Detail** tab.

4. Use the editing panel to change the report. For instructions, see "Customizing a Report" on page 282.

5. To also include tasks that have been marked as completed, click the **Include completed tasks** checkbox.

6. Click **Generate Report**.

LDS Ordinances Report

The LDS Ordinances Report is useful for members of The Church of Jesus Christ of Latter-day Saints (LDS church) and displays LDS-specific ordinances such as baptisms and sealings.

LDS Ordinances

Gedge, Herbert Bush
Birth:	10 Nov 1872 in Brighton, Salt Lake, Utah
Marriage:	20 Nov 1895 in Salt Lake City, Salt Lake, Utah
Death:	08 Sep 1942 in Salt Lake, Salt Lake City, Utah
Baptism (LDS):	10 Nov 1880
Endowment (LDS):	20 Nov 1895

Gedge, Phoebe Gold
Birth:	27 May 1900 in Salt Lake City, Salt Lake, Utah
Marriage:	15 Sep 1926 in Salt Lake City, Utah
Death:	28 Dec 1948 in Salt Lake City, Salt Lake, Utah
Endowment (LDS):	15 Sep 1926 in Salt Lake City, UT, USA

Gold, Sarah Hannah
Birth:	03 Dec 1873 in Salt Lake City, Utah
Marriage:	20 Nov 1895 in Salt Lake City, Salt Lake, Utah
Death:	05 Nov 1963 in Salt Lake City, Utah
Baptism (LDS):	03 Jan 1882

1. Go to the **Collection** tab on the Publish workspace.

2. In **Publication Types**, click **Person Reports**.

3. Double-click **LDS Ordinances**, or select its icon and then click the **Detail** tab.

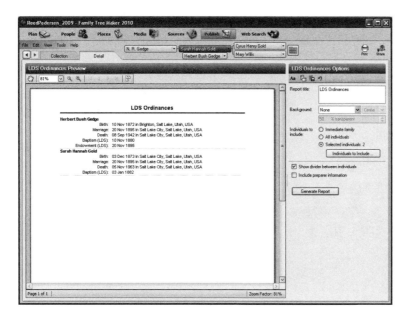

4. Use the editing panel to change the report. For instructions, see "Customizing a Report" on page 282.

5. Click **Generate Report**.

Data Errors Report

The Data Errors report lists all instances where there is missing data or where Family Tree Maker believes there may be a mistake. This includes nonsensical dates (e.g., an individual being born before his or her parents were born), empty fields, duplicate individuals, typos, and more.

Data Errors Report

Name	Birth Date	Potential Error
Anna Gedge	05 Sep 1865	The burial date occurred before his/her death.
Nathan Gedge	Abt. 1971	The birth date occurred after his/her mother was 60. The birth date occurred after his/her mother died. The birth date occurred after his/her father was 80. The birth date occurred more than one year after his/her father died.
Mette Katrina Pedersen		The individual has the same last name as her husband, Niels Pedersen.
Oliver Cowdrey Pedersen	Abt. 1891	Arrival date occurred before individual's birth date.

1. Go to the **Collection** tab on the Publish workspace.

2. In **Publication Types**, click **Person Reports**.

3. Double-click the **Data Errors Report** or click the report icon and then click the **Detail** tab.

4. Use the editing panel to change the report. For instructions, see "Customizing a Report" on page 282.

5. Click **Generate Report**.

Timeline Report

The Timeline report lists all the events you've entered for an individual. Each event shows the date and location of the event and the person's age at the time. You can also choose to include important events in an individual's immediate family (such as birth, marriage, and death) and historical events.

Timeline for John W. Bobbitt

Yr/Age	Event	Date/Place
1832	Birth	09 Jun 1832 Trigg, Kentucky, USA
1834 18 mos	Residence	1834 Hancock, Illinois, USA
1834 2	Birth (Spouse) Julia Hoyt	06 Sep 1834 Chillicothe, Ross, Ohio, USA
1852 20	Marriage Julia Hoyt	18 Oct 1852 Marshall County, Illinois
1854 21	Birth (Son) Seymour Bobbitt	Abt. 1854 Illinois
1856 23	Birth (Daughter) Cornelia Bobbitt	Abt. 1856 Illinois
1858 26	Birth (Son) James Clarence Bobbitt	28 Jul 1858 Illinois
1860 27	Census	1860 Roberts, Marshall, Illinois, USA
1861 28	Birth (Son) Willis R. Bobbitt	Abt. 1861 Illinois
1863 30	Birth (Daughter) Sarah Eleanor Bobbitt	Abt. 1863 Illinois
1865 32	Death (Father) Isham Drury Bobbitt Jr.	1865 Putnam, Illinois, USA
1869 36	Birth (Son) Francis M. Bobbitt	Abt. 1869 Illinois
1870 37	Census	1870 Roberts, Marshall, Illinois, USA
1873 40	Birth (Son) Jessie Bobbitt	Abt. 1873 Illinois
1877 44	Birth (Son) Eugene A. Bobbitt	Jan 1877 Illinois
1881 48	Marriage (Son) James Clarence Bobbitt	Abt. 1881 Fulton, Illinois, USA
1885 52	Census	1885 Liberty, Richardson, Nebraska, USA
1885 52	Death (Mother) Cynthia Haggard	26 Feb 1885 Missouri

1. Go to the **Collection** tab on the Publish workspace.

2. In **Publication Types**, click **Person Reports**.

3. Double-click the **Timeline Report** or click the report icon and then click the **Detail** tab.

4. Use the editing panel to change the report. For instructions, see "Customizing a Report" on page 282.

5. To display icons that identify the type of event, click the **Include event type icons** checkbox.

6. To include events for parents, siblings, spouses, and children, click the **Include family events** checkbox.

7. To include major world events that occurred during the individual's lifetime, click the **Include historical events** checkbox.

8. To include events that have been marked as private, click the **Include private facts** checkbox.

9. Click **Generate Report**.

> **Tip**
>
> All reports are based on the last individual you were viewing in your tree. To change the primary individual in the report, click his or her name in the mini pedigree tree above the report, or click the Index of Individuals button and choose the person you want.

Relationship Reports

Relationship reports are just what they sound like; they show the relationships between different individuals and families in your tree.

Kinship Report

The Kinship Report helps you determine how individuals in your database are related to a specific person.

Kinship Report for Maria Hitchcock

Name:	Birth Date:	Relationship:	Civil:	Canon:
(Hoyt), John Hait	24 Nov 1740	Father of father-in-law		
Bobbitt, Alta M.	09 Feb 1892	Great granddaughter	III	3
Bobbitt, Arthur L.	24 Aug 1897	Great grandson	III	3
Bobbitt, Bessie A.	14 Dec 1888	Great granddaughter	III	3
Bobbitt, Charity M.	10 Mar 1883	Great granddaughter	III	3
Bobbitt, Cornelia	Abt. 1856	Granddaughter	II	2
Bobbitt, Eugene A.	Jan 1877	Grandson	II	2
Bobbitt, Fern Edna	25 Feb 1909	Great granddaughter	III	3
Bobbitt, Francis M.	Abt. 1869	Grandson	II	2
Bobbitt, James Clarence	28 Jul 1858	Grandson	II	2
Bobbitt, James Leslie	19 Sep 1884	Great grandson	III	3
Bobbitt, Jessie	Abt. 1873	Grandson	II	2
Bobbitt, John W.	09 Jun 1832	Son-in-law		
Bobbitt, Lorine	04 Jun 1906	Great granddaughter	III	3
Bobbitt, Mary Eliza	10 Apr 1886	Great granddaughter	III	3
Bobbitt, Maurine	04 Jun 1906	Great granddaughter	III	3
Bobbitt, Sarah Eleanor	Abt. 1863	Granddaughter	II	2
Bobbitt, Seymour	Abt. 1854	Grandson	II	2
Bobbitt, Twila Margaret	18 Jul 1899	Great granddaughter	III	3
Bobbitt, Willis R.	Abt. 1861	Grandson	II	2
Crossman, William B.		Husband of great granddaughter		
Cullins, Clonnie		Husband of great granddaughter		
Hait, Abigail		Daughter of great grandfather of husband		
Hait, Abigail	09 Oct 1740	Mother of father-in-law		
Hait, Abraham	16 Jun 1704	Great grand uncle of husband		
Hait, Benjamin	02 Feb 1644	3rd great grandfather of husband		
Hait, Benjamin	09 Dec 1671	2nd great grandfather of husband		
Hait, Benjamin	24 Apr 1700	Great grand uncle of husband		
Hait, Benjamin	13 Jun 1718	Great grand aunt of husband		
Hait, David	23 Jun 1702	Great grand uncle of husband		
Hait, Deborah	09 Aug 1698	Great grand aunt of husband		
Hait, Deodate	14 Sep 1738	Uncle of father-in-law		
Hait, Ebenezer	Bet. 1712–1720	Great grand uncle of husband		

1. Go to the **Collection** tab on the Publish workspace.

2. In **Publication Types**, click **Relationship Reports**.

3. Double-click **Kinship Report**, or select its icon and then click the **Detail** tab.

4. Use the editing panel to change the report. For instructions, see "Customizing a Report" on page 282.

5. To include people who are not directly related to the primary individual, click **Show unrelated individuals**.

6. To show civil and canon numbers, click the **Show Civil and Canon** checkbox. (For more information on these numbers, see "Relationship Calculator" on page 382.)

7. To include individuals who have an "Also Known As" name (as a separate entry), click the **Show AKA** checkbox.

8. To show all the ways in which individuals are related (for example, two people may be married and third cousins), click the **Show all relationships** checkbox.

9. Click **Generate Report**.

> **Tip**
>
> If you choose to show all relationships, the report may take a long time to generate—from several minutes to over an hour. You may want to limit the number of individuals included in the report if you choose this option.

Marriage Report

The Marriage Report lists the names of husbands and wives, their marriage dates, and the relationship status for all marriages entered in your tree.

Marriage Report

Husband:	Wife:	Marriage Date:	Relation:
(Hoyt), John Hait	Hait, Abigail	31 Dec 1761	Spouse - None
Bobbitt, Isham	Haggard, Cynthia	21 Dec 1824	Spouse - None
Bobbitt, James Clarence	Shanklin, Margaret Rebecca	Abt. 1881	Spouse - Unknown
Bobbitt, John W.	Hoyt, Julia	18 Oct 1852	Spouse - None
Cothran, Claude M.	Reed, Florence L.		Spouse - None
Crossman, William B.	Bobbitt, Charity M.		Spouse - None
Cullins, Clonnie	Bobbitt, Fern Edna		Spouse - None
Gedge, Herbert Bush	Gold, Sarah Hannah	20 Nov 1895	Spouse - None
Gedge, William	Bush, Rachel	Abt. 1866	Spouse - None
Gold, Cyrus Henry	Newman, Louisa Fanny	08 Aug 1904	Spouse - None
Gold, Cyrus Henry	Willis, Mary	Abt. 1871	Spouse - None
Gold, Joseph	Thompson, Sarah	27 Jan 1845	Spouse - Ongoing
Hait, Benjamin	Jagger, Elizabeth	10 Jun 1697	Spouse - None
Hait, Benjamin	Weed, Hannah	05 Jan 1670	Spouse - None
Hait, Ebenezer	Hait, Mercy		Spouse - None
Hait, Samuel	Bell, Abigail	Bet. 08 Mar 1738–1739	Spouse - None
Hait, Samuel	Jagger, Mary	Bet. 29 Mar 1704–1705	Spouse - None
Hait, Samuel	Martha		Spouse - None
Hewitt, Edwin		Abt. 1853	
Hitchcock, David			
Hoyt, Benjamin	Reed, Elizabeth	23 Dec 1792	Spouse - None
Hoyt, James	Hitchcock, Maria	19 Sep 1833	Spouse - None
Hoyt, James	Mathis, Eliza Jane	28 Jul 1853	Spouse - None
Hoyt, Simon			
Jagger, Jeremiah			
Pedersen, Niels	Pedersen, Mette Katrina	04 Dec 1879	Spouse - None
Pedersen, Oliver Cowdery	Gedge, Phoebe Gold	15 Sep 1926	Spouse - None
Reed, Donal J			
Reed, George M.	Unknown, Ina E		Spouse - None
Reed, Harold Arthur	Bobbitt, Maurine	18 Aug 1923	Spouse - None
Reed, Isaac			

1. Go to the **Collection** tab on the Publish workspace.

2. In **Publication Types**, click **Relationship Reports**.

3. Double-click **Marriage Report**, or select its icon and then click the **Detail** tab.

4. Use the editing panel to change the report. For instructions, see "Customizing a Report" on page 282.

5. Click **Generate Report**.

Family Group Sheet

A family group sheet is one of the most commonly used reports in genealogy. It is a detailed report about a single family (primarily the parents and children of a family, although it also includes the names of the main couple's parents), including names, birth information, death information, marriage information, notes, and sources. If the individual has more than one spouse, a second family group sheet will show that family unit.

Family Group Sheet for William Gedge

Husband:	William Gedge	
Birth:	01 Jan 1830 in Old Buckenham, Norfolk, England	
Death:	30 Dec 1912 in Taylorsville, Salt Lake, Utah, USA	
Burial:	02 Jan 1913 in Salt Lake City, Salt Lake, Utah, USA; Salt Lake City Cemetery	
Marriage:	22 Nov 1855 in Guiltcross, Norfolk, England	
Father:	Reames Gedge	
Mother:	Lucy Kybird	
Wife:	Rachel Bush	
Birth:	10 Oct 1833 in Deopham, Norfolk, England	
Death:	15 Mar 1911 in Salt Lake City, Salt Lake, Utah, USA	
Burial:	17 Mar 1911 in Salt Lake City, Salt Lake, Utah, USA; Salt Lake City Cemetery	
Father:	Robb Bush	
Mother:	Mary Rush	

Children:

1 F	Name:	Leah Gedge
	Birth:	Abt. 1859 in Old Buckenham, Norfolk, England
2 F	Name:	Emma Gedge
	Birth:	30 Aug 1863 in Utah
	Death:	11 Dec 1906 in St George, Washington, Utah, USA
	Burial:	15 Dec 1906 in Salt Lake City, Salt Lake, Utah, USA; Salt Lake City Cemetery
3 F	Name:	Anna Gedge
	Birth:	05 Sep 1865 in Salt Lake City, Salt Lake, Utah, USA
	Death:	09 Jun 1945 in Salt Lake City, Salt Lake, Utah, USA
	Burial:	12 Jun 1942 in Salt Lake City, Salt Lake, Utah, USA; Salt Lake City Cemetery
4 M	Name:	William R. Gedge
	Birth:	30 Jun 1868 in Salt Lake City, Salt Lake, Utah, USA
5 M	Name:	Nathan Gedge
	Birth:	Abt. 1871 in Utah
	Death:	14 Jun 1902 in Brighton, Salt Lake, Utah, USA
	Burial:	14 Jun 1902 in Salt Lake City, Salt Lake, Utah, USA; Salt Lake City Cemetery
6 M	Name:	Herbert Bush Gedge
	Birth:	10 Nov 1872 in Salt Lake City, Salt Lake, Utah, USA
	Death:	09 Aug 1942 in Salt Lake City, Salt Lake, Utah, USA
	Burial:	12 Aug 1942 in Salt Lake City, Salt Lake, Utah, USA; Salt Lake City Cemetery
	Marriage:	20 Nov 1895 in Salt Lake City, Salt Lake, Utah, USA
	Spouse:	Sarah Hannah Gold

1. Go to the **Collection** tab on the Publish workspace.

2. In **Publication Types**, click **Relationship Reports**.

3. Double-click **Family Group Sheet**, or select its icon and then click the **Detail** tab.

4. Use the editing panel to change the report. For instructions, see "Customizing a Report" on page 282.

5. If the primary individual has more than one spouse, choose the spouse whose family group sheet you want to see from the **Spouse(s)** drop-down list.

6. To include blank rows for additional children, choose the number of rows you want from the **Extra children** drop-down list.

7. To include a photograph at the top of the report, choose a photo from the **Family picture** drop-down list. (You can choose any image that is linked to the primary individual's marriage.)

8. Click **Include thumbnails** to include small images of the individuals on the report.

9. Click **Include other spouses** to include the names of additional spouses on the report.

10. Click **Include LDS section** to display LDS-specific ordinances such as baptisms and sealings.

11. Click **Generate Report**.

Outline Descendant Report

This report starts with an ancestor and outlines each generation of descendants; you can even select the number of generations to show in the report.

Outline Descendant Report for Abigail Hait

..... 1 Abigail Hait (1740 - 1796) b: 09 Oct 1740, d: 27 Feb 1796
..... + John Hait (Hoyt) (1740 - 1825) b: 24 Nov 1740, m: 31 Dec 1761, d: 01 Mar 1825
.... 2 Samuel Hoyt (1762 - 1838) b: 08 Nov 1762, d: 22 Sep 1838 in Stamford, Fairfield,
            Connecticut, USA
.... 2 William Hoyt (1764 - 1828) b: 01 Aug 1764, d: 25 Aug 1828
.... 2 John Hoyt (1765 - 1812) b: 02 Dec 1765, d: 25 Dec 1812 in Burlington, Chittenden, Vermont,
            USA
.... 2 Abigail Hoyt (1767 - 1840) b: 31 Oct 1767, d: 26 Aug 1840 in Norwalk, Fairfield, Connecticut,
            USA
.... 2 Benjamin Hoyt (1769 - 1813) b: 19 Feb 1769, d: 21 Nov 1813
.... + Elizabeth Reed (1774 - 1818) b: 15 Nov 1774, m: 23 Dec 1792, d: 11 Jun 1818
.... 3 Sarah Hoyt (1794 -) b: 23 Feb 1794 in Tarrytown, New York
.... 3 Seymour Hoyt (1796 - 1866) b: 22 Mar 1796 in Stamford, Fairfield, Connecticut, USA, d:
            29 Oct 1866
.... 3 Benjamin Hoyt (1798 - 1801) b: 28 Jul 1798 in Stamford, Fairfield, Connecticut, USA, d:
            13 Feb 1801
.... 3 Elizabeth Hoyt (1800 -) b: 05 Aug 1800 in Stamford, Fairfield, Connecticut, USA
.... 3 Benjamin Hoyt (1802 -) b: 26 Nov 1802
.... 3 Emeline Hoyt (1805 - 1854) b: 02 Jun 1805 in Stamford, Fairfield, Connecticut, USA, d:
            09 Jan 1854
.... 3 James Hoyt (1807 -) b: 19 Sep 1807 in Stamford, Fairfield, Connecticut, USA
.... + Maria Hitchcock (1815 - 1850) b: 1815, m: 19 Sep 1833, d: 13 Mar 1850 in Illinois
.... 4 Julia Hoyt (1834 - 1923) b: 06 Sep 1834 in Chillicothe, Ross, Ohio, USA, d: 28 Jul
            1923 in Cortez, Montezuma, Colorado, USA
.... + John W. Bobbitt (1832 -) b: 09 Jun 1832 in Trigg, Kentucky, USA, m: 18 Oct 1852 in
            Marshall County, Illinois
.... 5 Seymour Bobbitt (1854 -) b: Abt. 1854 in Illinois
.... 5 Cornelia Bobbitt (1856 -) b: Abt. 1856 in Illinois
.... 5 James Clarence Bobbitt (1858 - 1929) b: 28 Jul 1858 in Illinois, d: 02 Jun 1929 in
            Balko, Beaver, Oklahoma, USA
.... + Margaret Rebecca Shanklin (1863 - 1944) b: 12 Jul 1863 in Illinois, m: Abt. 1881
            in Fulton, Illinois, USA, d: 29 Mar 1944 in Balko, Beaver, Oklahoma, USA
.... 6 Charity M. Bobbitt (1883 - 1982) b: 10 Mar 1883 in Nebraska, d: May 1982 in
            Gering, Scotts Bluff, Nebraska, USA
.... + William B. Crossman
.... 6 James Leslie Bobbitt (1884 - 1971) b: 19 Sep 1884 in Nebraska, d: 22 Mar
            1971 in Balko, Beaver, Oklahoma, USA
.... 6 Mary Eliza Bobbitt (1886 -) b: 10 Apr 1886 in Nebraska
.... 6 Bessie A. Bobbitt (1888 -) b: 14 Dec 1888 in Nebraska
.... 6 Alta M. Bobbitt (1892 - 1987) b: 09 Feb 1892 in Kansas, d: 04 Nov 1987 in
            Cherokee, Alfalfa, Oklahoma, USA
.... 6 Arthur L. Bobbitt (1897 - 1993) b: 24 Aug 1897 in Oklahoma, d: 05 Jun 1993
            in Oklahoma City, Oklahoma, Oklahoma
.... 6 Twila Margaret Bobbitt (1899 - 1991) b: 18 Jul 1899 in Oklahoma, d: 27 May
            1991 in Boise, Ada, Idaho, USA

1. Go to the **Collection** tab on the Publish workspace.

2. In **Publication Types**, click **Relationship Reports**.

3. Double-click **Outline Descendant Report**, or select its icon and then click the **Detail** tab.

4. Use the editing panel to change the report. For instructions, see "Customizing a Report" on page 282.

5. Choose the number of generations of descendants to include from the **Generations** drop-down list.

6. If you want to change the symbol that prints before each indented entry (the default is a period), enter the character in **Indentation character**.

7. To have each generation given a number, click the **Include generation number** checkbox and choose the beginning number from **Starting generation number**.

8. If you want the names of spouses to be included, click the **Include spouses** checkbox.

9. If you want to include an individual's date range after his or her name, click the **Include (B-D)** checkbox.

10. Click **Generate Report**.

Parentage Report

The Parentage Report lists each individual, the individual's parents, and the relationship between the individual and parents (e.g., natural, adopted, foster).

Parentage Report

Name	Parents	Relationship
(Hoyt), John Hait	Hait, Samuel	Natural
	Bell, Abigail	Natural
Bell, Abigail		
Bell, Permelia A.		
Bennington, Constance	Bennington, William Jr.	Natural
	Smith, Margaret	Natural
Bennington, Mary Elizabeth	Bennington, William Jr.	Natural
	Smith, Margaret	Natural
Bennington, Sarah	Bennington, William	Natural
	Smith, Margaret	Natural
Bennington, William		
Bennington, William Jr.		
Bobbitt, Alta M.	Bobbitt, James Clarence	Natural
	Shanklin, Margaret Rebecca	Natural
Bobbitt, Arthur L.	Bobbitt, James Clarence	Natural
	Shanklin, Margaret Rebecca	Natural
Bobbitt, Bessie A.	Bobbitt, James Clarence	Natural
	Shanklin, Margaret Rebecca	Natural
Bobbitt, Charity M.	Bobbitt, James Clarence	Natural
	Shanklin, Margaret Rebecca	Natural
Bobbitt, Cornelia	Bobbitt, John W.	Natural
	Hoyt, Julia	Natural
Bobbitt, Eugene A.	Bobbitt, John W.	Natural
	Hoyt, Julia	Natural
Bobbitt, Fern Edna	Bobbitt, James Clarence	Natural
	Shanklin, Margaret Rebecca	Natural
Bobbitt, Francis M.	Bobbitt, John W.	Natural
	Hoyt, Julia	Natural
Bobbitt, Isham Drury Jr.		
Bobbitt, James Clarence	Bobbitt, John W.	Natural
	Hoyt, Julia	Natural
Bobbitt, James Leslie	Bobbitt, James Clarence	Natural
	Shanklin, Margaret Rebecca	Natural
Bobbitt, Jessie	Bobbitt, John W.	Natural
	Hoyt, Julia	Natural
Bobbitt, John W.	Bobbitt, Isham Drury Jr.	Natural
	Haggard, Cynthia	Natural
Bobbitt, Lorine	Bobbitt, James Clarence	Natural
	Shanklin, Margaret Rebecca	Natural

1. Go to the **Collection** tab on the Publish workspace.

2. In **Publication Types**, click **Relationship Reports**.

3. Double-click **Parentage Report**, or select its icon and then click the **Detail** tab.

4. Use the editing panel to change the report. For instructions, see "Customizing a Report" on page 282.

5. Click **Generate Report**.

Place Usage Report

The Place Usage Report lists the locations you have entered into your tree and each person associated with that location. You can also choose to include the specific events, such as birth or marriage, that occurred in that location.

Place Usage Report

Aston, Warwickshire, England (con't)
Thompson, Sarah
    Marr: 27 Jan 1845

Balko, Beaver, Oklahoma, USA
Bobbitt, James Clarence
    Burial: 02 Jun 1929 Pleasant Hill Cemetery

Balko, Beaver, Oklahoma, USA
Bobbitt, James Clarence
    Death: 02 Jun 1929
Hewitt, Jessie Izetta
    Death: 04 Nov 1936
Shanklin, Margaret Rebecca
    Death: 29 Mar 1944
    Burial: 29 Mar 1944 Pleasant Hills Cemetery

Beaver, Beaver, Oklahoma, USA
Bobbitt, Maurine
    Marr: 18 Aug 1923
Reed, George M.
    Death: 01 Jan 1966
Reed, Harold Arthur
    Marr: 18 Aug 1923

Bedford County, Pennsylvania, USA
Smith, Margaret
    Birth: 16 Apr 1772

Bell Plain, Marshall, Illinois, USA
Shanklin, James
    Census: 1860

Benton, Arkansas, USA
Bobbitt, Maurine
    Res: 1924

Birmingham, Warwickshire, England
Thompson, George
    Baptism: 19 Sep 1791
Thompson, Sarah
    Birth: 1827

Boone County, Kentucky, USA
Bennington, Constance
    Birth: 1806
Bennington, William
    Death: 1817
Smith, Margaret
    Death: 08 May 1813

Boone, Kentucky, USA
Bennington, Sarah
    Birth: 17 Feb 1812

1. Go to the **Collection** tab on the Publish workspace.

2. In **Publication Types**, click **Place Reports**.

3. Double-click **Place Usage Report**, or select its icon and then click the **Detail** tab.

4. Use the editing panel to change the report. For instructions, see "Customizing a Report" on page 282.

5. If you want the report to include specific facts that are associated with a location, click the **Show facts** checkbox.

6. Click **Generate Report**.

Tip

All reports are based on the last individual you were viewing in your tree. To change the primary individual in the report, click his or her name in the mini pedigree tree above the report, or click the Index of Individuals button and choose the person you want.

Media Reports

The media reports in Family Tree Maker let you view media items individually or compiled into groups.

Media Item Report

You can create a report about any media item you have included in your tree, including its caption, date of origin, description, and any individuals associated with the item. This report is most useful for image files.

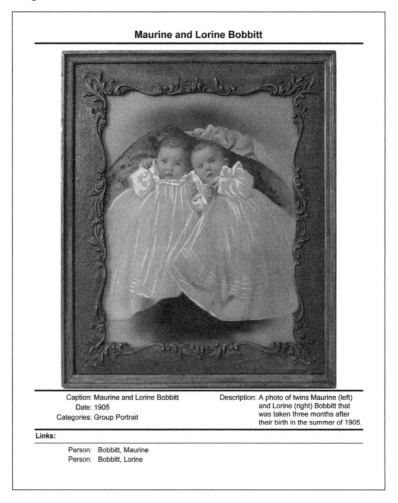

Maurine and Lorine Bobbitt

Caption: Maurine and Lorine Bobbitt
Date: 1905
Categories: Group Portrait

Description: A photo of twins Maurine (left) and Lorine (right) Bobbitt that was taken three months after their birth in the summer of 1905.

Links:

Person: Bobbitt, Maurine
Person: Bobbitt, Lorine

1. Go to the **Collection** tab on the Publish workspace.

2. In **Publication Types**, click **Media Reports**.

3. Double-click **Media Item**, or select its icon and then click the **Detail** tab.

4. Use the editing panel to change the report. For instructions, see "Customizing a Report" on page 282.

5. To choose the image displayed in the report, click the **Find Media** button next to the Media item field and locate the image.

6. Click **Generate Report**.

Media Usage Report

The Media Usage Report shows a thumbnail of every media item in your tree; lists each item's name and location; and shows which sources, facts, and individuals each item is linked to.

Media Usage Report

Records of the olden time, or, Fifty years on the prairies : embracing sketches of the discovery, exploration and settlement of
    File Location: C:\Documents and Settings\tlord\Desktop\Family Tree Maker\ReedPedersen_2009 Media\records.tmp
        Source Ancestry.com, Records of the olden time, or, Fifty years on the prairies : Citation: embracing sketches of the discovery, exploration and settlement of (Provo, UT, The Generations Network, Inc., 2005), www.ancestry.com, Database online. Record for.
        Source Ancestry.com, Records of the olden time, or, Fifty years on the prairies : Citation: embracing sketches of the discovery, exploration and settlement of (Provo, UT, The Generations Network, Inc., 2005), www.ancestry.com, Page 768.

Reed 1930 Census
    File Location: C:\Documents and Settings\tlord\Desktop\Family Tree Maker\ReedPedersen_2009 Media\Media0010.jpg
        Source 1930 United States Federal Census, www.ancestry.com. Citation:

Reed California Home c. 1930
    File Location: C:\Documents and Settings\tlord\Desktop\Family Tree Maker\ReedPedersen_2009 Media\Media0149.jpg
    Relationship: Harold Arthur Reed, Maurine Bobbitt

Reed Family
    File Location: C:\Documents and Settings\tlord\Desktop\Family Tree Maker\ReedPedersen_2009 Media\Media0163.jpg
    Relationship: Michael John Reed, Jessie Izetta Hewitt

Reed Family in 1968
    File Location: C:\Documents and Settings\tlord\Desktop\Family Tree Maker\ReedPedersen_2009 Media\ReedFamily60s.bmp
    Person: Bobbitt, Maurine

ReedMarriageCertificate.jpg
    File Location: C:\Documents and Settings\tlord\Desktop\Family Tree Maker\ReedPedersen_2009 Media\ReedMarriageCertificate.jpg
    Person: Bobbitt, Maurine

REEDsisters.bmp
    File Location: C:\Documents and Settings\tlord\Desktop\Family Tree Maker\ReedPedersen_2009 Media\REEDsisters.bmp
    [not linked to people, facts, or sources]

ReedSisters_FlorenceCoraLela.jpg
    File Location: C:\Documents and Settings\tlord\Desktop\Family Tree Maker\ReedPedersen_2009 Media\ReedSisters_FlorenceCoraLela.jpg
    [not linked to people, facts, or sources]

Sarah Age 16
    File Location: C:\Documents and Settings\tlord\Desktop\Family Tree Maker\ReedPedersen_2009 Media\Media0116.jpg
    Person: Gold, Sarah Hannah

---

1. Go to the **Collection** tab on the Publish workspace.

2. In **Publication Types**, click **Media Reports**.

3. Double-click **Media Usage Report**, or select its icon and then click the **Detail** tab.

4. Use the editing panel to change the report. For instructions, see "Customizing a Report" on page 282.

5. Click **Generate Report**.

Photo Album

The photo album shows a basic summary of an individual's life events, such as birth and death dates, and also includes all photos associated with the person.

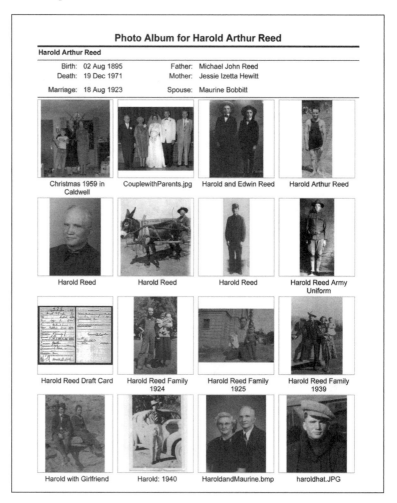

1. Go to the **Collection** tab on the Publish workspace.

2. In **Publication Types**, click **Media Reports**.

3. Double-click **Photo Album**, or select its icon and then click the **Detail** tab.

4. Use the editing panel to change the report. For instructions, see "Customizing a Report" on page 282.

5. Choose the number of images you want on each row in the report by choosing a number from the **Photos per row** drop-down list.

6. If you want to include only photos that are linked to the selected individual, click the **Show person photos only** checkbox. Images linked to sources or facts will not be included.

7. Click **Generate Report**.

Source Reports

Because making your family history accurate and complete is important, Family Tree Maker includes several reports that help you view how you've sourced facts in your tree.

Bibliography

The bibliography lists all the sources you used in your research.

Source Bibliography

1850 United States Federal Census, www.ancestry.com, Source Medium: Ancestry.com

1860 United States Federal Census, www.ancestry.com, Source Medium: Ancestry.com

1870 United States Federal Census, www.ancestry.com, Source Medium: Ancestry.com

1880 United States Federal Census, www.ancestry.com, Source Medium: Ancestry.com

1900 United States Federal Census, www.ancestry.com, Source Medium: Ancestry.com
Twelfth Census of the United States, 1900, Washington, D.C.: National Archives and Records
Administration, 1900

1910 United States Federal Census, www.ancestry.com, Source Medium: Ancestry.com

1920 United States Federal Census, www.ancestry.com, Source Medium: Ancestry.com
Fourteenth Census of the United States, 1920, Washington, D.C.: National Archives and Records
Administration, 1920

1930 United States Federal Census, www.ancestry.com, Source Medium: Ancestry.com
Fifteenth Census of the United States, 1930, Washington, D.C.: National Archives and Records
Administration, 1930

A Genealogical History of the Hoyt, Haight, and Hight Families (Chicago, Illinois, The S.J. Clarke
Publishing Company, 1886), Family History Library, 35 North West Temple Street
Salt Lake City, Utah 84150-3440.

Ancestry.com, Records of the olden time, or, Fifty years on the prairies : embracing sketches of the
discovery, exploration and settlement of (Provo, UT, The Generations Network, Inc., 2005),
www.ancestry.com, Ellsworth, Spencer., Records of the olden time, or, Fifty years on the prairies :
embracing sketches of the discovery, exploration and settlement of the country, the organization of the
counties of Putnam and Marshall, incidents and reminiscences connected therewith, biographies of
citizens, portraits and illustrations, Lacon, Ill.: Home Journal Steam Printing Establishment, 1880.

California Birth Index, 1905-10, www.ancestry.com, Source Medium: Ancestry.com

California Birth Index, 1905-1995, www.ancestry.com, Source Medium: Ancestry.com

California Death Index, 1940-1997, www.ancestry.com, Source Medium: Ancestry.com

Cemetery Records: Pleasant Hill, www.rootsweb.com/~okcemete/beaver/phill.htm.

Illinois State Archives, Illinois Statewide Marriage Index, 1763–1900,
http://www.cyberdriveillinois.com/GenealogyMWeb/MarriageSearchServlet.

Kentucky Marriages to 1850, Source Medium: Book

LDS IGI Records, Source Medium: Book

1. Go to the **Collection** tab on the Publish workspace.

2. In **Publication Types**, click **Source Reports**.

3. Double-click **Source Bibliography**, or select its icon and then click the **Detail** tab.

4. Use the editing panel to change the report. For instructions, see "Customizing a Report" on page 282.

5. Click **Generate Report**.

Documented Facts Report

The Documented Facts Report lists all of the events for which you have entered source information. Conversely, you can choose to show all of the events for which you do not have source information and use the report as a reminder of what you still need to research.

Documented Facts

Bennington, Mary Elizabeth
      1   Hester Geralding Lester Searl, *Hester Genealogy: A Story of Some Descendants of John Hester, an Early Settler of Fleming County, Kentucky, Who Arrived in America in the year 1740* (University of Wisconsin: Searl, 1972), Page 20. On March 17, 1814 in Fleming Co., Ky. John Hester married Mary Elizabeth (Polly) Bennington the daughter of William Bennington, Jr. and Margaret (Smith) Bennington.

Bennington, Sarah
Marr: 21 Mar 1837 in Fulton County, Illinois
      1   Illinois State Archives, Illinois Statewide Marriage Index, 1763-1900, http://www.cyberdriveillinois.com/GenealogyMWeb/MarriageSearchServlet, 00A/0034 00000033.

Bennington, William Jr.
Marr: 16 Apr 1793 in Bourbon County, Kentucky, USA
      1   "Bourbon County, Kentucky Marriage Records, 1786-1800", database, Ancestry.com, *Ancestry.com*, (www.ancestry.com), William Bennington and Margaret Smith Marriage. Name: Wm BenningtonSpouse: Margaret SmithMarriage Date: 16 Apr 1793.
Name: Bennington, William Jr.
      1   Hester Geralding Lester Searl, *Hester Genealogy: A Story of Some Descendants of John Hester, an Early Settler of Fleming County, Kentucky, Who Arrived in America in the year 1740* (University of Wisconsin: Searl, 1972), Page 20. On March 17, 1814 in Fleming Co., Ky. John Hester married Mary Elizabeth (Polly) Bennington the daughter of William Bennington, Jr. and Margaret (Smith) Bennington.

Bobbitt, Alta M.
Birth: 09 Feb 1892 in Kansas
      1   Ancestry.com, 1900 United States Federal Census (Provo, UT, USA, The Generations Network, Inc., 2004), www.ancestry.com, James Clarence Bobbitt household. Database online. Stone, Woods, Oklahoma, ED , roll , page. Record for James C Bobbitt. [Source citation includes media item(s)]
      2   Social Security Death Index, www.ancestry.com, Alta M. Ford SSN: 448-26-7828
           Last Residence: Cherokee, Alfalfa, Oklahoma.
Death: 04 Nov 1987
      1   Social Security Death Index, www.ancestry.com.
      2   Social Security Death Index, www.ancestry.com, Alta M. Ford SSN: 448-26-7828
           Last Residence: Cherokee, Alfalfa, Oklahoma.
Res: 1900 in Stone, Woods, Oklahoma
      1   Ancestry.com, 1900 United States Federal Census (Provo, UT, USA, The Generations Network, Inc., 2004), www.ancestry.com, James Clarence Bobbitt household. Database online. Stone, Woods, Oklahoma, ED , roll , page. Record for James C Bobbitt. [Source citation includes media item(s)]
Sex: Female
      1   Ancestry.com, 1900 United States Federal Census (Provo, UT, USA, The Generations Network, Inc., 2004), www.ancestry.com, James Clarence Bobbitt household. Database online. Stone, Woods,

1. Go to the **Collection** tab on the Publish workspace.

2. In **Publication Types**, click **Source Reports**.

3. Double-click **Documented Facts**, or select its icon and then click the **Detail** tab.

4. Use the editing panel to change the report. For instructions, see "Customizing a Report" on page 282.

5. Click **Generate Report**.

Source Usage Report

The Source Usage Report includes each source you have created
and lists the individuals and facts associated with that source. This
report helps you determine which recorded facts are supported
by sources. It can be useful in keeping track of the sources you've
researched and lets you compare notes with other researchers. You
can choose whether to include individuals and facts for sources or
only individuals.

Source Usage Report

Source Title:	**California Death Index, 1940-1997 (con't)**
Repository:	www.ancestry.com
Citation:	California Death Index, 1940-1997, www.ancestry.com, Ancestry.com. California Death Index, 1940-1997. [database online] Provo, UT: Ancestry.com, 2000. Original electronic data: State of California. California Death Index, 1940-1997. Sacramento, CA: State of California Department of Health Services, Center for Health Statistics, 19--.

Reed, Luzilla May
Birth: 09 Jun 1886 in Kansas
Death: 13 Apr 1940 in Tehama, California

Citation: California Death Index, 1940-1997, www.ancestry.com, Ancestry.com. California Death Index, 1940-1997. [database online] Provo, UT: Ancestry.com, 2000. Original electronic data: State of California. California Death Index, 1940-1997. Sacramento, CA: State of California Department of Health Services, Center for Health Statistics, 19--.

Reed, Lela M.
Name: WISE, Lela M.
Birth: 11 Sep 1887 in Kansas
Birth: 11 Sep 1887 in Kansas
Death: 03 Dec 1968 in FRESNO, California
Death: 03 Dec 1968 in FRESNO, California

Citation: California Death Index, 1940-1997, www.ancestry.com, Ancestry.com. California Death Index, 1940-1997. [database online] Provo, UT: Ancestry.com, 2000. Original electronic data: State of California. California Death Index, 1940-1997. Sacramento, CA: State of California Department of Health Services, Center for Health Statistics, 19--.

Reed, Edwin Ernest
Birth: 03 Dec 1893 in Kansas
Death: 05 Sep 1974 in Merced, California, USA

Citation: California Death Index, 1940-1997, www.ancestry.com, Ancestry.com. California Death Index, 1940-1997. [database online] Provo, UT: Ancestry.com, 2000. Original electronic data: State of California. California Death Index, 1940-1997. Sacramento, CA: State of California Department of Health Services, Center for Health Statistics, 19--.

Reed, Cora Evelyn
Name: WEST, Cora Evelyn
Birth: 31 Mar 1901 in Kansas
Death: 25 Jul 1982 in Tehama, California

Source Title:	**Cemetery Records: Pleasant Hill**
Repository:	www.rootsweb.com/~okcemete/beaver/phill.htm
Citation:	Cemetery Records: Pleasant Hill, www.rootsweb.com/~okcemete/beaver/phill.htm.

Bobbitt, James Clarence
Birth: 28 Jul 1858 in Illinois
Death: 02 Jun 1929 in Balko, Beaver, Oklahoma, USA
Hewitt, Jessie Izetta
Birth: 03 Jun 1858 in Pennsylvania
Death: 04 Nov 1936 in Balko, Beaver, Oklahoma, USA

Note: If you have not assigned a source to any facts, the report will include the fact and the message "Not associated with any facts."

1. Go to the **Collection** tab on the Publish workspace.

2. In **Publication Types**, click **Source Reports**.

3. Double-click **Source Usage Report**, or select its icon and then click the **Detail** tab.

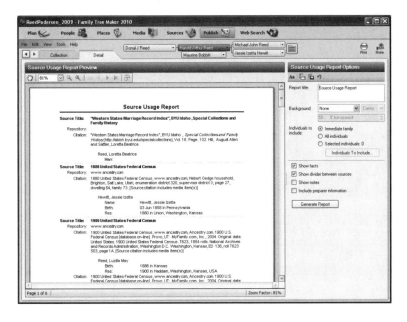

4. Use the editing panel to change the report. For instructions, see "Customizing a Report" on page 282.

5. To include the specific facts associated with each source, click the **Show facts** checkbox.

6. To include notes associated with each source citation, click the **Show notes** checkbox.

7. Click **Generate Report**.

Calendars

You can make a monthly calendar that displays all the birthdays and anniversaries included in your tree. Because you can choose which individuals to include, you can create a calendar for your own family or make one that celebrates your ancestors.

September 2009

September 2009	October 2009
S M T W T F S	S M T W T F S
1 2 3 4 5	1 2 3
6 7 8 9 10 11 12	4 5 6 7 8 9 10
13 14 15 16 17 18 19	11 12 13 14 15 16 17
20 21 22 23 24 25 26	18 19 20 21 22 23 24
27 28 29 30	25 26 27 28 29 30 31

Sunday	Monday	Tuesday	Wednesday	Thursday	Friday	Saturday
		1	2	3	4 Joseph W. HOYT - 234	5 Anna GEDGE - 143
6 Julia HOYT BOBBITT - 175 James SHANKLIN - 199	7	8 Hannah HAIT - 293	9	10 Mary E. GOLD - 129	11 Leander HOYT - 226 Lela M. REED WISE - 122	12
13	14 Deodate HAIT - 271	15 Phoebe G. and Oliver C. PEDERSEN - 83	16	17 Melancthon HOYT - 239	18 Susanna HAIT - 255	19 James L. BOBBITT - 125 Maria and James HOYT - 176 James HOYT - 202 Julia HOYT - 202
20 Mary HAIT - 336	21	22 Niels PEDERSEN - 160	23 Charles E. HOYT - 163	24	25	26 Elizabeth HAIT - 299
27 George M. REED - 120	28	29	30			

1. Go to the **Collection** tab on the Publish workspace.

2. In **Publication Types**, click **Other**.

3. Double-click **Calendar Report**, or select its icon and then click the **Detail** tab.

4. To customize the calendar, click the **Calendar Options** button in the report toolbar. The Calendar Options window opens.

5. Change the calendar as necessary:

In this section	Do this
Begin	Choose the starting month and year for the calendar. You can also choose the number of months to include—up to thirty-six.
People	Click **Use married names for female birthdays** to include a woman's married and maiden names on her birthday.
	Click **Use married names for female anniversaries** to include a woman's married and maiden names on her wedding anniversary.
	Click **Use AKA if available** to include names you've entered in the AKA field for an individual.
	Click **Display last name in all caps** to display surnames in capital letters.
	Click **Print only if still living** to include individuals who don't have a death date or whose birth date is less than 120 years ago.
Event items to include	Click **Birthdays** to display birth dates you've entered in your tree. To change the color of the text, choose a color from the drop-down list. Click **Include age for birthdays** to display the individual's age on their birthday.
	Click **Anniversaries** to display marriage dates you've entered in your tree. To change the color of the text, choose a color from the drop-down list. Click **Include years for anniversaries** to display the number of years married on anniversaries.
Anniversaries after death of one spouse	Click the checkbox to exclude anniversaries in cases where the relationship status has been marked as "Deceased."
Background color	Choose a color for the days of the calendar from the drop-down list.

6. Click **OK**.

Customizing a Report

You can customize the contents and format of many reports in Family Tree Maker. For example, you can determine which individuals and facts are included in the report and choose background images and text options.

Changing General Customization Options

A few customization options can be changed for every report in
Family Tree Maker. This task explains how to modify these options.

1. Access the report you want to change. The editing panel displays
   the options you can change.

2. Use this chart to help you customize a report:

In this field	Do this
Report title	Enter a new title for the report.
Background	Change the background image for the report. For instructions, see "Adding a Background Image" on page 287.
Individuals to include	Change which people are included in the report. For instructions, see "Choosing Individuals to Include in a Report" on page 284.
Show divider	Click this box to include a graphical dividing line between individuals in the report.
Include preparer information	Click this box to include your personal information on the report.

Choosing Individuals to Include in a Report

In many reports, you can choose which individuals will be included. You might want to choose a specific ancestor and only his or her descendants, or you may choose to include everyone in the tree. You can also choose individuals by picking specific criteria (for example, you may want to generate a report that shows all individuals who were born in a particular city).

1. Access the report you want to change. You can choose individuals for the report in the editing panel.

2. Do one of these options:

   • If you want to include the individual's immediate family members, click **Immediate family**.

   • If you want to include everyone in your tree in the report, click **All individuals**.

   • If you want to choose specific individuals to include in the report, click **Selected individuals**. The Filter Individuals window opens. Click a name and then click **Include** to add the person. When you're finished choosing individuals click **OK**.

Tip

For more instructions on selecting individuals, see "Using the Filter Individuals Window" on page 25.

Choosing Facts to Include in a Report

When customizing your report, you can often choose which facts you'd like to include.

1. Access the report you want to change.

2. In the editing toolbar, click the **Items to include** button.

Items to include button

The Items to Include window opens. The default facts for the report are shown in the Included facts list. You can add and delete facts for a report and also change display options for each fact. For example, you can change the order in which a name displays.

3. Do one of these options:

- To delete a fact from a report, click the fact in the Included facts list and click the red (**X**) button.

- To add a fact to the report, click the blue (**+**) button. The Select Fact window opens. Choose a fact from the list and click **OK**.

4. In the Items to Include window, complete these fields as necessary:

In this section	Do this
Fact options	You may have multiple facts for the same event. Click **Include only preferred facts** to include only the facts designated as "preferred."
	Click **Include private facts** to include facts designated as "private."
	Click **Include blank facts** to include a fact field even if the fact has not been entered for an individual.
	If you have entered shortened place names for locations, click **Display user-defined short place name** to use these locations in the report.
Notes	Click **Include person notes** to include person notes linked to individuals.
	Click **Include research notes** to include research notes linked to individuals.
	Click **Include relationship notes** to include person notes linked to relationships.
	Click **Include fact notes** to include notes linked to specific facts.
	Click **Include private notes** to include any note that has been designated as "private."

5. To change the display options for a fact, click the fact in the Included facts list. Then click the **Options** button. The Options window opens.

Note: The options for each fact vary. For example, with births, marriages, and deaths, you can include dates and locations.

6. Change the options for the fact and click **OK**.

7. Click **OK**.

Changing the Formatting of a Report

You can change the text styles and background images for reports. (You can also change page setup options such as margins and page size. For instructions, see "Changing Printing Options" on page 292.)

Adding a Background Image

Family Tree Maker comes with several attractive images you can use as your report's background, or you can select your own images stored on your computer or family pictures you've already added to your tree.

1. Access the report you want to change.

2. In the **Background** field, choose an image from the drop-down list:

   - To choose a Family Tree Maker background picture, click the image's name.

   - To choose an image you've already added to your tree, click **Select a media item**. The Find Media Item window opens. Choose an image and click **OK**.

   - To look for an item on your computer's hard drive, click **Browse for an image**. The Select Report Background Image window opens. Choose an image and click **Open**.

3. Choose where the image will be displayed on the report. If you want the image centered in the background, click **Center**. If you want the image stretched to fit the entire page, click **Stretch**. If you want a close-up of the image, click **Zoom**. If you want a series of the same image to fill the background, click **Tile**.

4. In the transparency drop-down list, choose the intensity of the image. At zero percent, the image will appear at its usual intensity, while a higher percentage will fade the image so the report is easier to read.

Changing Fonts

You can change the appearance of the text in reports to make it more formal, more fun, or maybe just more readable.

1. Access the report you want to change.

2. In the editing toolbar, click the **Fonts** button.

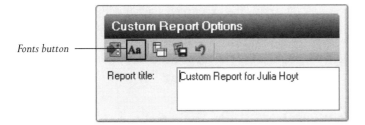

Fonts button

The Fonts window opens.

3. In the **Items to format** list, click the text element you would like to change, such as the report title.

4. Choose a font from the **Font** drop-down list. You can also change the size of the text, its style, color, and alignment. The Sample box shows you how your font choices will appear in the report.

5. Click **OK** to save your changes.

Saving Reports

You can save reports you've created in two ways: within Family Tree Maker and as an exported file.

Saving a Report in Family Tree Maker

After you've modified or customized a report you may want to save it. That way you can access the exact report again without having to recreate it.

1. After you have modified the report, click the **Save report** button in the editing toolbar.

The Save Report window opens.

Tip

To open a saved report, go to the **Collection** tab on the Publish workspace. In **Publication Types**, click **Saved Reports**. Then double-click the report you want to open.

290

2. Enter a name for the report in the **Report name** field. Be sure to use a name that will distinguish the report from others. For example, don't use generic terms like "Family Group Sheet" or "Custom Report."

3. Click **Save**.

Saving a Report as a File

You may want to save a report to a file format compatible with software other than Family Tree Maker; for example, a spreadsheet or word-processing program. These files can be easily shared with others, posted on a website, or have additional facts and data added to them.

1. Access the report you want to save.

2. Click the **Share** button above the editing panel.

3. From the drop-down list, choose one of these options:

   • **Export to PDF.** An Adobe PDF (Portable Document Format) is useful because PDFs keep the formatting you select. That way, if you print your report or send it to a relative, the report will look exactly as you see it on your monitor. You cannot make changes to the PDF within Family Tree Maker, and you need the Adobe *Reader* in order to view it. (Adobe *Reader* can be downloaded for free from the Adobe website.)

   • **Export to CSV.** This format organizes information into fields (comma-separated values) and is meant to be imported into spreadsheet programs. Only reports that use column formats can be exported to CSV.

   • **Export to RTF.** This word-processor format is based on a basic text file, but it can include information such as text style, size, and color. Also, this is a universal format, so it can be read by nearly all word processors.

- **Export to HTML.** The Hypertext Markup Language format is the standard language for creating and formatting Web pages.

Each format has its own export options you can choose from. After you choose a format type, you may be able to choose options such as page borders and text separators. Once you've made your selections, the Save As window opens.

4. Use the **Save in** drop-down list to find the location where you want to save the report.

5. Enter a name for the report in the **File name** field.

6. Click **Save**.

Printing Reports

When you are done creating and customizing a report, you may want to print it out. Family Tree Maker makes it easy to choose setup options and print a report.

Changing Printing Options

Before you print a report, you might want to change the margins, print orientation, or paper size. Changes you make to the print setup will apply only to the report you're accessing.

1. Access the report you want to change.

2. In the editing toolbar, click the **Page setup** button.

The Page Setup window opens.

3. Click the **Size** drop-down list to change the size of the paper if your printer is capable of printing larger sheets of paper. Otherwise, leave the selection at letter size, which is a standard 8 ½" x 11" sheet of paper.

4. If necessary, choose a paper type or paper tray from the **Source** drop-down list.

5. In the **Orientation** section, click **Portrait** if you want your document to print with the short edge of the paper at the bottom (the way a letter normally prints). This is the default setting. Click **Landscape** if you want your document to print with the long edge of the paper at the bottom.

6. In the **Margins** section, make any necessary changes to the margin size of your report. By default, each page prints with one-inch margins on the left and right, and half-inch margins on the top and bottom.

7. Click **OK**.

Printing a Report

1. Access the report you want to print.

2. Click the **Print** button above the editing panel. The Print window opens.

   Just like printing from any other application, you can choose a printer, select the number of copies, and choose a page range.

3. Click **Print**.

Sharing a Report

Family Tree Maker lets you share reports with others—via e-mail—in a variety of formats.

> Note: You must be connected to the Internet and have e-mail access to use this feature.

1. Access the report you want to e-mail.

2. Click the **Share** button above the editing panel.

3. From the drop-down list, choose one of these options:

   • **Send as PDF.** The Adobe PDF retains printer formatting and graphical elements so it resembles how the printed document will appear.

   • **Send as CSV.** This format organizes information into fields (comma-separated values) and is meant to be imported into spreadsheet programs. Only reports that use column formats can be exported to CSV.

- **Send as RTF.** This word-processor format is based on a basic text file, but it can include information such as text style, size, and color. Also, this is a universal format, so it can be read by nearly all word processors.

- **Send as Image.** This option lets you create an image of the report as a bitmap, JPEG, and other image formats.

Each format has its own export options you can choose from. After you choose a format type, you may be able to choose options such as page borders and text separators. Once you've made your selections, the Save As window opens.

4. Use the **Save in** drop-down list to find the location where you want to save the report.

5. Enter a name for the report in the **File name** field.

6. Click **Save**. Family Tree Maker opens a new e-mail (with the file attached) in your default e-mail program.

7. Send the e-mail as you would any other.

Chapter 9

Creating a Family History Book

For many family historians the ultimate goal—and reward—is to publish a record of their ancestry. And what could be more convenient than using the same software to organize your family history *and* create a book to tell your ancestral story?

Family Tree Maker gives you access to two publishing tools that will help you create a quality family history book that you and your family will enjoy for many years to come. The first tool is a desktop book-building feature built into the Family Tree Maker software. It's a great way to assemble a traditional genealogy using the images, facts, charts, and reports you've already entered in your tree; you can also use the text-editing features to add stories and additional information. The second tool is MyCanvas, a Web-based publishing service. It's perfect for creating scrapbooks, photo books, memorial books, and more informal family histories.

Desktop Book-Building or MyCanvas?

Family Tree Maker includes a desktop book-building tool integrated into the Family Tree Maker software and access to an online self-publishing service called MyCanvas. Before starting your family history book, you should decide which tool is best for the type of book you're creating. Here's a side-by-side comparison of their features:

- **Text.** The desktop tool handles text like any word processing program. You can choose fonts and formatting, change spacing and margins, and flow text from page to page. MyCanvas also lets you add and format text; however, you cannot flow text from page to page and your font and formatting choices are limited.

- **Images.** Both tools let you add photos and images of records. However, MyCanvas has photo-editing capabilities that help you crop and resize images, rotate pictures on a page, and even add finishing touches like drop-shadows and borders.

- **Charts and reports.** MyCanvas can generate standard pedigree charts, descendant charts, and timelines. The desktop tool lets you include any trees, charts, and reports available in Family Tree Maker.

- **Print options.** The desktop tool allows you to print your book on a home printer or export it as a PDF, which you can take to a copy shop to be professionally printed and bound. MyCanvas also allows you to print your book pages at home; however, the quality of the printout will be low. For a fee MyCanvas will professionally print and bind your book and send it to you.

- **Book size.** The desktop tool lets you choose a landscape or portrait layout, and you can include as many pages as you'd like. MyCanvas books are available in 8" x 8", 14" x 11", and 11" x 8 1/2". And while you can include as many pages as you'd like, you pay a flat fee for the first twenty pages and a fee for each additional page.

- **Accessibility.** Because a MyCanvas book is stored online you can work on your project anywhere you have a computer and an Internet connection. You can also allow others to access your book and add their own stories. A book created in Family Tree Maker can only be worked on in the software. However, if you have gathered all the records, photos, and text files you need on your computer, you don't have to worry about uploading these to an online site.

Planning Your Book

You want to capture your ancestry in a book. But how do you get started? Before you grab a pen and paper or your keyboard, you can make some decisions that will simplify the process.

Creating the Book You Want

Family history books come in many forms. As you start sketching out your book, there are a few questions you might want to ask yourself.

- What type of book do you want to create? A biography? Auto-biography? A standard family history? A scrapbook? As you're sorting through material to use, knowing what the final product will be can help you weed out irrelevant information and images.

- Who is your audience? For example, if you're creating a book to be submitted to a local genealogy society, you'll need to plan on including a variety of charts and reports and numerous sources. However, if your book is for your grandchildren, you might want to fill your pages with photos and personal stories.

- Who is your book about? A book that mentions every individual in your tree could be overwhelming for a reader—and take forever to create, depending on the size of your tree. You may want to focus on a specific family line or a certain number of generations.

- What will you do with the book when you're done? If you're planning on having the book printed and bound at a copy shop or publishing company, start looking now to find the company that best fits your needs.

For advice on writing your family history, you may want to read Patricia Law Hatcher's *Producing a Quality Family History* or *Writing Up Your Family History: A Do-It-Yourself Guide* by John Titford.

Preparing Your File

Perhaps the best thing you can do to give your book project a good start is to make sure that your Family Tree Maker file is as complete and accurate as possible. Take some time to go through your file with a critical eye and evaluate your information. Remember, in a book, your research will likely be scrutinized by others. Here are some tips to get you started:

- Review your sources. Are your facts documented and sourced? Have you checked for inaccurate dates and spelling errors?

- Make sure you have been consistent when entering data. Are individuals' names spelled the same throughout your tree? Have you entered counties and countries for locations (where known)?

- Create customized reports or charts and save them. Although you can create a report within a book, you can save time by making a list of all the reports and charts you want to use in your book and creating them beforehand.

- Gather your photos, records, and images. If you haven't already, scan any photos or records you want to include in the book and have them accessible from your computer's hard drive.

- Run the Data Errors report. This will show you which fields have been left blank, discover duplicate individuals, find capitalization errors, and more.

The Desktop Book-Building Tool

Family Tree Maker lets you create a family history right on your own desktop using its book-building tool. Getting started is easy because you can use the facts, photos, charts, and reports already in your file. Add some personal stories and anecdotes, and you're ready to combine all the pieces together into a real book you can share with others electronically or take to a copy shop to be printed and bound.

The Book-Building Workspace

The book-building workspace (see figure 9-1) lets you write stories, add charts and images, and develop your family history book without leaving Family Tree Maker. The Detail tab has two main sections: the display area, where the book's content appears; and the book panel, which shows an outline of your book.

Use the book panel toolbar to add or delete sections and change their properties.

You can show or hide the rulers and toolbars using the View menu.

The button bar has standard options such as saving a document and spell checking.

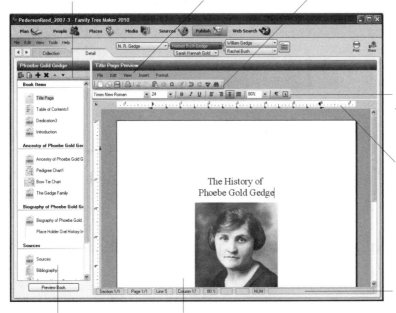

The editing toolbar helps you format text. It works like any word processing program.

Horizontal and vertical rulers display margins, paragraph indents, and tabs.

The status bar shows information about the current document such as page and section numbers.

The book panel shows your book in outline form.

Display area. If you're working with a chart or report, this area will have an additional editing panel.

Figure 9-1. The book-building workspace

Starting a New Book

1. Go to the **Collection** tab on the Publish workspace.

2. In **Publication Types**, click **Books**.

3. Double-click **Genealogy Book**. The Save Book window opens.

4. Enter a title for the book in the **Book name** field.

5. Click **Save**. The book opens in the text editor.

Importing a Book from a Previous Version

If you created a book in Family Tree Maker 2006 or Version 16, you can import the book into your 2010 file. However, because of differences between the old and new software formats, some items won't transfer over, such as images, text formatting, and NGSQ reports (placeholder pages show you where reports and charts have been left out).

Before you import a book, you should make a backup of your current tree. For instructions, see "Backing Up a File" on page 377.

Note: When you import a book, Family Tree Maker adds an explanatory page as the first item in your book. You should delete this before you share or print the book.

1. Choose **File>Import Books**. The Select File with Books window opens.

2. Click the **Look in** drop-down list and find the folder where the file is located.

3. Click the Family Tree Maker (.ftw) file that contains the book you want to import.

Note: The Import Books option imports *only* books that have been created in Family Tree Maker.

4. Click **Open**. When the import is complete, you'll see the Success window, which shows how many books and book items were imported.

5. Click **OK**. The books are added to your Saved Books list.

6. To view your imported book, go to the **Collection** tab on the Publish workspace.

7. In **Publication Types**, click **Saved Books**.

8. Double-click the book you imported, or select its icon and then click the **Detail** tab. The book opens in the text editor.

   If Family Tree Maker was unable to import an item (such as a timeline, map, or report), click on the missing item in the outline, and its placeholder text will explain what book item has been left out—and in some cases, who the item was attached to.

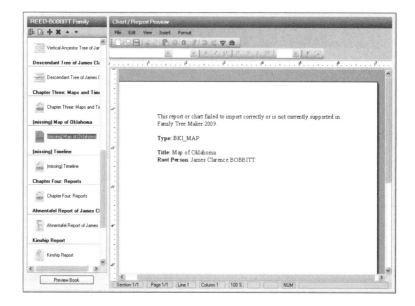

Accessing a Saved Book

1. Go to the **Collection** tab on the Publish workspace.

2. In **Publication Types**, click **Saved Books**.

3. Double-click the book you want to open, or select its icon and then click the **Detail** tab. The book opens in the text editor.

What's in a Book?

You're an expert on your family. You've spent years entering facts, gathering photos, and analyzing records, but you probably haven't given much thought to the actual pieces that go into creating a book. As you get ready to put it all together, consider adding one or more of these elements to make your family history book complete and professional.

- **Title page.** A title page is automatically created for your book in Family Tree Maker. However, you might want to add a subtitle, edition number, or author names to it.

- **Copyright.** Although you do not have to include a copyright notice in order to be protected from unauthorized usage, you should consider adding this information, especially if you want to submit your book to a library, society, or association.

- **Dedication or Acknowledgments.** A dedication is usually a short inscription dedicating the book to an individual or group. If you have many people who have contributed to your book, you can create an acknowledgments page to thank them.

- **Table of Contents.** In any book, a table of contents is an essential element that helps your readers quickly access the items they're interested in. Family Tree Maker can automatically generate a table of contents for you.

- **List of Illustrations.** If you are including photos and records that you want people to be able to find easily, you might want to include a list of their titles and the pages they're located on.

- **Preface.** A preface contains information about you, the author, such as your research methods or your reasons for writing the book.

- **Introduction.** An introduction explains what readers will find in the book and why you've included—and excluded—specific content.

- **Content.** The contents of your book can include charts, reports, stories, photos, record images, and more.

- **Index.** An index of individuals is automatically created for your book in Family Tree Maker. It lists the names of every individual included in a chart or report and the page numbers where they appear.

Setting Up a Book's Properties

1. Access the book you want to change.

2. In the book panel toolbar, click the **Book Properties** button. The Book Properties window opens.

3. Complete these fields as necessary:

In this field	Do this
Book title	Enter the name of your book. This is the name that will appear in the book's headers and footers.
Author	Enter the name of the individual who wrote the book.
Header	Choose a header type from the drop-down list. Headers are typically the title of a book, but you can choose to have no header, or a combination of the book title, chapter name, and page number. To change the header's font, click **Font** and choose a style from the drop-down list. Note: You can change the header for a specific page using Item Properties.

In this field	Do this
Footer	Choose a footer type from the drop-down list. Footers are typically page numbers, but you can choose to have no footer, or a combination of the book title, chapter name, and page number. To change the footer's font, click **Font** and choose a style from the drop-down list. Note: You can change the footer for a specific page using Item Properties.
Starting number	Choose what page you want the body of the book to start on (the front matter—title page, table of contents, dedication, etc.—will be numbered separately).
Use Roman numerals	Click this checkbox to use Roman numerals (i, ii, iii, iv) for the book's front matter—title page, table of contents, dedication, etc.

4. Click **OK**.

Adding Content to a Book

You can include stories, photos, reports, charts, and even an automatically generated table of contents and index to your book.

Adding a Text Item to a Book

When you add a new text item to a book, you open a blank sheet of paper in the book text-editor, much like you would when you open a new document in any word processing program. A text item can be anything from an entire chapter to a simple page with a photo and a caption.

1. Access the book you want to add a text item to.

2. In the book panel toolbar, click the **Add Book Item** (+) button. The Add Book Item window opens.

3. In **Publication type**, click **Other**.

4. Double-click **Text Item**, or select its icon and then click **OK**. A blank page opens in the text editor.

Entering Text Manually

Don't let your family history book become a dry recitation of facts. Add interest and personality by including family stories and memories. If your grandfather immigrated to America when he was young, don't just list this fact in an individual report. Include a photo of the ship your grandfather arrived on and an excerpt from his journal that tells how he felt when he saw the Statue of Liberty for the first time.

1. Access the text item you want to add text to by clicking its name in the book panel.

2. Place your cursor where you want the text to begin.

3. Type in the text you want to add.

Tip

You can also copy and paste text from within Family Tree Maker (for example, from an individual's notes).

Importing Text from Another Document

If you've already written your book in another text program, you don't have to re-type your text or copy and paste sections into Family Tree Maker. You can import the entire document at once—without losing formatting.

1. Access the text item you want to import text into by clicking its name in the book panel.

2. Place your cursor where you want the text to begin.

3. Choose **File>Open**. The Open window opens.

4. Use the **Look in** drop-down list to find the folder where the document is located. When you find the correct folder, double-click the folder to open it.

5. Choose your document type from the **Files of type** drop-down list.

6. Click the document you want to import.

7. Click **Open**. The document opens in the text editor.

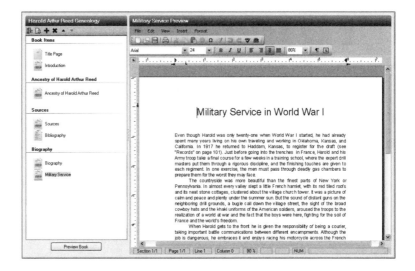

Adding an Image to a Text Item

What family history book would be complete without family photos, personal correspondence, record images, and maps? Family Tree Maker lets you add any image you've included in your family tree to your book. You can also add images you've stored elsewhere on your computer that you don't necessarily want to keep in your family tree, for example, clip art embellishments.

1. Access the text item you want to add an image to by clicking its name in the book panel.

   Note: In the book-building tool you cannot wrap text around images. If you don't want the image to be inline with the text, you may want to add space before and after the object.

2. Place your cursor where you want the image to appear.

3. Do one of these options:

   • To add an image you've uploaded to Family Tree Maker, choose **Insert>Image from Media Collection**. The Find Media Item window opens. Select the image and click **OK**.

   • To add an image from your computer, choose **Insert>Image from File**. The Open window opens. Use the **Look in** drop-down list to locate the image. Select the image and click **Open**.

4. To align the image, right-click it. Then choose "Left," "Center," or "Right" from **Justify Image**. You can also move the image by clicking on it and dragging it to a new location.

5. If you need to resize the image, click on the image to highlight it. Then drag one of the square handles to change the size. To maintain the image's proportions, drag the image from one of the corners.

Adding a Chart or Report

You can add as many charts and reports to a book as you'd like. Make sure you choose ones that are appropriate for your audience. For example, you may want to share more personal and informal trees and reports in a book meant for your children, but you'll want to remove information about living relatives if you plan on sharing your book with other genealogists.

1. Access the book you want to add a chart or report to.

2. In the book panel toolbar, click the **Add Book Item** (+) button. The Add Book Item window opens.

3. In **Publication type**, click the category for the chart or report you want to use. Then double-click the chart/report, or select its icon and click **OK**.

Tip
In **Publication type** you can also click **Saved Charts** or **Saved Reports** to use items you've already created.

The chart or report opens. You can use the editing panel to change the chart or report just as you would if you were creating it outside of the book.

Adding a Placeholder

If you want to incorporate a story, chart, or photo from outside Family Tree Maker, you can use a placeholder to reserve a specific number of pages until you're ready to add the information.

1. Access the book you want to add a placeholder to.

2. In the book panel toolbar, click the **Add Book Item** (+) button. The Add Book Item window opens.

3. In **Publication type**, click **Other**.

> **Tip**
> Give the place-holder a descriptive name so you won't forget what you were going to use it for.

4. Double-click **Place Holder**, or select its icon and then click **OK**. A blank page opens in the text editor.

5. Choose the number of pages you want to reserve from the **Number of pages** field.

Creating a Table of Contents

Family Tree Maker can automatically generate a table of contents for your book. If you make changes to your book (such as adding a new chart or moving a text item) Family Tree Maker will update the table of contents and its page numbers to reflect the changes.

> Note: The table of contents is automatically added after the title page. You can change the order of the front matter—table of contents, dedication, preface, etc.—but you cannot move the table of contents out of the front matter.

1. Access the book you want to add a table of contents to.

2. In the book panel toolbar, click the **Add Book Item** (+) button. The Add Book Item window opens.

3. In **Publication type**, click **Other**.

4. Double-click **Table of Contents**, or select its icon and then click **OK**. The table of contents opens. Although you cannot directly edit the table of contents, you can customize the text's font, size, and color by clicking the Fonts button under the "Table of Contents Options" heading.

Creating an Index of Individuals

Family Tree Maker can automatically generate an index that lists all the individuals included in your book's reports and charts (names mentioned in text items will *not* be included). If you make changes to your book (such as adding a new chart) Family Tree Maker will update the index to reflect the change.

> Note: The index cannot be moved; it must be the last item in your book.

1. Access the book you want to add an index to.

2. In the book panel toolbar, click the **Add Book Item** (+) button. The Add Book Item window opens.

3. In **Publication type**, click **Other**.

4. Double-click **Index**, or select its icon and then click **OK**. The index opens. Although you cannot edit the index, you can customize the text's font, size, and color by clicking the Fonts button under the "Table of Contents Options" heading.

Formatting Text

The text formatting options available in a Family Tree Maker book are similar to those in any word processing program. You can change fonts, text size, alignment, tabs, indents, and more.

1. Access the text item you want to format.

2. Use this chart to help you format your text:

To do this	Do this
Change the font color, size, or style	Select the text you want to change. Click **Format>Character.** The Font window opens. Make the necessary changes and click **OK**.
Change the amount of space between lines of text	Select the paragraph that has line spacing you want to change. Click **Format>Paragraph.** On the **Formatting and Indents** tab, choose a spacing option from the **Line spacing** drop-down list. Click **OK**.
Change the indent of a paragraph	Select the paragraph you want to change the indent for. Click **Format>Paragraph.** On the **Formatting and Indents** tab, choose new indents from the **Left** and **Right** drop-down lists. Click **OK**.
Add a page break	Place your cursor where you want the page break to occur. Click **Format>Paragraph.** Click the **Frame and Page Breaks** tab. Click the **Page break before** checkbox and click **OK**.
Add a frame around a paragraph	Select the paragraph you want to add a frame to. Click **Format>Paragraph.** Click the **Frame and Page Breaks** tab. Choose the type of frame you want and click **OK**.
Change the tabs for a document	Click **Format>Tabs.** The Tabs window opens. Make the necessary changes and click **OK**.

Organizing a Book

As your book grows, you may find that it has changed from the project you originally envisioned and that you need to make some adjustments. Perhaps you've uncovered additional records and photos and you want to rearrange a couple of chapters to include them. Or maybe you decided that it wasn't necessary to include a Research Note report. Family Tree Maker makes it easy to change titles, rearrange the order of how things appear in your book, or even delete sections you don't need.

Changing an Item's Settings

A Family Tree Maker book is made up of a variety of different book items: text items, charts, reports, etc. You can change settings for each book item.

1. Access the book you want to change.

2. Access the item you want to change.

3. In the book panel toolbar, click the **Book Item Properties** button. The Item Properties window opens.

4. Use this chart to change the item's settings:

To do this	Do this
Change the item's title	Enter a title in the **Item name** field. This is the title that will appear in the book's table of contents and this item's headers and footers.
Make this item start a new chapter	Click the **This item begins a chapter** checkbox.
Make the first page of this item start on an odd-numbered (right-facing) page	Click the **Start this item on an odd numbered page** checkbox. Typically each chapter starts on an odd-numbered page.
Prevent a page number from appearing on the first page of an item	Click the **Do not print page number on the first page** checkbox. Typically chapter openers do not include a page number. You may also want to use this option for reports, charts, and full-page images.
Display headers in the item	Click the **Include the header in this item** checkbox.
Display footers in the item	Click the **Include the footer in this item** checkbox.

5. Click **OK**.

Rearranging Book Items

The book panel shows you all the items you've included in a book. The order in which they're displayed in this outline is the order in which they'll print. You can change this order at any time.

1. Access the book you want to change.

2. Click on the item you want to move in the book panel.

3. To move the item up in the outline, click the **Move Up Book Item** button in the book editing panel. To move the item down in the outline, click the **Move Down Book Item** button in the book editing panel.

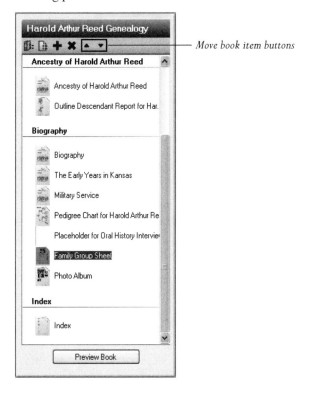

Move book item buttons

Note: The title page must always be the first item in the book and the index page must always be the last.

Deleting a Book Item

If you decide you don't want a text item, report, or chart you've included in your book, you can delete it.

1. Access the book you want to delete an item from.

2. Click on the item in the book panel.

3. Click the **Delete Book Item** button.

Printing a Book at Home

When you are done creating your book, you can make copies on your home printer.

> Note: If you want to see what your book will look like when it is printed, click the Preview Book button below the book outline.

1. Access the book you want to print.

2. Click the **Print** button below the main toolbar.

   The Print window opens. Just like printing from any other application, you can choose a printer, select the number of copies to print, and choose a page range.

3. Click **Print**.

Exporting a Book

You can export your book as a PDF and take it to a copy shop to be printed and professionally bound or e-mail it to family members.

1. Access the book you want to export.

2. Click the **Share** button below the main toolbar.

3. Choose **Export to PDF** from the drop-down list. The PDF Export Options window opens.

4. Change format options as necessary and click **OK**. The Save As window opens.

5. Click **OK**.

Deleting a Book

> Warning: Deleting a book from a tree is permanent. You might want to create a backup of your tree before completing this task. (For instructions, see "Backing Up Files" on page 377.)

1. Go to the **Collection** tab on the Publish workspace.

2. In **Publication Types**, click **Saved Books**.

3. Right-click the book you want to delete, and choose **Delete Item** from the drop-down list. A message asks you to confirm that you want to delete the book.

4. Click **OK**. The book is deleted.

MyCanvas

MyCanvas is a Web-based publishing program and printing service provided by Ancestry.com that you can use to create a family history book using your Family Tree Maker tree.

When you upload your tree to Ancestry.com, the publishing tool gets you started by automatically generating pages (pedigree trees, family group sheets, and even timelines) based on information in your tree. You can then use its intuitive features to modify these pages by adding photos, stories, historical records, and more. You can also add more pages to your book or delete pages you don't like. When you're finished, you can have your book professionally printed and bound—an heirloom to be enjoyed and shared for years to come.

> Note: This section explains how to upload your Family Tree Maker tree to MyCanvas, the Ancestry publishing tool; it does not explain how to use its features. To learn more about the tool, go to <**www.ancestry.com**> and click the Publish button on the main toolbar. Then click the Help tab at the top of the page. You'll find FAQs (Frequently Asked Questions), tips and tricks for using the tool, and even a book-building guide.

Creating a MyCanvas Book

When you're ready to create a MyCanvas book, you will upload your tree to MyCanvas and create a project. You can choose which individuals you want to include in your projects. That way, you can create as many books as you'd like—maybe even one book for each branch of your family.

> Note: You must be a registered user or have a subscription to Ancestry to upload your tree. You must also be connected to the Internet to use this feature.

Tip
You can also start a project by clicking the **Share** button in the upper, right corner of the window and choosing **Upload to Ancestry**.

What Is MyCanvas?

MyCanvas is one of the many offerings from Ancestry.com Inc.—the parent company of Family Tree Maker. MyCanvas is a Web-based tool that allows you to create your own family history books, photo albums, posters, and more. If you have already created a family tree using Ancestry.com or Family Tree Maker, you can use this tree for your project and let MyCanvas start the work for you. The information in your tree will be placed in professionally designed templates. You can leave the pages "as is" or use the interactive tools to add additional photographs and text.

When you complete your book, you may want to print some pages on your desktop printer. Keep in mind, if you choose to print at home, pages will have a low resolution (meaning the text and images won't look sharp), and if you have lots of colorful photographs and backgrounds, you can go through quite a bit of ink or toner. Through MyCanvas, you can buy a high-resolution copy of your book and have it printed, professionally bound, and sent to your door.

Each unique book you create preserves your heritage and is an exciting way to share your discoveries with family and friends. And these books also make great gifts for anniversaries, birthdays, and reunions.

1. Go to the **Collection** tab on the Publish workspace.

2. In **Publication Types**, click **Books**.

3. Double-click **Create a Professionally Printed Book Online**. The Upload to MyCanvas window opens.

   You can choose which individuals are included in the tree you're uploading.

4. Do one of these options:

   - If you want to include all the individuals in your tree, click **Entire file**.

   - If you want to choose only a few specific individuals to include in the tree, click **Selected individuals**. The Filter

> **Tip**
> For more instructions on selecting individuals, see "Using the Filter Individuals Window" on page 25.

Individuals window will open. Click a name and then click **Include** to add the person. When you're finished choosing individuals click **OK**.

5. If you're going to be sharing your book with people other than immediate family members, you might want to leave out private facts and notes. To do so, make sure the **Include private facts** and **Include private notes** checkboxes are not selected.

6. If you want media items linked to a tree to be uploaded to your book project, click the **Include media files** checkbox.

7. Click **OK**.

8. If necessary, log in to your Ancestry account.

While the tree is being uploaded, you'll see the Upload to My-Canvas window, which shows the number of individuals, families, etc. that are being uploaded.

A browser window will open. First, you will upload your tree to Ancestry.com, and then the information will be transferred to the publishing tool.

9. Enter a name for your tree in the **Tree Name** field.

10. If you want your tree to be viewable to all Ancestry members, click the **Allow others to see my tree** checkbox.

   Note: If you choose to keep your tree private, Ancestry members can still see names, birth dates, and birthplaces from your tree in search results. However, if they want to see the full tree or any attached photos and records, they will have to use the Ancestry Connection Service to contact you. Then you can choose to give them access to your tree or not.

11. Click the checkbox to accept the submission agreement.

12. Click **Upload**. The MyCanvas window opens.

13. Click the book icon for the type of book you want to create
(standard, combination, or descendant). You can click the "Learn
more" link if you want more information about each book type
before you choose one.

You can now choose a few options for your family history book.

14. Choose the book's size and the number of generations included.

15. Choose the family tree you want to use. (Because you just uploaded your tree from Family Tree Maker, this should be the default tree selected.)

16. Start typing the name of the individual you want to be the "root" person in your tree. The tool will try to recognize the name as you enter it. To use the suggested name, click it in the drop-down list.

17. Enter a name for your book project in the **Name your project** field.

18. Click **Continue**. Your book project opens.

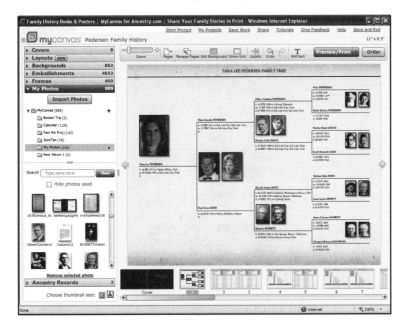

You can now use the MyCanvas publishing tool to create your book. Your book project is saved automatically every five minutes; however, make sure you save your project each time before you close the tool.

Tip
You can also access your book project by going to <www.ancestry.com> and clicking the **Publish** button tab. Then click the "My Projects" link.

Accessing a MyCanvas Book

Once you've created a MyCanvas book, whether through this software or Ancestry.com, it's easy to access it from Family Tree Maker.

Note: You must be connected to the Internet to access a MyCanvas book.

1. Go to the **Collection** tab on the Publish workspace.

2. In **Publication Types**, click **Books**.

3. Double-click **Go to Existing Online Projects**. A Web browser opens, and the My Projects page is displayed.

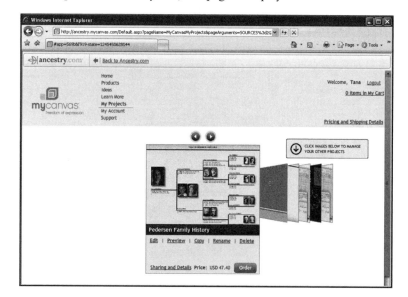

4. In the center of the window, you will see thumbnail images of your projects. Use the arrow buttons to scroll through the projects. When you find the project you want to open, click its thumbnail. The MyCanvas publishing tool opens in a new window.

Chapter 10

Researching Your Tree Online

As you have entered your family stories and facts into Family Tree Maker, you have probably noticed that more information about your family is waiting to be discovered—perhaps it's the burial location of your grandfather or the wedding certificate for your aunt and uncle. Family Tree Maker can help you fill in these gaps in your research. If you are connected to the Internet, Family Tree Maker will automatically perform behind-the-scenes searches of Ancestry.com and alert you when it has found information that seems to match individuals in your tree. View the results when it's convenient, and if the information is relevant, you can merge it into your tree.

You can also use Family Tree Maker to search the vast number of family history resources available on the Web. Search for information on RootsWeb.com, Genealogy.com, or any of your favorite websites. And if you find information that matches a family member in your tree, you can quickly add it to your tree—all without leaving Family Tree Maker.

Using the Web Search

The Web Search in Family Tree Maker automatically searches thousands of Ancestry.com databases—census records; birth, marriage, and death records; court and land records; immigration records; military records; family trees; and more—looking for information that matches people in your tree. When a possible match is found, a green leaf appears next to the individual's name in the pedigree view and editing panel on the People workspace.

You can move the mouse over the leaf to see how many records and trees were found on Ancestry.com. To view the search results, simply click the leaf. If you find a record that matches the individual, you can quickly merge the results into your tree. If a search result doesn't match anyone in your tree, you can choose to ignore it—it will no longer show up as a hint on the pedigree view.

Starting a Web Search

If Family Tree Maker has found records on Ancestry.com that might match an individual in your tree, you'll see a green leaf next to the individual's name on the People workspace.

> Note: To use the Web Search feature and see search results on Ancestry.com, you must register Family Tree Maker and have an Internet connection. To view the actual records, you must have a subscription to Ancestry.com.

1. Go to the **Family** tab on the People workspace.

2. In the pedigree view or editing panel, move the mouse over the leaf icon next to the individual you want to see search results for. You will see the number of records and trees that possibly match the individual in your tree.

Tip

If you don't want Family Tree Maker to automatically search Ancestry.com when you are connected to the Internet, you can turn this feature off. For instructions, see "Online Searching Preferences" on page 412.

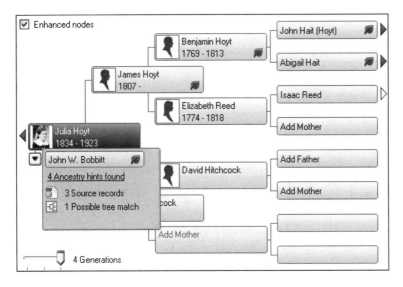

3. Click the **Ancestry hints found** link. The Web Search workspace opens. In the browser you can see the Ancestry.com search results that are possible matches for your ancestor. You may need to scroll down the window to see all available results.

4. Click on any search results that interest you.

5. Do one of these options:

   • If the record matches someone in your family, you can merge the information into your tree. For instructions, see "Merging Web Search Results into a Tree" on page 335.

   • If the record does not match anyone in your tree, you can choose to ignore the record. For instructions, see "Ignoring Web Search Results" on page 333.

Tip

If you want to search for the individual using different spellings or perhaps using a maiden name, click **New Search** in the browser toolbar. Then enter the alternate information and click **Search**.

Ignoring Web Search Results

If one of the Web Search results you've accessed is not relevant to anyone in your tree, you can choose to ignore it. That way the record won't show up in the Web Search hints list on the People workspace again.

1. Access the Web Search results for an individual. For help, see the previous task, "Starting a Web Search."

2. Click the search result that you want to ignore.

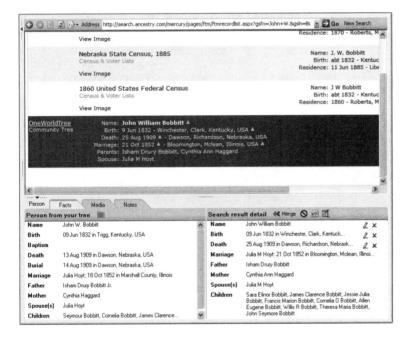

3. On the Search Result Detail toolbar, click the **Ignore record** button.

Search result detail	◀◀ Merge 🚫	— Ignore record button
Name	John William Bobbitt	
Birth	09 Jun 1832 in Winchester, Clark, Kentuck...	
Death	25 Aug 1909 in Dawson, Richardson, Nebrask...	
Marriage	Julia M Hoyt: 21 Oct 1852 in Bloomington, Mclean, Illinoi...	
Father	Isham Drury Bobbitt	
Mother	Cynthia Ann Haggard	
Spouse(s)	Julia M Hoyt	
Children	Sara Elinor Bobbitt, James Clarence Bobbitt, Jessie Julia Bobbitt, Francis Marion Bobbitt, Cornelia O Bobbitt, Allen Eugene Bobbitt, Willis R Bobbitt, Theresa Maria Bobbitt, John Seymore Bobbitt	

The Ignore record button changes to yellow to show that the record is being ignored. When you return to the Person workspace this record will not appear in the Ancestry hints list.

Viewing Ignored Web Search Results

If you've chosen to ignore a Web Search result for an individual, you can still access the results at a later time.

1. Click the **Web Search** button on the main toolbar.

2. Using the mini pedigree tree or Index of Individuals button, choose the individual whose ignored search results you'd like to view.

3. Click **Web Search>View Ignored Records**. If this individual has no ignored records, a message appears; click **OK** and choose another individual.

4. If you want to take the search result off the Ignore list, click the **Ignore record** button again.

The Ignore record button changes back to blue. When you return to the Person workspace this record will appear in the Ancestry hints list.

Merging Web Search Results into a Tree

If you find Web Search results on Ancestry.com that you would like to add to your tree, you can merge them into your file with the Family Tree Maker Web Merge Wizard. You can merge specific individuals and facts as well as an individual's parents, spouses, and children, as long as those family members are associated with the record that Web Search found.

Source information will automatically be included for each fact you add to your tree, unless you opt to ignore the fact or individual.

> Note: The Web Merge process does not overwrite any of the data in your tree. However, it is always a good idea to save a backup of your file before making major changes. (For instructions, see "Backing Up Files" on page 377.)

1. Access the Ancestry.com record that you want to merge into your tree. For instructions, see "Starting a Web Search" on page 331.

2. In the browser, click the individual search result you would like to merge into your tree. The information you currently have in your tree is listed in the Person from Your Tree section; the information available in the online record appears in the Search Result Detail section.

Note: If you want to merge the record with a person in your tree who is different from the currently selected individual, click the Select a Different Person button next to the Person from Your Tree heading. Choose an individual and click OK.

3. Click **Merge** on the **Facts** tab. The Web Merge Wizard will launch.

The left side of the window lists the names of all the people included in the record you are merging. As you move through the wizard, each individual will be highlighted as you make decisions about his or her information. Next to the individuals' names, you'll see three columns: the Person from My Tree column shows the information you already have in your tree; the Person from Web Search column shows the information from the record and lets you choose how to handle the information (i.e., ignore, make preferred, make alternate); and the Merged Result column shows how the information will be added to your tree.

4. In the Person from Web Search column, choose how you want the information found on Ancestry.com to be merged into your tree:

- **Make preferred.** Enter the information as the "preferred" fact for the individual.

- **Make alternate.** Enter the information as an alternate fact for the individual.

- **Discard this fact.** Do not merge the information into your tree. (You may choose to ignore some facts from a record, although it is usually a good idea to include all facts from a particular record in case they turn out to be relevant.)

    Click the **Keep sources** checkbox if you want to add the source information but not the fact. For example, you may already have the same fact listed in your tree, but you want to add this record's source information to further validate the existing fact.

5. Click **Next**.

> **Tip**
>
> If you do not want to go through each name in the Web Merge Wizard, click **Summary**; then click **Merge Now**. The additional family members will automatically be added to your tree if no equivalent family members exist. However, if the family member already exists in the tree, Family Tree Maker will ignore the person.

Tip

If you don't want to use the Wizard to systematically move through each individual on the record, you can click on a name to skip to a specific individual.

6. Do one of these options:

   - If the individual you want to merge has parents, spouse(s), or children associated with the record, the Web Merge Wizard asks you if you want to add the information found for the first additional family member. Continue with the next step.

   - If the individual does not have siblings or parents associated with this source, click the **Next** button to go to the Summary window and skip to step 10.

7. Choose what you want to do with each family member. You can ignore the person, add the person as a new individual in your tree, or merge the person with an existing individual in your tree.

   The details about the additional family members appear in the Person from Web Search column, while the information you already have in your tree appears in the Person from My Tree column. You can compare the information you have with what Family Tree Maker has found on Ancestry.com. If more than one individual appears in the Person from My Tree column, you will need to select the individual with whom you want to merge the new information.

8. Click **Next** and complete step 7 for every name in the record until all additional family members have been looked through. When you have made decisions for each family member, the Summary window opens.

9. If you want to include an image of a record as a media item, click the **Media** checkbox.

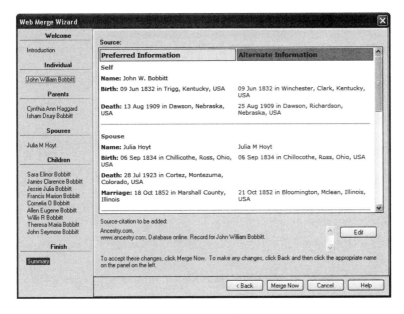

10. Verify your selections in the Summary window and click **Merge Now**. A message tells you when the Web Search result has been successfully merged into your tree.

11. Click **OK** to close the message.

Note: You *cannot* undo a merge. However, none of your existing information will be overwritten, so if you decide you made a mistake, you can simply delete the fact or source that you added during the merge.

Searching Online with Family Tree Maker

With Family Tree Maker, you have a convenient starting point
for researching and expanding your family history—without
interrupting your work. You can explore the Web using any of your
favorite search engines or genealogy websites. Although Family Tree
Maker won't automatically search websites other than Ancestry.com,
it does provide a "Web clipping" tool that lets you select text you're
interested in and add it to an individual in your tree.

1. Click the **Web Search** button on the main toolbar.

2. Using the mini pedigree tree or Index of Individuals button,
    choose the individual whose information you want to search for.

3. In **Search Locations**, click the website that you want to
    search, or enter a website address in the **Address** field of the
    Web browser. (For instructions on adding websites to this list,
    see "Adding a Website to Your Favorites List" on page 352.) The
    website opens in a browser window.

4. Look for information on your ancestors just as you would if you were performing any kind of online search.

5. If you find facts that you want to add to your tree, continue with the next task, "Saving Online Facts to a Tree."

Saving Online Facts to a Tree

If you find family facts such as a birth date or birthplace on a website that you'd like to add to your tree, you can use the Family Tree Maker "Web clipping" tool to select the information. In some cases, Family Tree Maker will recognize the type of information you're trying to add and will give you relevant fields to choose from. For example, if you try to add information from the Social Security Death Index, you'll have the option to add the selected text to a name, Social Security Number, birth fact, death fact, or Social Security Issued fact.

1. Access the online facts you want to add to your tree. For instructions, see the previous task, "Searching Online with Family Tree Maker."

2. If you want to link the facts to a person in your tree who is different from the currently selected individual, click the **Select a different person** button in the Person from Your Tree section. Choose an individual and click **OK**.

3. Click the **Facts** tab at the bottom of the window. On the Search Result Detail toolbar, click the **Enable web clipping** button.

— Enable web clipping button

When you move the mouse over text in the browser, the pointer will turn into a cursor.

4. Highlight the text you want to add to an individual. The Insert Fact drop-down list appears.

5. Choose a fact from the **Insert Fact** drop-down list. For example, you can choose the birthplace fact. The information now appears in the Search Result Detail section.

6. Repeat steps 4 and 5 to select any additional facts you want to add to your tree.

7. When you have selected all the information you want from the website, click **Merge**. The Web Merge Wizard will launch. (For more information on the Web Merge Wizard, see "Merging Web Search Results into a Tree" on page 335.)

8. In the Person from Web Search column, choose how you want the information to be merged into your tree:

    •   **Make preferred.** Enter the information as the "preferred" fact for the individual.

    •   **Make alternate.** Enter the information as an alternate fact for the individual.

    •   **Discard this fact.** Do not merge the information into your tree. Click the **Keep sources** checkbox if you want to keep the source information (the URL where the information was located) but not the fact. (You can also enter the source information yourself on the Summary page.)

9. Click **Summary** to see how the information will be added to your tree.

> **Tip**
> You can add multiple facts to your tree before merging the information; you don't need to merge each fact separately.

10. If necessary, click **Edit** to enter a source citation for the information. (The default source citation added by Family Tree Maker is the URL where the information was located.)

11. Click **Merge Now**. A message tells you when the Web Search result has been successfully merged into your tree.

12. Click **OK** to close the message.

Saving an Online Image to a Tree

You may find family photos or images of historical documents online that will enhance the family history you're compiling. Family Tree Maker makes it easy to add these directly from a website to your tree.

> Note: Before downloading any images from the Web, make sure you aren't violating any copyright restrictions or get permission from the owner.

1. Access the online image that you want to add to your tree. For instructions, see "Searching Online with Family Tree Maker" on page 340.

2. If you want to link the image to a person in your tree who is different from the currently selected individual, click the **Select a different person** button in the Person from Your Tree section. Choose an individual and click **OK**.

3. Click the **Media** tab at the bottom of the window.

4. Move the cursor over the browser window until the image you want is highlighted by a green dotted line.

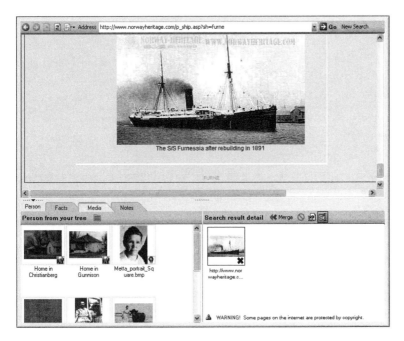

5. Click the highlighted image. A thumbnail of the image appears in the Search Result Detail section.

6. Repeat steps 4 and 5 to select any additional images you want to add to the individual.

   Note: A red X in the bottom corner of an image shows that it has not yet been merged into the tree.

7. Click **Merge**. A message tells you when the image has been successfully merged into your tree.

8. Click **OK** to close the message. A thumbnail of the image now appears in the Person from Your Tree section.

   Note: The image will be linked to the person displayed in the Person from Your Tree section. If you want to link the image to a different person in your tree, see "Linking a Media Item to an Individual" on page 136. To view the item, click the Media button on the main toolbar to access the Media workspace.

Saving Additional Notes to a Tree

While you're online looking for information about your family, you may come upon interesting stories about the founding of your grandfather's hometown or a description of the ship your great-grandparents sailed to America on. Or you might find clues that will help you further your research goals. You can easily preserve this type of information on the Notes tab using the "Web clipping" tool.

1. Access the online content that you want to add to your tree. For instructions, see "Searching Online with Family Tree Maker" on page 340.

2. If you want to link the notes to a person in your tree who is different from the currently selected individual, click the **Select a different person** button in the Person from Your Tree section. Choose an individual and click **OK**.

3. Click the **Notes** tab at the bottom of the window.

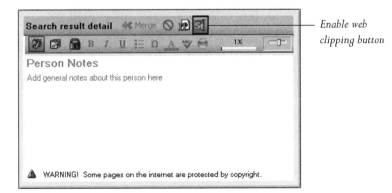

4. Do one of these options:

- If you want to add the information as a personal note, click the **Person note** button on the Notes toolbar.

- If you want to add the information as a research note, click the **Research note** button on the Notes toolbar.

   Note: To learn more about the differences between Person notes and Research notes, see "Adding Notes" on page 53.

5. On the Search Result Detail toolbar, click the **Enable web clipping** button.

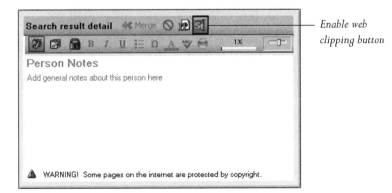

— Enable web
clipping button

When you move the mouse over text in the browser, the pointer will turn into a cursor.

6. Highlight the text you want to add to the note. The Insert note button appears.

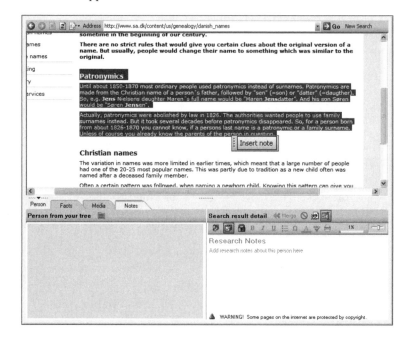

7. Click **Insert note**. The information now appears in the Search Result Detail section.

Note: The notes will be linked to the person displayed in the Person from Your Tree section. To view the notes later, click the People button on the main toolbar; then click the Person tab for the individual. The notes appear on the Notes tab at the bottom of the window.

Archiving a Web Page

If you find a website that contains too much information for you to read in one sitting, you might want to "archive" the Web page so that you can view its contents later—without being connected to the Internet. When you archive a Web page, Family Tree Maker will save a "snapshot" of the page in HTML format that can be opened in any Web browser. This makes it easy to read the page's contents and continue your research when it's convenient for you.

1. Access the Web page you want to archive. For instructions, see "Searching Online with Family Tree Maker" on page 340.

2. If you want to link the archived page to a person in your tree who is different from the currently selected individual, click the **Select a different person** button in the Person from Your Tree section. Choose an individual and click **OK**.

3. Click the **Facts**, **Media**, or **Notes** tab.

4. In the Search Result Detail toolbar, click the **Create page archive** button. A thumbnail of the page appears in the Search Result Detail section.

Create page archive button

> **Tip**
> Because websites are constantly changing and even disappearing, you might want to archive a Web page if it contains information you'll want to refer to multiple times.

Genealogy Websites

Some of the most popular and useful resources for researching your family on the Web are free. Here are some websites you might want to visit:

- **www.rootsweb.com.** RootsWeb contains genealogy-related message boards and mailing lists, thousands of user-contributed trees (WorldConnect Project), and user-contributed databases of historical records.

- **www.archives.gov.** The official site for the U.S. National Archives and Records Administration, this site contains genealogy how-to guides and is your link to ordering copies of the many original records housed in the National Archives.

- **www.familysearch.org.** Sponsored by the LDS Church, this site contains a catalog to more than 2.4 million microfilmed genealogical records held at the Family History Library in Salt Lake City. It also contains millions of names in pedigree charts submitted by users.

- **www.usgenweb.org.** USGenWeb is a portal page with links to all the U.S. state genealogy websites. The state websites have links to all the county genealogy websites. USGenWeb also hosts special genealogy projects.

- **www.findagrave.org.** Find a Grave contains more than 34 million tombstone and cemetery record transcriptions (many with photographs) from the United States and countries around the world.

- **www.worldgenweb.org.** Besides message boards, mailing lists, and historical data, WorldGenWeb hosts websites for locations around the world. Websites contain lists of local resources.

- **www.familyrecords.gov.uk.** This site is a great starting point for conducting research in the UK. Besides giving general research guides, it lists types of records and where to access them.

- **www.interment.net.** Interment.net contains thousands of tombstone and cemetery record transcriptions from cemeteries in the United States, Canada, England, Ireland, Australia, New Zealand, and elsewhere.

5. Click **Merge**. A message tells you when the archived Web page has been successfully merged into your tree.

6. Click **OK** to close the message. A link to the page now appears in the Person from Your Tree section.

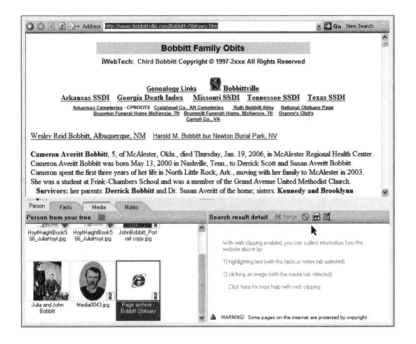

> Note: The archived page will be linked to the person displayed in the Person from Your Tree section. To view the archived page, click the Media button on the main toolbar to access it on the Media workspace.

Managing Research Websites

As you discover websites that contain valuable information for your family tree, you'll want to add them to your list of favorite websites so they're easy to visit again. And once you've gathered quite a few favorite sites, you can sort the list so the websites appear in an order that's useful to you. For example, if you visit certain websites daily, you may want to put these websites at the top of the list.

Adding a Website to Your Favorites List

Each website will be added to your favorites list that appears on the left side of the Web Search workspace under the Personal Favorite Sites heading.

1. Click the **Web Search** button on the main toolbar.

2. In **Search Locations**, click the **New** button. The New Search Favorite window opens.

3. Enter the address for the website in the **URL address** field. For example, for the Kentucky GenWeb site, you would enter "www.kygenweb.net".

4. Enter a name for the website in the **Favorite name** field. This can be any name that helps you identify the website.

5. Click **OK**. The new website now appears in your list of personal favorites.

Sorting Your Website Favorites List

1. Click the **Web Search** button on the main toolbar.

2. Click **Manage Favorites**. The Manage Favorites window opens.

3. Do one of these options:

    *   To display the websites in alphabetical order, click **Sort favorites alphabetically**.

    *   To choose your own display order for the websites, click a website in the Personal favorites list and then click the up and down arrows.

4. Click **OK**.

Chapter 11

Working with Trees

A "tree" in Family Tree Maker is the file where you gather and enter all your family data and information. Depending on your own personal preferences, you may have several separate trees or just one tree for all branches of your family history.

Family Tree Maker makes it easy to get started. If you have received a family history file from another family member or researcher, you can import the file, creating a new tree. You can then begin adding your own information. You can also create a tree by entering a few quick facts about an individual or by downloading a tree you've created at Ancestry.com.

At some point, you may also want to share your hard work and files with others. Perhaps you've met someone on a message board who has common ancestors. You can export your tree in several different file types that will work with almost any genealogy software.

This chapter will explain the many tools Family Tree Maker has to help you manage, share, and protect your trees.

In This Chapter

- Creating a Tree
- Managing Your Trees
- Exporting a File
- Merging Two Files
- Backing Up Files
- Compressing a File

How Many Trees Should I Create?

When most beginners create a family history tree, their first question is, "Should I create one large, all-inclusive file or several small files, one for each family?" The truth is, there is no right answer. Here are some things to consider as you decide how you want to organize your trees.

The advantages to having one large tree are pretty simple. One computer file is easier to keep track of than many files—one file to enter your information in, one file to back up, one file to share. You also won't have to duplicate your efforts by entering some data, sources, and media items in multiple files.

Multiple trees can be useful too. The more trees you have, the smaller the files will typically be. If you have concerns about your computer's performance or have storage issues, smaller files might work best for you. Smaller files also make it easier to collaborate with other family members; you can send them only the family lines they're interested in.

Regardless of which way you choose to organize your trees initially, don't feel like you're stuck with a permanent decision. The flexible nature of Family Tree Maker lets you merge multiple files at any time; you can even export parts of your tree to create a brand new file.

Creating a Tree

Family Tree Maker makes it easy to create new trees, whether you're a first-time user or you have family files you've worked on for years. You have three options for creating new trees:

- **Enter what you know.** If this is your first time working on a family tree, you'll want to use this option. Enter a few brief facts about yourself and your parents, and you're on your way.

- **Import a tree from an existing file.** If you already have a file you've created or received from another family member, you can import it. You can import files from previous versions of Family Tree Maker, GEDCOM (GEnealogical Data COMmunications format) files, FamilySearch™ Personal Ancestral Files (PAFs), *Legacy Family Tree*, and *The Master Genealogist*.

- **Download a tree from Ancestry.** If you have a tree you've created on Ancestry.com, you can download the file and either create a new tree or merge the information with another tree. The tree will include all the facts, sources, and images you have *manually* attached to individuals. If you have linked Ancestry.com records to your tree, the downloaded tree will include only the information and sources associated with the records, not the actual record images.

> Note: In order to download an Ancestry tree, you must be the tree's owner; even if you have been invited to view or share a tree, you will not be able to download it. If you do find a tree you want to download but don't have rights to it, consider using the Ancestry Connection service to politely request that the owner download a GEDCOM for you.

Entering Your Information from Scratch

1. Go to the **New Tree** tab on the Plan workspace.

2. Click **Enter what you know**.

3. Enter your name, gender, and birth date and place; then enter your parents' names.

4. By default, your tree will be saved to a Family Tree Maker folder located in your My Documents folder. If you want to save the file to another location, click **File Location** and choose a new location for your tree.

5. Enter a name for the file in the **New tree name** field.

6. Click **Continue**. The tree opens to the People workspace. You can start adding your family information to the file at any time.

Importing an Existing File

1. Go to the **New Tree** tab on the Plan workspace.

2. Click **Import a tree from an existing file**.

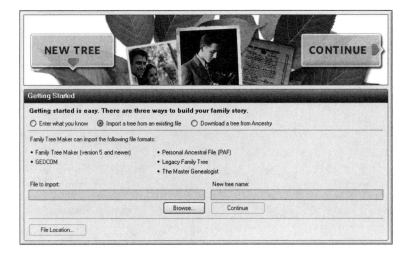

3. Enter the path to the file you're importing in the **File to import** field, or click **Browse** to locate the file.

4. By default, your tree will be saved to a Family Tree Maker folder located in your My Documents folder. If you want to save the file

to another location, click **File Location** and choose a new location for your tree.

5. If necessary, change the file's name in the **New tree name** field.

6. Click **Continue**. When the import is complete, you'll see the Import Complete window, which shows statistics for the new tree, including the number of individuals, families, and sources that were imported.

7. Click **Close**. The tree opens to the People workspace. You can start adding your family information.

Downloading an Ancestry.com Family Tree

1. Go to the **New Tree** tab on the Plan workspace.

2. Make sure you are logged in to your Ancestry.com account (if necessary click the log in link in the Web Dashboard).

3. Click **Download a tree from Ancestry**. A list of your trees appears.

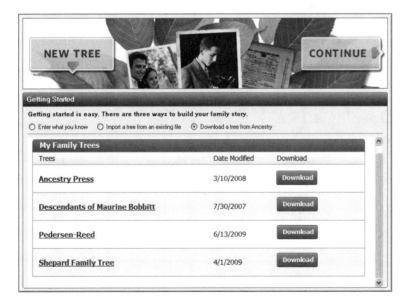

4. Click the **Download** button. A message asks you whether you want to merge the Ancestry tree with an existing tree or create a new one.

5. Click **Import** to save the file as a new tree; click **Merge** to merge the file with an existing tree.

   If you choose to import the tree, you will be prompted to enter a name for the tree and save it; if you choose to merge the file with an existing tree, the Merge Wizard will open and guide you through merging the trees. A message tells you when the process is complete.

Managing Your Trees

Whether you have one comprehensive tree or multiple trees you're working on, Family Tree Maker helps you organize them all. This section explains the basic tasks you'll need to know to manage your trees effectively.

Opening a Tree

When you launch Family Tree Maker, it automatically opens the last tree you were working in. If you want to work on a different tree, you'll need to open it first.

Note: If you try to open a Family Tree Maker file from a previous version, a GEDCOM, or another non-Family Tree Maker file, the software will automatically open the New Tree tab and you will need to import the file.

1. Click the **Plan** button on the main toolbar. The Trees section on the right side of the window lists the trees that you've recently worked on.

2. Do one of these options:

   - If you see a tree in the list that you want to open, double-click the tree name, or highlight the tree and click **Options>Open Tree**. The tree opens.

   - If the tree you want to open isn't in the list, you can look for the file on your hard drive. Click **Options>Browse**. The Select Family Tree Maker Tree File window opens.

> **Tip**
> You can have two trees open at once, which can be helpful if you want to compare your trees side by side. Highlight a tree and click **Options>Open Tree in New Window**.

3. Click the **Look in** drop-down list and find the folder where the file is located.

4. If you are looking for a certain category of file, for example from a previous version of Family Tree Maker, choose a type from the **Files of type** drop-down list.

5. Click the file you want to open.

6. Click **Open**.

Renaming a Tree

You can change the name of a tree at any time.

1. Click the **Plan** button on the main toolbar.

2. In the Trees section, highlight a tree and click **Options>Rename Tree**. The Rename Tree window opens.

3. Enter a new name for the tree in the **New tree name** field.

4. Click **OK**.

Viewing Information About a Tree

The Current Tree tab on the Plan workspace contains a summary about the tree you're working on. You can learn information about the actual computer file, such as its size and the last day you saved or backed it up. You can also view information about the people in your tree, for example, the number of marriages, individuals, surnames, and sources in your tree.

1. Go to the **Current Tree** tab on the Plan workspace. A basic summary of your file appears at the top of the tab.

2. To see additional statistics, click the **More** button. The File Statistics window opens.

3. When you've finished viewing the statistics, click **Close**.

Comparing Two Trees

You may have more than one family tree. For example, you might have one tree that you are working on and another tree that you received from a family member that you want to evaluate. Family Tree Maker makes it easy to switch back and forth between these two trees to compare information. And when you have two trees open, you can easily copy and paste information between them.

1. Click the **Plan** button on the main toolbar. In the Trees section, you'll see the tree that you are currently working on.

2. Highlight the second tree you want to open and click **Options>Open Tree in New Window**. Both trees are now available—each in its own window.

3. To switch back and forth between trees, simply click the tree's window.

Securing a Tree

Your tree probably contains personal details about family members who are still living or even confidential information about you. Before you export your tree to share with others, you might want to "privatize" it. When you privatize your tree, you can print and share charts and reports; however, you cannot edit the tree or add any additional information. Also, the names, birth dates, and additional facts for living individuals are not displayed. These changes will be in effect until you turn off the privatize option.

1. Click **File**>**Privatize File**. You can tell that the tree is secured because the word "Privatized" appears in the window's title bar, and a check mark appears next to the Privatize File option in the File menu.

2. When you want to continue working with your tree, you'll need to turn the privatize option off; click **File**>**Privatize File** again.

Deleting a Tree

If necessary, you can delete an entire tree at once.

1. Click the **Plan** button on the main toolbar.

2. In the Trees section, highlight a tree and click **Options>Delete Tree**. The Delete Tree window opens.

3. If you want to delete the media files that are linked to the tree, click **Move selected linked files** and select the files you'd like to delete.

4. Click **OK**.

Exporting a File

If you want to share your family tree with someone, you can export all or part of a file as a GEDCOM—the standard file format used to transfer data between different genealogy software. You can also export your tree as a Family Tree Maker file; however, it will be compatible only with Family Tree Maker 2010.

> Note: While Family Tree Maker lets you add digital images, sound, and videos to your tree, these items are not included when you export to a GEDCOM.

Tip

Before you make any major changes to a file, it's a good idea to make a backup of your tree. For instructions, see "Backing Up a File" on page 377.

1. Click **File>Export**. The Export window opens.

2. Do one of these options:

    • If you want to export the entire tree, click **Entire file**.

    • If you want to choose only a few specific individuals to include in the file, click **Selected individuals**. The Filter Individuals window will open. Click a name and then click **Include** to add the person. When you're finished choosing individuals, click **OK**.

Tip

For help selecting individuals, see "Using the Filter Individuals Window" on page 25.

GEDCOM

Because your great-aunt may not use the same software that you use, you'll need to share your family history in a file format that anyone can open. That format is GEDCOM. GEDCOM stands for GEnealogical Data COMmunications; it allows genealogy files to be opened in any genealogy software program. Even genealogists using Macintoshes can share their GEDCOMS with PC users.

3. Choose "GEDCOM" or "Family Tree Maker" from the **Output format** drop-down list.

4. Complete these fields as necessary:

In this field	Do this
Privatize living people	Click this checkbox if you do not want to include in your tree information about individuals who are still living. Names will be included, but facts and relationship information will not be exported at all.
Include private facts	Click this checkbox to include facts you have designated as private.
Include private notes	Click this checkbox to include notes you have designated as private.
Include media files	Click this checkbox to include all media files that are linked to a tree. Note: This option is not available for GEDCOMs.
Include tasks	Click this checkbox to include tasks you've added to your Research To-Do list. Note: This option is not available for GEDCOMs.
Include charts, reports, and books	Click this checkbox to include saved charts and reports and books you've created.
Include only items linked to selected individuals	Click this checkbox to include only tasks, notes, and media items that are linked to the individuals you're exporting. Note: This option is not available if you are exporting your entire file.

5. Click **OK**. The Export To window opens.

6. In the **Save in** field, choose the location where the exported file will be saved.

Note: Family Tree Maker automatically names the exported file with the same name as the tree. If you want to use a different name, you can change it in the File name field.

7. Click **Save**. A message tells you when your file has been exported successfully.

Merging Two Files

If you receive a family history file that has information you would like to include in one of your trees, you can merge the two files together instead of manually typing in the new information. It's a good idea to evaluate the file for accuracy before you merge it with your own tree. Make sure that the information is sourced, reliable, and relevant to the people in your tree. When you merge the files together, you'll have further opportunities to determine whether the new data in the new file matches individuals in your tree.

Before you merge a file into your tree, you should make a backup of your original tree. For instructions, see "Backing Up a File" on page 377.

> Note: Although merging files is not difficult, if the file you are merging into your tree contains many people, it can take some time to go through each individual and decide how you want to handle the information. Make sure you plan an adequate amount of time to go through each individual.

1. Open the tree that you want to merge the new file to.

2. Click **File>Merge**. The Open window opens.

3. Click the **Look in** drop-down list and find the folder where the new file is located.

4. Click the file you want to merge and click **Open**. After a mo-
ment, the Merge Wizard window opens. At the top of the window you'll see the name of the original tree (the host file) and
the name of the tree that is being merged into the original (the
import file).

Note: Make sure these are the trees you want to
merge together; if they aren't, click Cancel.

5. Do one of these options:

• If you want to merge all individuals in the file into your
tree, click **Include all individuals**.

• If you want to choose specific individuals to merge into your
tree, click **Include only selected individuals**. The Filter
Individuals window will open. Click a name and then click
Include to add the person. When you're finished choosing
individuals click **OK**.

Tip

For help selecting
individuals, see
"Using the Filter In-
dividuals Window"
on page 25.

Merging Unrelated Individuals into Your Tree

When you are merging two trees together, you have the option to add individuals to your tree without merging them with anyone. You might wonder why you would do this. Perhaps you haven't determined a connection between your family and a specific individual in the tree you're merging with. You don't want to merge this individual with anyone currently in your tree, but you don't want to lose his or her information in case you discover a relationship with the person at a later time.

Once the individual has been added to your file, he or she will not be connected to other individuals in your tree. In order to navigate to the person, you'll need to find his or her name in the Index panel of the People workspace.

6. Do one of these options:

   • If you want to merge the information for individuals whose information matches, click **Merge matching individuals**.

   • If you want to add individuals to your file instead of merging them with others, click **Add individuals without merging**.

   Note: You might want to add the individuals as new people in your tree—instead of merging them—if you're not sure that they match individuals already in your tree.

7. To choose how closely records need to match, click the **Advanced** button. Then drag the **Match threshold** slider to choose how similar records must be before they are considered a "match." The higher the match number you set, the more new individuals you will create and the fewer merged individuals you will add to your tree.

8. Click **Next**. A status window appears as the files are being "matched up." Then the Merge Wizard reappears.

The name list on the left side of the window shows the individuals who have been "flagged" (meaning that you will need to decide what will happen to these individuals), the individuals who will be merged with people in your original tree, and the new individuals who will be added to your tree. You cannot merge the two files until all the flagged individuals have been resolved.

9. Click on an individual's name in the "Flagged" list.

Notice that the window now reflects this specific individual's information. The Person from Host File column shows the facts about the individual that are in your original tree; the Person from Import File column shows the facts about the "matching" individual in the merged tree; the Merged Result column shows how you want the information to be merged into your tree.

> **Tip**
>
> You can also follow these steps to choose how "New" or "Merged" individuals are handled.

In the bottom, right corner, you will see the selected individuals' match score—a zero means that the individuals do not match at all; a 1,000 means the individuals are extremely similar.

10. To view a mini pedigree tree for the individual, click **View Pedigree**. Click **Host** to view the individual from your original tree; click **Import** to view the individual from the tree that is being merged into the original.

11. Use this chart to resolve any issues for flagged individuals:

To do this	Do this
Choose which individual's facts will be kept during the merge	Click **Accept host person** to use the facts associated with the individual from your host tree; or, click **Accept import person** to use the facts associated with the individual from the imported tree.
	If you want to keep the other individual's facts as alternates, click **Save differences as alternate facts**. If you want to discard facts from the other individual that don't match, click **Discard differences**.

To do this	Do this
Choose how specific facts for an individual will be merged into your tree	In the Person from Import File column, choose how you want specific facts for the individual in the merging tree to be added to your tree: • Click **Make preferred** to merge the information as the "preferred" fact for the individual. • Click **Make alternate** to merge the information as an alternate fact for the individual. • Click **Discard this fact** to *not* merge the information into your tree. You may choose to discard some facts for a person, although it is usually a good idea to include all facts in case they turn out to be relevant. Click the **Keep sources** checkbox to merge the source information for the discarded fact. Note: Don't forget to use the scroll bar on the right side of the window; there may be additional facts for the individual that cannot be viewed on just one screen.
Choose a different host person to merge your import individual with	If you want to merge the flagged individual with a person other than the one Family Tree Maker has matched them with, click **Merge to Other Person**. The Index of Individuals opens. Select the person you want to merge with the imported individual and click **OK**.
Prevent the selected individuals from merging	Click **Do Not Merge These People**. The Merge Wizard will add the imported individual to your host tree as a new person.
Accept all facts in your original tree as "preferred" facts	Click **Accept All Host** to mark all facts in the original tree as "preferred." The Accept All Host Facts window opens. Do one of these options: • Click **Save import differences** to keep facts from the merging tree but mark them as "alternate." In the Person from Import File column, the "Make alternate" option will be marked for each individual. • Click **Discard import differences** to ignore all facts from the merging tree. In the Person from Import File column, the "Discard this fact" option will be marked for each individual.
Accept all facts in the merging tree as "preferred" facts	Click **Accept All Import** to mark all facts in the merging tree as "preferred." The Accept All Import Facts window opens. Do one of these options: • Click **Save host differences** to keep facts from the original tree but mark them as "alternate." In the Person from Import File column, the "Make preferred" option will be marked for each individual. • Click **Discard host differences** to ignore all facts from the original tree.

12. When you have resolved an individual's conflicting facts, click the **Resolved** checkbox. The individual will be moved from the "flagged" list to the "resolved" list.

13. Click **Select Next** at the top of the window to move to the next individual. (You can also choose an individual by clicking his or her name in the panel on the left side of the window.)

    Note: If you find an individual is not related to someone in your tree, you can click the Do Not Merge These People button to add the person to your tree as an unrelated individual. Also, if you think the individual matches an individual not suggested by Family Tree Maker, you can click the Merge to Other Person button and choose the person you want the individual to be merged with.

14. When you've made all the selections you want for the merging files, click **Merge**.

Multiple Copies of a File

You might notice several different copies of your trees on your hard drive—all with the same name. If you look closely, you'll see that each one has a different file extension (the letters after the file name). These extensions help the computer distinguish between different files with the same name. Here are the extensions you might notice on your tree files:

.FTM—This is the "regular" Family Tree Maker extension. All Family Tree Maker trees you create will have this extension.

.FTMB—This is the file extension used when you create a compressed backup file using the Family Tree Maker Backup command.

.GED—This is the file extension for a GEDCOM file.

Backing Up Files

Your family trees are important; not only do they contain your family's history, but they also represent hours of your hard work. Family Tree Maker automatically saves your information while you are working and also creates backups of your tree. Unfortunately, all computer files are vulnerable and can be corrupted by viruses or accidentally deleted or destroyed. You can preserve your family history through regular manual backups of your tree files. For example, you can back up your trees to a CD every month and archive the CD. Then, if your original tree is damaged or you want to revert to a previous copy, you can restore it from the CD backup.

Backing Up a File

1. Make sure the tree you want to back up is open.

2. Click **File>Backup**. The Backup window opens.

3. If you want a new name to distinguish your backup file from your original tree, enter a new name for the tree in the **Backup file name** field. For example, if you back up your trees to the same rewriteable CD every time, and this backup file has the same

name as the file that is already on the CD, then this backup will write over the original file.

4. Choose one of these backup locations:

To back up your file to this	Do this
Floppy disk	Click **Removable Media**. In the drop-down list, choose your floppy disk drive. Note: If you are backing up a large file, Family Tree Maker will ask you to insert new diskettes as needed. When the backup requires multiple diskettes, be sure to label them in the order in which they are used.
CD, DVD, or flash drive	Click **Removable Media**. In the drop-down list, choose your CD-ROM drive, DVD drive, or flash drive. Note: The first time you back up a file to a CD-ROM, you may get a message asking you to install a driver—this message will appear only once.
Hard drive	Click **Working Directory** to save your file to the directory where your current tree is saved on your hard drive; click **Custom directory** to choose a new location on your hard drive.

5. Click **Include media files** to also back up media files you've added to your tree.

6. Click **OK**. A message tells you when the file has been backed up successfully.

Note: Backup files cannot be exchanged between genealogy software programs like GEDCOMs can. They can only be opened with the version of Family Tree Maker in which they were created.

Restoring a File from a Backup

1. Disable any anti-virus software you may be using.

2. If your backup file has been copied to a CD or other removable media, copy it back to your hard drive.

3. Click **File**>**Restore**. The Choose File to Restore window opens.

4. Click the **Look in** drop-down list and find the folder where the backup file is located.

5. Click the file you want to open.

6. Click **Open**.

   Your tree will open. Any data you entered in your tree since you created this backup will not be included in the tree.

   Note: Don't forget to reenable your anti-virus software.

Compressing a File

As you work in your trees you will add and delete quite a bit of data. However, even when the data has been removed from the file, the file may still remain at a larger size. You should compress your tree files periodically to optimize performance, remove unnecessary items, and reindex the file.

1. Click **Tools>Compact File**. The Compact File window opens.

2. If you want to back up your file before you compress it, click the **Back up file before compacting** checkbox.

3. Click **Compact**. If you have chosen to back up your file, the Backup window opens. Change any options as necessary and click **OK**.

4. When Family Tree Maker is finished, a message shows how much Family Tree Maker reduced the size of your file. Click **OK**.

    Because file compression happens behind the scenes, you won't see any changes to your tree, but you should notice better performance and a smaller overall file size.

Chapter 12

Using Family Tree Maker Tools

While entering information about your family in a tree, you may need some extra help calculating approximate birth dates, understanding how individuals are related to each other, or creating a research to-do list. Family Tree Maker has several calculators and tools to help you with these tasks and more.

Soundex Calculator

Soundex is a term familiar to most family historians. Soundex is a coding system that was used by the government to create indices of U.S. census records (and some passenger lists) based on how a surname sounds rather than how it is spelled. This was done to accommodate potential spelling and transcription errors. For example, "Smith" may be spelled "Smythe," "Smithe," or "Smyth." Using Soundex, these "Smith" examples are all identified by the same Soundex code (S530). Family Tree Maker can determine the Soundex code for any surname. You can use this information to find other surnames that use that same code and then search for ancestors using all surname variations.

1. Click **Tools**>**Soundex Calculator**. The Soundex Calculator opens.

2. Enter a surname in the **Name** field, or click **Index** to select a name.

    The Soundex number beneath the Name field changes automatically as you enter information in the field.

Relationship Calculator

The Relationship Calculator helps you identify the relationship between any two individuals in your tree, shows an individual's nearest common relatives, and gives his or her canon and civil numbers.

> Note: Canon and civil numbers indicate the degree of relationship between individuals. Canon laws (used in the United States) measure the number of steps back to a common ancestor. Civil degree measures the total number of steps from one family member to another.

1. Click **Tools>Relationship Calculator**. The Relationship Calculator opens. In the first field, you will see the name of your home person. In the second field, you will see the name of the individual who is the focus of your tree currently.

2. To change the individuals whose relationship you are calculating, click the **Person from people index** button next to a name (the button with an index card). In the Index of Individuals window, select a new person and click **OK**.

    The individuals' relationship is listed in the "Relationship" section. If they have multiple connections (for example when cousins marry), you can click the drop-down list to see each relationship. You can also see how the individuals are related in the "Path" section.

> **Tip**
>
> To print a relationship chart for the displayed individuals, click **View Relationship Chart**. Then click **Print**.

Date Calculator

You can use the Date Calculator to calculate an individual's birth year, his or her age at the time of a specific event, or the date of an event.

Calculating a Birth Date

If you know the date your grandmother was married and you know how old she was when she got married, you can determine approximately the year she was born.

1. Click **Tools>Date Calculator**. The Date Calculator opens.

2. Click **Birth date**.

3. Enter a date in the **Date of known event** field (in this example it would be the marriage date).

4. Enter the individual's age in the **Age at time of event** field (in this example it would be her approximate age on the date of her marriage).

5. Click **Calculate**. The Calculated birth date field will show the calculated date.

Calculating the Date of a Specific Event

If you know your mother's birth date and her age when she was married, you can determine approximately the year she was married.

1. Click **Tools>Date Calculator**. The Date Calculator opens.

2. Click **Other event date**.

3. Enter a date in the **Known birth date** field (in this example it would be your mother's birth date).

4. Enter the individual's age in the **Age at time of event** field (in this example it would be her approximate age at the time of her marriage).

5. Click **Calculate**. The Date of calculated event field will show the calculated date.

Calculating an Individual's Age on a Specific Date

If you know when your great-aunt was born and you know the year she was married, you can figure out her approximate age when she was married.

1. Click **Tools>Date Calculator**. The Date Calculator opens.

2. Click **Age**.

3. Enter a date in the **Known birth date** field (in this example it would be your great-aunt's birth date).

4. Enter a date in the **Date of known event** field (in this example it would be her wedding day).

5. Click **Calculate**. The Age at time of event field will show the calculated date.

Convert Names Tool

If you import another person's genealogy file into your tree, you may find that each file has recorded names differently; for example, your surnames may all be capitalized. You can use the Convert Names tool to format all the names in your tree consistently.

1. Click **Tools>Convert Names**. The Convert Names window opens.

2. Do one of these options:

   • To capitalize the first letter in each name, click **First Middle Surname**.

   • To capitalize the first letter of the first and middle names and capitalize the entire surname, click **First Middle SUR-NAME**.

3. Click **OK**.

Find and Replace Tool

You may have mistakenly spelled an individual's name wrong throughout your tree, or perhaps you have abbreviated a place name that you want to spell out. You can use the Find and Replace feature to quickly correct these mistakes.

1. Click **Edit>Find and Replace**. The Find and Replace window opens.

2. Enter the term you want to change in the **Find** field.

3. Enter the new term you want to use in the **Replace with** field.

4. Choose one or more of these options:

    - If you want to find words that match your search exactly (uppercase and lowercase), select the **Match case** checkbox.

    - If you want to find entire words that match your search, select the **Find whole words only** checkbox. (For example, a search for Will would not show results for William or Willton.)

    - If you want to search using wildcards, click the **Use wildcards** checkbox. Wildcards allow you to search for one or more "missing" characters. An asterisk (*) lets you search for multiple characters; a search for "Mas*" could find Massachusetts, Masonville, or Masterson. A question mark (?) lets you search for one character; a search for Su?an could find Susan and Suzan.

5. Choose which parts of your file you want Family Tree Maker to search in. If you're not sure where the information is, you might want to leave all the "Search in" checkboxes selected. Otherwise, choose the checkbox you want.

6. Click **Find**. You will see the first search result that matches your terms.

7. If you want to replace the current match, click **Replace**.

   Note: You can also replace all matching search results by clicking the Replace All button. Before you do so, you should back up your file because you cannot undo these changes.

8. To find the next matching term, click **Find Next**.

9. Continue searching and replacing terms, as necessary.

Find Individual Tool

You can use any of the facts in your tree (such as occupation, immigration, or burial) to locate either a specific individual or a group of individuals who fit specific criteria. For example, you can do a search for everyone in your tree that lived in Illinois at the time of the 1850 census. Or, you might find out which individuals are all buried in the same cemetery.

> Note:The Find Individual tool searches Place and
> Description fields; information contained in a fact's
> Date field cannot be searched.

1. Click **Edit>Find Individual**. The Find Individual window opens.

2. Choose the type of fact you want to search from the drop-down list.

3. Enter your search term in the next field and click **Find**.

4. If you want to access an individual's information, click his or her name in the search results and click **Go To**.

Find Individual			X
Death	illinois		Find

Name	Birth Date	Death Date
Isham Drury Bobbitt Jr.	Abt. 1790	1865
Sarah Bennington	17 Feb 1812	13 Aug 1863
Maria Hitchcock	1815	13 Mar 1850
Ann Maria Hoyt	20 Jul 1843	20 Jul 1843
Albert Hoyt	10 Feb 1848	10 Feb 1848
Susan Caroline Hoyt	22 Apr 1849	22 Aug 1849
Ann Hart	1776	18 Mar 1855
James Shanklin	06 Sep 1810	29 Oct 1887

Count: 8   Go To   Close   Help

Global Spell Checker

The global spell checker lets you search for spelling errors in specific text fields in your file: the Description fields for all facts, the Caption and Description fields for media items, the Citation Detail and Citation Text fields for sources, and notes and to-do tasks.

> Note: You can customize how spell check works in Family Tree Maker. For more information, see "Spell Checking Preferences" on page 415.

1. Click **Edit>Global Spell Check**. The Spell Check window opens.

2. Click the checkbox for each part of the file you want Family Tree Maker to search.

3. Click **Begin Checking**. The Spell Check window opens and begins checking the note for spelling errors. If Family Tree Maker detects a potential spelling error, it displays the word in the Not in dictionary field.

4. Correct or ignore the word using the Spell Check buttons. When a dialog box tells you that the spell check is complete, click **OK**.

Research To-Do List

Whether you are a new user or an experienced family historian, the To-Do list can help you keep track of the research you've already done and let you create tasks for the next steps you need to take. You can add research tasks for specific individuals or general tasks for your entire tree; tasks can be as simple as sending an e-mail to a cousin or as complicated as locating an entire branch of your family in the 1930 census.

Creating a To-Do Task

When you create a task, you can choose the priority of the task, the category it fits in, and its due date.

> Note: This section explains how to add tasks for specific individuals. You can also add general tasks to the To-Do list. To do this, click the Plan button on the main toolbar; click the Current Tree tab; then enter a new to-do item in the Tasks section.

1. Go to the **Person** tab for a specific individual (on the People workspace).

2. Click the **Tasks** tab.

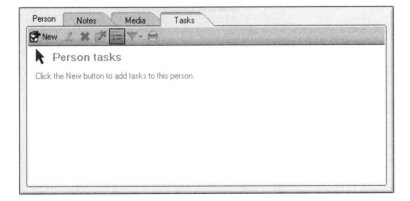

3. Click the **New** button in the Tasks toolbar. The Add Task window opens.

```
┌──────────────────────────────────────────────────────┐
│ Add Task For John W. Bobbitt                     [X] │
│                                                        │
│ Description:                              ┌─────────┐  │
│ ┌──────────────────────────────────────┐ │   OK    │  │
│ │ Look for burial information in Dawson, │ └─────────┘  │
│ │ Nebraska.                              │ ┌─────────┐  │
│ │                                        │ │ Cancel  │  │
│ │                                        │ └─────────┘  │
│ │                                        │ ┌─────────┐  │
│ │                                        │ │  Help   │  │
│ │                                        │ └─────────┘  │
│ └──────────────────────────────────────┘              │
│ Category / Location:          Due date:                │
│ ┌───────────────┐ ┌──────┐   ┌──────────────┐         │
│ │ Death records │ │Edit..│   │☑11/30/2009 ▼│         │
│ └───────────────┘ └──────┘   └──────────────┘         │
│ ┌ Priority ─────────────────────────────────┐         │
│ │  ○ ❗ High    ◉ ▭ Medium   ○ ⬇ Low         │         │
│ └────────────────────────────────────────────┘         │
│ ☐ Completed                                            │
└──────────────────────────────────────────────────────┘
```

4. Enter the to-do task in the **Description** field. For example, enter "Look for burial information in Dawson, Nebraska."

5. Click **Edit** to choose a category for the task. The Category/Location window opens. Choose a category or create a category and click **OK**. (For more information, see the next section, "Creating Task Categories.")

6. Choose a deadline date for the task from the **Due date** drop-down list.

7. Click a priority for the task. Assign a high priority to the tasks you want to accomplish first.

8. Click **OK**.

Creating Task Categories

Each task you create can be assigned to a category. Categories can be helpful when you want to sort your To-Do list or simply for choosing tasks to work on. Because everyone conducts research a little differently, you can create category topics that are useful for

> **Tip**
> You can print the task list for this individual by clicking the **Print** button on the Tasks toolbar. To print a list of all tasks in your tree, see "Task List" on page 248.

you. Examples of categories are the type of research, such as census or church records, or surnames, such as the Smiths and the Lees.

1. Go to the **Current Tree** tab on the Plan workspace. In the Tasks section, you can see any items currently in your Research To-Do list.

2. Click **New**. The Add Task window opens.

3. Click **Edit**. The Category/Location window opens, showing all the currently available categories.

4. Click **Add**. The Add Category Name window opens.

5. Enter a name in the **Category name** field and click **OK**.

6. Click **OK**.

Marking a Task as Complete

When you finish a task on your To-Do list, you'll want to mark it as complete.

1. Go to the **Current Tree** tab on the Plan workspace.

2. In the Tasks section, click the checkbox next to the task.

Tip

To delete a To-Do task, click the task in list and click the red (X) button in the tasks toolbar.

		Task Description	Task For	Category / Location	Due	Created
		Tasks: 9				Go To
High Priority						
☐	!	Locate Edwin Hewitt in the 1860 census.	General Task	Hewitts		5/21/2008
☑	!	Order a copy of Milton Hewitt's marriage...	General Task	Hewitts, Marriage rec...	6/13/2009	6/9/2008
☐	!	Take photos at Fairview Pioneer Cemet...	General Task	Photographs	5/26/2009	6/9/2008
Medium Priority						
☐	⊂⊃	Find death records for William Benningt...	General Task	Death records, Shank...		5/21/2008
☐	⊂⊃	Look for burial information in Dawson, N...	John W. Bobbitt	Death records	11/30/2009	7/9/2009
☐	⊂⊃	Scan the Bell Plain, Illinois, map.	General Task	Scan	1/27/2009	6/9/2008
☑	⊂⊃	Scan Mom's photos before reunion.	General Task	Photographs, Scan	6/13/2008	5/21/2008

Sorting the To-Do List

The Research To-Do list is your road map to the research you have completed and the tasks you still have to do. You can filter the list in various ways. For example, you can sort the list to show which tasks are done or are still pending.

1. Go to the **Current Tree** tab on the Plan workspace.

2. Click the **Filter tasks** button and choose one of these options from the drop-down list:

- To show every task you've entered, choose **Show All Tasks**.

- To show tasks that haven't been completed yet, choose **Show Uncompleted Tasks**.

- To show tasks that belong to a specific category, choose **Filter by Task Categories**.

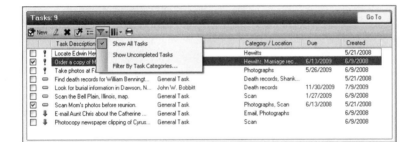

Note: You can also change the information that displays for each task (such as due date) by showing or hiding columns. Click the Show/Hide columns button in the Tasks toolbar. Then, from the drop-down list, select or deselect specific columns.

Additional Tools

You might have noticed two additional tools on the Tools menu that haven't been covered in this chapter; these tools are explained in other chapters with similar tasks. For information on the Resolving All Place Names tool, see "Standardizing Locations" on page 165. For information on the Compacting File tool, see "Compressing a File" on page 380.

Chapter 13

Setting Up Preferences

Family Tree Maker is a powerful program that offers you many features and options. To help you get the most out of the software, you might want to take a minute and define a few key preferences. You can add and modify facts, determine the display of some windows, choose how common tasks are performed, add user information, change date formats, and even decide how Family Tree Maker handles data entry.

Managing Facts

Facts are the essential building blocks of your tree, where you record the details about your family that are important to you. In order to capture the information you care about, you might want to create your own facts or change which fields appear for the predefined facts that come with Family Tree Maker.

In addition, Family Tree Maker makes it easy to edit a group of facts in one simple process.

Creating a Custom Fact

Although Family Tree Maker comes with a variety of default facts, you may want to create custom facts that work for your family tree. For example, if you are trying to track your ancestors by censuses, you may want to create a custom fact for each census year. Or, if you have many ancestors who served in the Korean War or other conflicts, you can create a fact for each war.

1. Click **Edit>Manage Facts**. The Manage Facts window opens.

Facts	Type
Address	Individual
Adoption	Individual
Age	Individual
Also Known As	Individual
Ancestral File Number	Individual
Annulment	Shared
Arrival	Individual
Baptism	Individual
Baptism (LDS)	Individual
Bar Mitzvah	Individual
Bat Mitzvah	Individual
Birth	Individual
Blessing	Individual
Burial	Individual
Caste	Individual
Cause of Death	Individual
Census	Individual
Christening	Individual
Christening (adult)	Individual

Buttons: Close, Help, New..., Properties..., Data Options..., Delete

Fact label: Address
Short label: Addr
Abbreviation: ADR
Fact type: Individual, Predefined
Fact elements: Date, Place, Description

2. Click **New**. The Add Custom Fact window opens.

3. Complete these fields as necessary:

In this field	Do this
Fact label	Enter the name of the fact as it will appear on the Person tab.
Short label	Enter a short name for the fact that will appear on the Family Tab editing panel; you can enter up to six characters.
Abbreviation	Enter an abbreviation for the fact that will appear in reports; you can enter up to three characters.
Fact type	Choose **Individual fact** if the fact applies to only one person, such as birth or death. Choose **Shared fact** if the fact applies to more than one individual, such as marriage.
Fact elements	Choose the fields that you want to appear for the fact: Date and Place; Date, Place, and Description; or Description only.

4. Click **OK**.

Modifying a Predefined Fact

Family Tree Maker comes with many predefined facts. While you can't rename or delete any of these facts, you can choose which fields are included as part of the fact. For example, the default Cause of Death fact has three fields: Date, Place, and Description; you can modify the fact so that only the Description field is included.

1. Click **Edit>Manage Facts**. The Manage Facts window opens.

2. Click the predefined fact that you want to modify.

3. Click **Properties**. The Fact Properties window opens.

4. In **Fact elements**, choose which fields you want to appear for the fact.

5. Click **OK**.

Editing Facts as a Group

If you need to modify the same fact for every person in your tree (for example, you want to make the Social Security Number fact private) it can take a lot of time to access each individual and then update the fact. Instead, you can edit a fact as a group. Family Tree Maker lets you group-edit facts in these ways: move data from one fact to another; move data from one field to another (within the same fact); make a fact private or public.

You might find group editing particularly useful when you import or merge another family member's tree with your own. Perhaps the facts from the new tree don't match how you've recorded information in yours. You can move all data in their "Job" fact to your

"Occupation" fact. Or maybe they've included hospital names in the Place field of the Birth fact. You can move that information to the Description field instead.

> Note: When you edit a group of facts, you will be prompted to back up your tree. It is always a good idea to back up your tree before making major changes. (For more information, see "Backing Up Files" on page 377.)

1. Click **Edit>Manage Facts**. The Manage Facts window opens.

2. Click the fact that you want to edit.

3. Click **Data Options**.

4. If you want to back up your file before you update your facts, click **Yes**. The Backup window opens. Change any options as necessary and click **OK**.

The Fact Data Options window opens. Now you can choose which individuals you want included in the edit.

5. Do one of these options:

- If you want to include all individuals in your tree who have this fact, click **All individuals**.

- If you want to include only specific individuals in your tree who have this fact, click **Selected individuals**. The Filter Individuals window will open. Click a name and then click **Include** to add the person. When you're finished choosing individuals click **OK**.

> **Tip**
>
> For more instructions on selecting individuals, see "Using the Filter Individuals Window" on page 25.

You can also deselect the checkbox next to an individual's name to prevent his or her fact from being edited.

6. Use this chart to modify the fact:

To do this	Do this
Move data from one fact to another fact	Click the **Change selected facts to this fact type** checkbox. Then choose the fact you want to move the information to from the drop-down list.
Move data from one field to another field (in the same fact)	Click the **Move data in the selected facts** checkbox. Then choose "From place to description" or "From description to place."
Change the privacy status of the fact	Click the **Mark the selected facts as** checkbox. Then choose "Private" or "Not private" from the drop-down list.

7. Click **OK**. The Manage Facts window reopens.

Customizing the Family Tab Editing Panel

By default, these fields appear on the editing panel of the Family tab in the People workspace: Name, Sex, Birth Date, Birth Place, Death Date, Death Place, Marriage Date, and Marriage Place. If you often include burial information or christening dates for people in your tree, you can add these facts to the editing panel so you can enter the information more easily.

1. Go to the **Family** tab on the People workspace. The editing panel appears with its default fields.

2. In the editing panel, click **Customize View**. The Customize View window opens.

3. In the Individual facts section or the Shared facts section, click on the fact you'd like to add to the panel; then click the right arrow button to add the fact to the Selected facts sections.

4. To change the order in which the fields will display on the panel, click a fact in the Selected facts section and click the up or down arrows on the right side of the window.

   You can also create new facts. For instructions, see "Creating a Custom Fact" on page 400.

5. Click **OK**. The editing panel now includes the new fields.

> **Tip**
>
> Any facts you add to the editing panel will also appear on the Add fact drop-down list on the Person tab.

Margaret Rebecca Shanklin
Mother of
Maurine Bobbitt

Name:	Margaret Rebecca Shanklin
Sex:	Female Age: 80
Birth:	12 Jul 1863
	Illinois
	Description
Chr:	Date
	Place
Death:	29 Mar 1944
	Balko, Beaver, Oklahoma, USA
	Description
Burial:	31 Mar 1944
	Balko, Beaver, Oklahoma, USA
	Pleasant Hills Cemetery

Marriage to James Clarence Bobbitt

Marr:	Abt. 1881
	Fulton, Illinois, USA

Next: Charity M. Bobbitt
Press Ctrl+Enter to add or edit the next person

Customize View...

Changing Your Preferences

Some of the default settings in Family Tree Maker—such as Fastfields, date formats, and the spell checker—can be changed.

General Preferences

You can set some preferences that affect the interface and general workings of Family Tree Maker.

1. Click **Tools>Options**.

2. Click the **General** tab.

3. Change these preferences as necessary:

In this field	Do this
Default directory for new tree files	Shows the default location where tree files are saved on your hard drive. If you want to change the default location, enter a new destination or click **Browse** to choose where you want trees to be saved.
Automatically check for program updates when connected to the Internet	Click this checkbox if you want Family Tree Maker to automatically look for software updates when you're online. You will be alerted if an update exists.
Show LDS information	Click this checkbox if you want LDS fields such as sealings and baptisms to be displayed.
Use Windows system colors	Click this checkbox if you want Family Tree Maker to base its display colors on the program colors of your Windows operating system.
Automatically back up family file	Click this checkbox if you want Family Tree Maker to automatically create backups of your projects when you exit the program. If your original tree is ever lost or damaged, you can use the backup to restore your information. However, because the backup file takes up space on your hard drive, you may not want to use this option if your hard drive space is limited.
Check place authority when entering place names	Click this checkbox if you want Family Tree Maker to check each place you enter against its database of locations. This option helps you keep your locations in standard formats and consistent throughout the project.
Crop portrait displays	If you have assigned a portrait to an individual, a thumbnail version of the photo appears in the pedigree view and editing panel. Click this checkbox if you want to resize thumbnail images so they fill their frames. Note: The actual images in your file will not be modified. Also, you cannot choose to resize individual thumbnails. This option resizes every thumbnail image in your file.
Use large fonts	Click this checkbox to make the fonts in Family Tree Maker larger and more readable.
Use caption instead of filename for media display	Click this checkbox if you want to sort media items by the captions you have assigned them in Family Tree Maker. If you don't select this checkbox, media items will be sorted and displayed by filename.

4. Click **OK**.

Fastfields Preferences

Fastfields speed up data entry by automatically filling in repetitive data as you type. For example, if you type "San Jose, California" into a location field, then go to another location field and begin to type "San," Family Tree Maker will recognize the similarity and suggest "San Jose, California." By default, all Fastfields are selected, but you can turn off any that you'd like to.

1. Click **Tools>Options**.

2. Click the **General** tab.

3. In the "Use fastfields for" section, click the checkbox for each type of field you want to turn off Fastfields for: names, places, and/or sources.

4. Click **OK**.

Online Searching Preferences

The Family Tree Maker Web Search feature can automatically search the databases at Ancestry.com for records that match individuals in your tree. You can determine whether or not you want Family Tree Maker to search every time you connect to the Internet.

Note: You must have a subscription to view records in the Web Search on Ancestry.com.

1. Click **Tools>Options**.

2. Click the **General** tab.

3. Click **Search online automatically** if you want Family Tree Maker to automatically search Ancestry.com for more information on individuals in your tree when your Internet connection is available.

Family Tree Maker will conduct a behind-the-scenes search on each person and alert you when it has found relevant search results. You will see a green leaf next to an individual's name on the pedigree view when possible matches have been found.

If you deselect this feature, you can still search online for your family members if you have an Internet connection by going to the Web Search workspace and entering your own website and search criteria.

4. Click **Show Web Search help dialog** if you want to display a window that explains how to use the Web Merge when you begin an online search.

5. Click **OK**.

Fact Display Preferences

On the Person tab of the People workspace, you'll see an editing panel on the right side of the window. This panel shows an individual's name and dates and information about the currently selected fact. Below this, you'll see a Sources tab. If you want, you can use the Fact display preferences to also display a Media tab and a Notes tab in the editing panel.

1. Click **Tools>Options**.

2. Click the **General** tab.

3. In the "Fact display" section, click the checkbox for each type of tab you want to display on the People tab's editing panel: Media tab and Notes tab.

4. Click **OK**.

Spell Checking Preferences

You can determine how the spell check in Family Tree Maker should work, specifically what words it should ignore. The default setting is to ignore words in uppercase and to ignore HTML tags. Most likely you will want to leave the default setting for ignoring uppercase words; in family history, some individuals use capital letters for surnames to distinguish them from first and middle names.

1. Click **Tools>Options**.

2. Click the **General** tab.

3. Click **Spell Check Options**. The Spell Checker Options window opens.

4. Change any preferences as necessary.

    Note: You can use the dictionary to add words that you want the spell checker to ignore. You might want to add unusual family surnames or place names that will appear often in your tree.

5. Click **OK**.

Date Preferences

Family Tree Maker allows you to change the way dates are formatted.
If you do not like the selections you've made, you can always reset
your preferences by clicking the Use Defaults button.

1. Click **Tools>Options**.

2. Click the **Dates/Names** tab.

3. Change these preferences as necessary:

Preference	Explanation
Date display format	Choose how you want Family Tree Maker to display dates. Click **Day Month Year** if you want the day to appear before the month (e.g., 07 January 2010). By default, Family Tree Maker displays dates in this accepted genealogical date standard. Click **Month Day Year** if you want the month to appear before the day (e.g., January 07, 2010).
	Click the drop-down lists to choose different formats for the day, the month, and the date separator.
Date input format	Choose how you want Family Tree Maker to interpret dates you enter: day, month, year, or month, day, year. For example, if you enter "6/7/10" Family Tree Maker can read this as June 7th or July 6th.
Double dates	Change the year in this field to change the default double date cutoff year. If you do not want double dates to print, set the double date cutoff year to zero.
	Note: Calendars used in Europe and the United States changed systems in 1752, moving from Julian to Gregorian. In the Julian system, the first day of the year was 25 March. In today's Gregorian system, 1 January is the first day of the year. A date that falls between January and March before 1752 can be interpreted in two ways, and some genealogists prefer to show both dates. For example, February 22 could fall in the year 1750 according to the Gregorian calendar, so the date would be noted as 22 February 1750/51. You can set the year at which you want to display both date interpretations.
Fact labels	To display a different abbreviation for the term "About" (meaning "Circa"), enter your preferred label in the field.
	Note: If you change these labels, they will apply from this time forward. Dates that have already been entered using a different label will remain unchanged.
Ancient date notation	Choose whether you want dates before 100 AD to be displayed with BC and AD or BCE and CE.

4. Click **OK**.

Name Preferences

Family Tree Maker lets you determine how names are displayed in the Index panel on the People workspace. (The Index panel is explained in depth on page 24.) You can include titles, alternative names, and married names for females. If you do not like the selections you've made, you can always reset your preferences by clicking the Use Defaults button.

1. Click **Tools>Options**.

2. Click the **Dates/Names** tab.

3. Change these preferences as necessary:

Preference	Explanation
Use AKA if available after middle name	If you enter a name for an individual in the Also Known As fact, click this checkbox to have the alternate name included with the preferred name (for example, Bobbitt, Mary Eliza "Mollie").
Use AKA if available as an additional entry	If you enter a name for an individual in the Also Known As fact, click this checkbox to have the alternate name appear as its own entry in the Index panel (for example, Hannah "Anna" Willis).
Use titles if available	If you enter a title for an individual in the Title fact, click this checkbox to have the title included with the preferred name (for example, Hait, Captain Samuel).
Use married names for females	Click this checkbox to have a woman's married name included in addition to her maiden name (for example, Hoyt, Maria Hitchcock).

4. Click **OK**.

Warning and Alert Preferences

Family Tree Maker can automatically check your tree for errors and alert you if it detects a possible error, such as an illegal character or unusual dates.

1. Click **Tools>Options**.

2. Click the **Warnings** tab.

3. Change these preferences as necessary:

Preference	Explanation
Show warnings for non-critical errors	Choose how you want Family Tree Maker to handle these minor errors: • **Double dates.** If Family Tree Maker detects double dates, you can choose to leave the dates as they are, use special formatting to show both dates, or be prompted for instructions. (For more information on double dates, see "Date Preferences" on page 416.) • **Titles in name fact.** If Family Tree Maker detects titles such as Jr. or Sr. in a name field, you can choose to leave the title in the name field, move the title to the title field, or be prompted for instructions. • **One- or two-digit years.** If Family Tree Maker detects years entered with one or two digits, you can choose to accept the date as it is, change the date to the most recent century, or be prompted for instructions. • **Text in quotes.** If Family Tree Maker detects nicknames (indicated by quotes) in a name field, you can choose to leave the nickname in the name field, move the nickname to the nickname field, or be prompted for instructions. • **Copy media files.** When you add a media file to your tree, you can choose whether or not to automatically copy the file to a Family Tree Maker media folder or be prompted for instructions.
Show alerts for unlikely birth, death, and marriage dates	Click this checkbox if you want to be alerted when dates you enter don't seem accurate (for example, a death date that occurs earlier than a birth date).
Show unrecognized place name indicators	Click this checkbox if you want to be alerted when Family Tree Maker doesn't recognize a location you have entered. Note: This checkbox is grayed out if you have deselected the "Check place authority" option on the General tab.
Show informational alerts	Click this checkbox if you want to be alerted when you update your Family Tree Maker project; for example, when you change the home person or update an individual's name.

4. Click **OK**.

Entering User Information

You can enter your personal information so that you will be identified as the person who created a tree. This information is then automatically added to your file if you contribute your tree to an online collection or export it and send it to another family member or researcher.

1. Click **Tools>User Information**. The User Information window opens.

User Information	✕

First name: _____ Middle: _____

Last name: _____

Address: _____

_____

City: _____

State or province: _____

Postal code: _____

Country: _____

Telephone: _____

Email address: _____

[Clear Information]   [OK]   [Cancel]   [Help]

Note: If you are viewing another person's tree, the fields may already be completed. You can click the Clear Information button to clear the fields.

2. Enter your information.

3. Click **OK**.

Appendix A

Installing the Software

Installing Family Tree Maker 2010

Family Tree Maker has been designed to be easy to install. Most computers will auto-run the install as soon as you insert the CD into your CD-ROM drive—you shouldn't have to do a thing.

> Note: If you have any programs running on your computer, close them before you begin the installation.

1. Insert the Family Tree Maker 2010 CD into your computer's CD-ROM drive. An automatic installer will launch. Click **Install** to start the installation. The Family Tree Maker 2010 Setup Wizard will open.

   > Note: You can stop the installation at any time by clicking the Cancel button.

In This Appendix

- Installing Family Tree Maker 2010
- Uninstalling Family Tree Maker 2010
- Registering the Software
- Activating Your Subscription

2. Read the message and click **Next**. The license agreement will open.

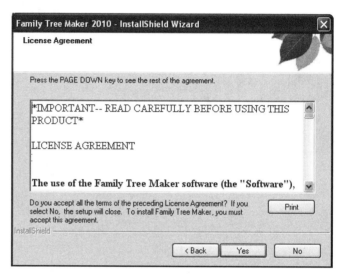

3. Read the license agreement. You can use the scroll bar to view the entire agreement. Click **Yes** to accept the agreement. The Choose Destination Location window will open.

4. Click **Next** if you want to install Family Tree Maker in the default location (recommended), or click **Browse** to choose a new location. The Setup Status window will open and Family Tree Maker will begin to install.

5. Click **Finish**. The installation window will close.

Uninstalling Family Tree Maker 2010

Family Tree Maker can be uninstalled just as you would any other Windows software program.

> Note: If you experience problems running Family Tree Maker, you may want to try reinstalling the program instead of uninstalling it. To do this, choose the Repair option in the Setup Wizard.

1. Click **Start>Control Panel**. The Control Panel window opens.

2. Double-click **Add or Remove Programs**. The Add or Remove
   Programs window opens.

3. Click "Family Tree Maker 2010" in the list of installed programs.

4. Click the **Change/Remove** button. The Setup Wizard opens.

5. Click **Remove**, then click **Next**. The InstallShield will verify that you want to remove the program.

6. Click **Yes**. The program will begin to uninstall.

7. When the uninstall is complete, click **Finish**.

Registering the Software

Registered users of Family Tree Maker receive special benefits: the ability to merge Ancestry.com records into a tree, access to online mapping tools, discounts on future versions of Family Tree Maker, and notifications of software updates. When you first install Family Tree Maker, you are given the option to register the software; if you do not, you can always register the software at a later time.

Note: You must be connected to the Internet to register Family Tree Maker.

1. Click **Help>Register Family Tree Maker**. The Welcome window opens.

2. Click the **Terms and Conditions** checkbox and then click **Register Program**.

3. Enter your name and e-mail address. If you have an Ancestry.com membership, use the e-mail address for that account.

4. Click **Continue**.

5. Enter your zip code. You can also choose to receive newsletters and special offers and allow Family Tree Maker to save your Ancestry.com login information.

6. Click **Continue**.

7. Click **Finish** to complete your registration.

Activating Your Subscription

In order to use the Web Search feature and merge records found on Ancestry.com into your tree, you must have a current Ancestry.com subscription—and you must activate your subscription within Family Tree Maker.

> Note: You must be connected to the Internet to activate your Ancestry.com subscription.

1. Click **Help>Activate Ancestry Subscription**. The Welcome window opens.

2.   Click **Activate Subscription**.

3.   Enter the name and e-mail address you use for your Ancestry membership and click **Continue**.

4. If you have more than one Ancestry account, you will need to choose the account you want to use.

5. Enter the password associated with your Ancestry account and click **Continue**.

6. Click **Finish** to complete the activation.

Appendix B

Using Keyboard Shortcuts

You may prefer to use the keyboard instead of the mouse when you're entering information in Family Tree Maker. Keyboard shortcuts make this possible. Although the guide focuses on using the mouse to do tasks, this appendix teaches you how to use keyboard shortcuts and lets you see some of the most commonly used options at a glance.

In This Appendix

- Using the Keyboard to Access a Menu Option
- Keyboard Shortcuts

Using the Keyboard to Access a Menu Option

1. Press the **ALT** key. Notice that the File menu option turns yellow and one letter in each menu is underlined now.

2. Press the key for the underlined letter of the menu that you want to open. For example, after you press the **ALT** key, the V in "View" is underlined. Press the **V** key to open the View menu. Notice that each menu option in the View menu also has one underlined letter.

3. Press one of the underlined letters in the menu. For example, press **P** to open the People workspace. Now you know that pressing **ALT, V, P** in succession will open the People workspace in Family Tree Maker.

Keyboard Shortcuts

Here are some of the Family Tree Maker shortcuts that you will use most often:

Getting Help

Task	Shortcut
View Help for the displayed window	F1
Open Family Tree Maker Help	ALT, H, H

Navigation

Task	Shortcut
Go back to the previous window	ALT+left arrow
Go forward to a window you've already accessed	ALT+right arrow
Open the Plan workspace	ALT, V, A or CTRL+1
Open the People workspace	ALT, V, P or CTRL+2
Open the Places workspace	ALT, V, C or CTRL+3
Open the Media workspace	ALT, V, M or CTRL+4
Open the Sources workspace	ALT, V, S or CTRL+5
Open the Publish workspace	ALT, V, U or CTRL+6
Open the Web Search workspace	ALT, V, W or CTRL+7

Working in Trees

Task	Shortcut
Open a tree	CTRL+O
Close Family Tree Maker	ALT+F4
Undo a change	CTRL+Z
Go to the home person	CTRL+Home
Use the Find and Replace tool	CTRL+F
Bookmark an individual	CTRL+B
Open the Date Calculator	CTRL+D
Access the index of individuals (on People workspace)	F2
Add a media item (on Media workspace)	CTRL+M
Add a source citation (on Source workspace)	CTRL+S

Working with Text

While most text entries in Family Tree Maker are made in fields, there are a number of windows for entering notes. This table shows you some useful shortcuts for selecting and changing text.

Task	Shortcut
Highlight the character right of the cursor	SHIFT+right arrow
Highlight the character left of the cursor	SHIFT+left arrow
Highlight an entire word right of the cursor	CTRL+SHIFT+right arrow
Highlight the entire word left of the cursor	CTRL+SHIFT+left arrow

Task	Shortcut
Highlight an entire line	SHIFT+End
Highlight a paragraph one line at a time	SHIFT+down arrow
Highlight all lines above the cursor	CTRL+SHIFT+home
Copy text	CTRL+C
Cut text	CTRL+X
Paste text	CTRL+V
Delete highlighted text	CTRL+Delete

Appendix C

Chart Templates

Family Tree Maker comes with several custom templates you can use to quickly dress up your family tree charts. Each has its own background, creative color scheme, formatted text boxes and borders, and more.

Accessing a Chart Template

1. Access the chart you want to apply a template to.

2. Click the **Use saved settings** button in the editing toolbar. The Use Settings Template window opens.

3. Click **Custom template**; then click **OK**.

4. Choose a template from the list and click **Open**.

Landscape Mountain Template

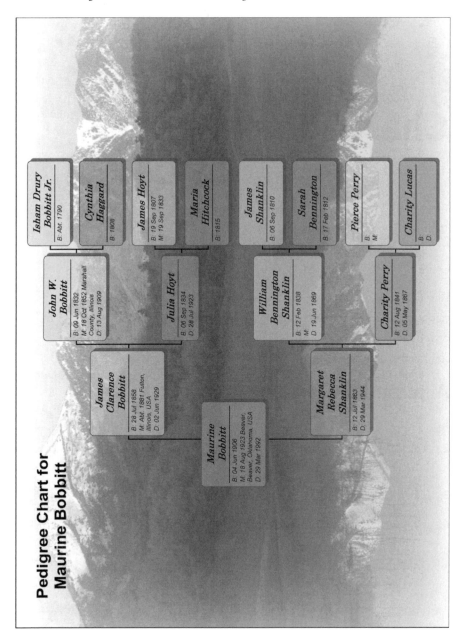

Pedigree Chart for Maurine Bobbitt

Isham Drury Bobbitt Jr.
B: Abt. 1790

Cynthia Haggard
B: 1808

James Hoyt
B: 19 Sep 1807
M: 19 Sep 1833

Maria Hitchcock
B: 1815

James Shanklin
B: 06 Sep 1810

Sarah Bennington
B: 17 Feb 1812

Pierce Perry
B:
M:

Charity Lucas
B:
D:

John W. Bobbitt
B: 09 Jun 1832
M: 18 Oct 1852 Marshall County, Illinois
D: 13 Aug 1909

Julia Hoyt
B: 06 Sep 1834
D: 28 Jul 1923

William Bennington Shanklin
B: 12 Feb 1838
M:
D: 19 Jun 1869

Charity Perry
B: 12 Aug 1841
D: 05 May 1867

James Clarence Bobbitt
B: 28 Jul 1858
M: Abt. 1881 Fulton, Illinois, USA
D: 02 Jun 1929

Margaret Rebecca Shanklin
B: 12 Jul 1863
D: 29 Mar 1944

Maurine Bobbitt
B: 04 Jun 1906
M: 18 Aug 1923 Beaver, Beaver, Oklahoma, USA
D: 29 Mar 1992

Landscape Tree Template

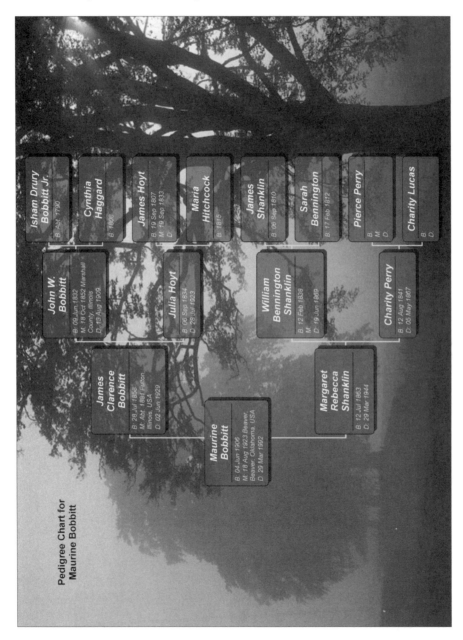

Pedigree Chart for Maurine Bobbitt

Isham Drury Bobbitt Jr.
B. Abt 1790

Cynthia Haggard
B. 1808

James Hoyt
B. 19 Sep 1807
M. 19 Sep 1833
D.

Maria Hitchcock
B. 1815

James Shanklin
B. 06 Sep 1810

Sarah Bennington
B. 17 Feb 1812

Pierce Perry
B.
M.
D.

Charity Lucas
B.
D.

John W. Bobbitt
B. 09 Jun 1832
M. 18 Oct 1852 Marshall County, Illinois
D. 13 Aug 1909

Julia Hoyt
B. 06 Sep 1834
D. 28 Jul 1923

William Bennington Shanklin
B. 12 Feb 1836
M.
D. 19 Jun 1869

Charity Perry
B. 12 Aug 1841
D. 05 May 1867

James Clarence Bobbitt
B. 28 Jul 1858
M. Abt 1881 Fulton, Illinois, USA
D. 02 Jun 1929

Margaret Rebecca Shanklin
B. 12 Jul 1863
D. 29 Mar 1944

Maurine Bobbitt
B. 04 Jun 1906
M. 18 Aug 1923 Beaver, Beaver, Oklahoma, USA
D. 29 Mar 1992

Light Tree Template

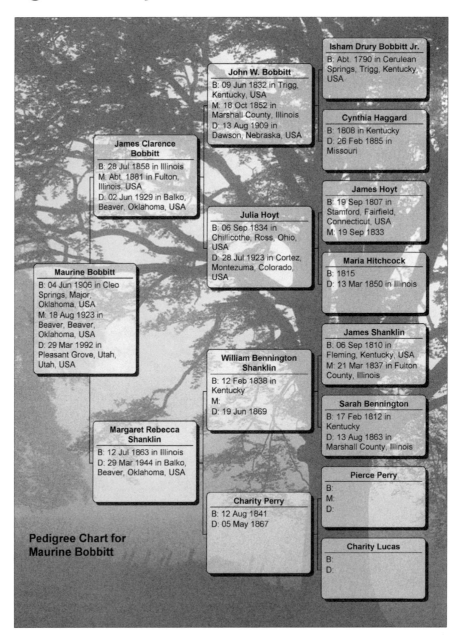

Isham Drury Bobbitt Jr.
B: Abt. 1790 in Cerulean Springs, Trigg, Kentucky, USA

Cynthia Haggard
B: 1808 in Kentucky
D: 26 Feb 1885 in Missouri

John W. Bobbitt
B: 09 Jun 1832 in Trigg, Kentucky, USA
M: 18 Oct 1852 in Marshall County, Illinois
D: 13 Aug 1909 in Dawson, Nebraska, USA

James Hoyt
B: 19 Sep 1807 in Stamford, Fairfield, Connecticut, USA
M: 19 Sep 1833

James Clarence Bobbitt
B: 28 Jul 1858 in Illinois
M: Abt. 1881 in Fulton, Illinois, USA
D: 02 Jun 1929 in Balko, Beaver, Oklahoma, USA

Maria Hitchcock
B: 1815
D: 13 Mar 1850 in Illinois

Julia Hoyt
B: 06 Sep 1834 in Chillicothe, Ross, Ohio, USA
D: 28 Jul 1923 in Cortez, Montezuma, Colorado, USA

James Shanklin
B: 06 Sep 1810 in Fleming, Kentucky, USA
M: 21 Mar 1837 in Fulton County, Illinois

Maurine Bobbitt
B: 04 Jun 1906 in Cleo Springs, Major, Oklahoma, USA
M: 18 Aug 1923 in Beaver, Beaver, Oklahoma, USA
D: 29 Mar 1992 in Pleasant Grove, Utah, Utah, USA

Sarah Bennington
B: 17 Feb 1812 in Kentucky
D: 13 Aug 1863 in Marshall County, Illinois

William Bennington Shanklin
B: 12 Feb 1838 in Kentucky
M:
D: 19 Jun 1869

Pierce Perry
B:
M:
D:

Margaret Rebecca Shanklin
B: 12 Jul 1863 in Illinois
D: 29 Mar 1944 in Balko, Beaver, Oklahoma, USA

Charity Perry
B: 12 Aug 1841
D: 05 May 1867

Charity Lucas
B:
D:

Pedigree Chart for Maurine Bobbitt

Simple Bold Template

Pedigree Chart for
Maurine Bobbitt

Isham Drury Bobbitt Jr.
B: Abt. 1790 in Cerulean Springs, Trigg, Kentucky, USA

John W. Bobbitt
B: 09 Jun 1832 in Trigg, Kentucky, USA
M: 18 Oct 1852 in Marshall County, Illinois
D: 13 Aug 1909 in Dawson, Nebraska, USA

Cynthia Haggard
B: 1808 in Kentucky
D: 26 Feb 1885 in Missouri

James Clarence Bobbitt
B: 28 Jul 1858 in Illinois
M: Abt. 1881 in Fulton, Illinois, USA
D: 02 Jun 1929 in Balko, Beaver, Oklahoma, USA

James Hoyt
B: 19 Sep 1807 in Stamford, Fairfield, Connecticut, USA

Julia Hoyt
B: 06 Sep 1834 in Chillicothe, Ross, Ohio, USA
D: 28 Jul 1923 in Cortez, Montezuma, Colorado, USA

Maria Hitchcock
B: 1815
D: 13 Mar 1850 in Illinois

Maurine Bobbitt
B: 04 Jun 1906 in Cleo Springs, Major, Oklahoma, USA
M: 18 Aug 1923 in Beaver, Beaver, Oklahoma, USA
D: 29 Mar 1992 in Pleasant Grove, Utah, Utah, USA

James Shanklin
B: 06 Sep 1810 in Fleming, Kentucky, USA

William Bennington Shanklin
B: 12 Feb 1838 in Kentucky
M:
D: 19 Jun 1869

Sarah Bennington
B: 17 Feb 1812 in Kentucky

Margaret Rebecca Shanklin
B: 12 Jul 1863 in Illinois
D: 29 Mar 1944 in Balko, Beaver, Oklahoma, USA

Pierce Perry
B:
M:
D:

Charity Perry
B: 12 Aug 1841
D: 05 May 1867

Charity Lucas
B:
D:

Simple Elegant Template

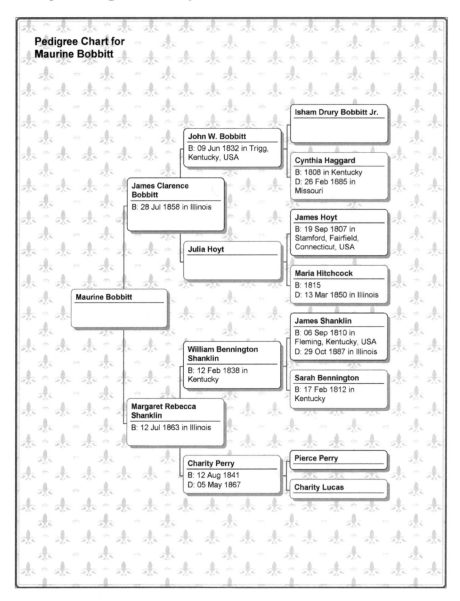

Pedigree Chart for
Maurine Bobbitt

Isham Drury Bobbitt Jr.

John W. Bobbitt
B: 09 Jun 1832 in Trigg,
Kentucky, USA

Cynthia Haggard
B: 1808 in Kentucky
D: 26 Feb 1885 in
Missouri

**James Clarence
Bobbitt**
B: 28 Jul 1858 in Illinois

James Hoyt
B: 19 Sep 1807 in
Stamford, Fairfield,
Connecticut, USA

Julia Hoyt

Maria Hitchcock
B: 1815
D: 13 Mar 1850 in Illinois

Maurine Bobbitt

James Shanklin
B: 06 Sep 1810 in
Fleming, Kentucky, USA
D: 29 Oct 1887 in Illinois

**William Bennington
Shanklin**
B: 12 Feb 1838 in
Kentucky

Sarah Bennington
B: 17 Feb 1812 in
Kentucky

**Margaret Rebecca
Shanklin**
B: 12 Jul 1863 in Illinois

Pierce Perry

Charity Perry
B: 12 Aug 1841
D: 05 May 1867

Charity Lucas

Simple Portrait Template

Simple Scenic Template

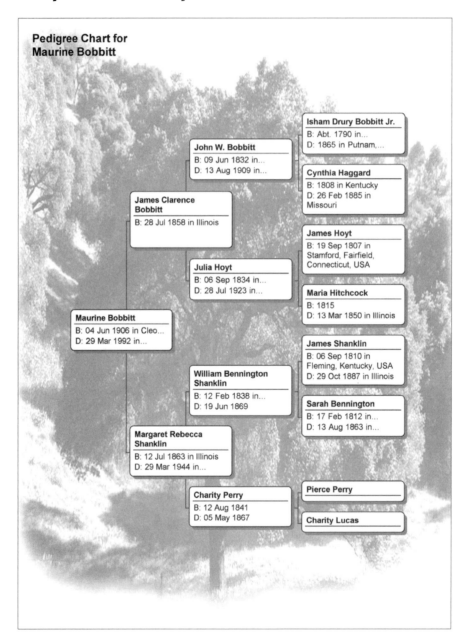

Pedigree Chart for
Maurine Bobbitt

Isham Drury Bobbitt Jr.
B: Abt. 1790 in…
D: 1865 in Putnam,…

John W. Bobbitt
B: 09 Jun 1832 in…
D: 13 Aug 1909 in…

Cynthia Haggard
B: 1808 in Kentucky
D: 26 Feb 1885 in
Missouri

**James Clarence
Bobbitt**
B: 28 Jul 1858 in Illinois

James Hoyt
B: 19 Sep 1807 in
Stamford, Fairfield,
Connecticut, USA

Julia Hoyt
B: 06 Sep 1834 in…
D: 28 Jul 1923 in…

Maria Hitchcock
B: 1815
D: 13 Mar 1850 in Illinois

Maurine Bobbitt
B: 04 Jun 1906 in Cleo…
D: 29 Mar 1992 in…

James Shanklin
B: 06 Sep 1810 in
Fleming, Kentucky, USA
D: 29 Oct 1887 in Illinois

**William Bennington
Shanklin**
B: 12 Feb 1838 in…
D: 19 Jun 1869

Sarah Bennington
B: 17 Feb 1812 in…
D: 13 Aug 1863 in…

**Margaret Rebecca
Shanklin**
B: 12 Jul 1863 in Illinois
D: 29 Mar 1944 in…

Pierce Perry

Charity Perry
B: 12 Aug 1841
D: 05 May 1867

Charity Lucas

Appendix D

Source Templates

Family Tree Maker 2010 includes 174 source templates based on the QuickCheck models used in Elizabeth Shown Mills's book *Evidence Explained*—the premier reference for citing genealogy sources. Source templates take the guesswork out of citing facts: no more wasted time entering irrelevant information; no more hoping that you've captured the right data; and no more wondering whether other family members will be able to follow your research paths. And templates also ensure that your sources are consistent.

This appendix lists all the source templates that are available, organized by source group and category.

> Note: For instructions on using these templates, see "Using Source Templates" on page 93.

In This Appendix

- Archives and Artifacts
- Business and Institutional Records
- Cemetery Records
- Census Records
- Church Records
- Courts and Governance
- Registrations, Rolls, and Vital Records
- Property and Probate
- National Government Records
- Books, CDs, DVDs, Maps, Leaflets, and Videos
- Legal Works and Government Documents
- Periodicals, Broadcasts, and Web Miscellanea

Archives and Artifacts

Category	Templates
Archived Material	Artifact Digital Archive Manuscript Record by Collection Manuscript Record by Document Manuscript Record by Series Personal Bible Portrait Research Report Unpublished Narrative Vertical File
Preservation Film	FHL-GSU Preservation Film In-House Film
Private Holdings	Artifact Diary or Journal Family Bible Records Family Chart or Group Sheet Historic Letter Interview Tape and Transcript Legal Document—Unrecorded Family Copy Personal Correspondence Personal E-mail Research Report Tradition, Recorded

Business and Institutional Records

Category	Templates
Corporate Records	Bound Volume Document—Loose Record Extract Supplied by Staff Microfilm Online Database Online Image
Lineage Society Records	Application File Online Database
Organizational Records	Archived In-House Archived Off-Site

Category	Templates
Professional Reports	Genetic Testing Historical Research—Corporate Historical Research—Online
School Records	Administrative Material Student Transcript

Cemetery Records

Category	Templates
Cemetery Office Records	Personally Used Supplied by Staff Online Image Preservation Film, FHL-GSU
Grave Markers	Rural Location Urban Location Online Image
Memorial Plaques	Memorial Plaque
Derivatives	Cemetery Abstract—Vertical File Cemetery Abstract—Card File Online Database

Census Records

Category	Templates
Original Manuscripts	Local Copy—United States Federal Census National Archives Copy
Digital Images	CD/DVD—United States Online Commercial Site—United States by Census Year and Location Online Commercial Site—United States by Census Year Online Archive—France Online Archive—United Kingdom and Wales Online Commercial Site—Generic by Census Year and Location Online Commercial Site—Generic by Census Year

Category	Templates
Microfilm	Native American Tribal Census Non-population Schedule—NARA Film Non-population Schedule—FHL-GSU Film Non-population Schedule—UNC Film Population Schedule—United States, 1790–1840 by Census Year and Location Population Schedule—United States, 1790–1840 by Census Year Population Schedule—United States, 1850–70 by Census Year and Location Population Schedule—United States, 1850–70 by Census Year Population Schedule—United States, 1850–60 Slaves by Census Year and Location Population Schedule—United States, 1880–1930 by Census Year and Location Population Schedule—United States, 1880–1930 by Census Year Population Schedule—U.S. State-Level Copy: In-House Preservation Film State-Sponsored Census—FHL-GSU Preservation Film
Derivatives	Database, CD/DVD Database, Online SOUNDEX and Miracode, Microfilm Statistical Database, Online, User-Defined Report

Church Records

Category	Templates
Church Books	Named Volume—Held by Church Numbered Volume—Held by Church Named Volume—Archived Off-Site Numbered Volume—Archived Off-Site
Image Copies	Digitized Online Microfilm—FHL-GSU Preservation Copy Microfilm—LDS Records at the FHL Microfilm—Publication
Derivatives	Church-Issued Certificate Church Record Book, Recopied Church Records Database, Online

Local and State Records—Courts and Governance

Category	Templates
Original Records	Local—Case File Local—Record Book Local—Case File, Archived Off-Site Local—Record Book, Archived Off-Site State Level—Appeals Court Record Book State Level—Legislative Petitions and Files
Image Copies	CD/DVD Microfilm—Archival Preservation Copy Microfilm—FHL-GSU Preservation Copy Online Image
Derivatives	Database Online

Local and State Records—Registrations, Rolls, and Vital Records

Category	Templates
Local Records	File Item File Moved to State Archives Registers—Named Volume Registers—Numbered Volume Vital Records Certificate Vital Records Register Vital Records, Amended Vital Records, Delayed
State-Level Records	Miscellaneous Files Vital Records Certificate Vital Records Register Vital Records, Amended

Local and State Records—Property and Probate

Category	Templates
Original Records	Local—Case File Local—Registers Local—Tract (Plat) Book State Level—Land-Grant Registers State Level—Land Warrants, Loose
Image Copies	CD/DVD Microfilm Online
Derivatives	Abstracts, Online Database, Online

National Government Records

Category	Templates
Original Materials (United States)	Audio Recordings—National Archives Manuscript—Library of Congress Manuscript—National Archives Manuscript—National Archives, Regional Map—National Archives Photograph—Library of Congress Railroad Retirement Board Pension File Social Security Administration Forms SS-5
Databases	CD-ROM Publication Database Online—National Archives (Australia) Database Online—National Archives (Canada) Database Online—National Archives (United Kingdom) Database Online—National Archives (United States) Database Online—Generic (any country; any database) Database Online—Social Security Death Index
Image Copies	NARA Microfilm—NARA-Style Citation NARA Microfilm—Publications-Style Citation
Images Online	Online Image—Library of Congress Online Image—National Archives (U.S.) Online Image—Patent and Trademark Office (U.S.)

Publications—Books, CDs, DVDs, Maps, Leaflets, and Videos

Category	Templates
Print Publications	Book—Basic Format Book—Chapter Book—Edited Book—Multi-volume Set Book—Reprint Book—Revised Edition Leaflet Map
Electronic Publications	Audio book CD/DVD Book—Text Video Website as Book
Image Copies	CD/DVD Publication Microfilm—FHL-GSU Preservation Copy Microfilm Publication Online Publication

Publications—Legal Works and Government Documents

Category	Templates
Book—Basic Format	Book—Basic Format
Legal Reference Works	Case Reporter—Series Named for Editor Case Reporter—Standardized Series Codes and Statutes, Online—State Database Codes and Statutes, Online—United States Code Slip Law—Federal Statutes—Federal Statutes—State

Category	Templates
Printed Government Documents	Congressional Records—Citing Volume from Title Page Congressional Records—Traditional Academic Style Congressional Records—Online Images National Archives (U.S.) Guides—Descriptive Pamphlet, Online National Archives (U.S.) Guides—Preliminary Inventory, Microfilmed

Publications—Periodicals, Broadcasts, and Web Miscellanea

Category	Templates
Periodicals	Journal Article—Print Edition Journal Article—Online Archive of Print Journal Journal Article—Online Journal Magazine Article—Print Edition Magazine Article—Online Reprints, Random Title Newspaper Article—Print Edition Newspaper Article—Print Edition by Location Newspaper Article—Print Edition by Newspaper Name Newspaper Article—Online Archive by Author Name Newspaper Article—Online Archive by Newspaper Name
Broadcasts and Web Miscellanea	Blog Discussion Forum or List Podcast Radio or Television Clip

Glossary

Ahnentafel   German for ancestor table. In addition to being a chart, it also refers to a genealogical numbering system.

ancestor   A person from whom one descends.

ancestor tree   Also known as a pedigree chart, this chart begins with a specific individual and displays the direct lineage of all of the individual's ancestors.

Ancestry.com family tree   A family tree you have created on or uploaded to Ancestry.com.

bibliography   A report that shows a list of sources used to compile the information included in a genealogy. The sources follow an accepted format that Family Tree Maker has built into the program.

BMP   Bitmap. A file format for graphics.

browser   See Web browser.

citation   The accepted notation of the source of information.

cite   The act of noting the proof that supports a conclusion or claimed fact in genealogy.

click The action of pressing and releasing a mouse button. Usually, when a program instructs you to click an item, it is referring to the left side of the mouse. A program may specify "left-click" or "right-click." You can also double-click by pressing and releasing the mouse button twice in rapid succession.

CSV Comma Separated Value(s). A file that separates data by commas, which then allows importing into a spreadsheet program.

descendant A person who descends lineally from another.

descendant chart A chart that lists an individual and his or her descendants.

editing panel A section of a workspace that lets you easily edit and view information for a specific individual or item you have entered in Family Tree Maker.

endnotes Source citations and explanatory notes that appear at the end of a document, specifically a tree or report.

export To transfer data from one computer to another or from one computer program to another.

family group sheet A form that displays information on a single, complete family unit.

family group view Shows a single family unit—parents and their children—in Family Tree Maker.

file format The file format in which you save a document indicates what program will open the file. Each file format can be opened only by certain programs. The file formats are automatically attached to the end of a file name, but you can change the file format when you are saving it. Family Tree Maker uses the .FTM extension to indicate file format, or, for backup copies, it uses .FTMB.

Fastfields Family Tree Maker remembers the names of the locations and people you have typed in so that when you begin to type a place in a new location field or a surname in a name field, Family Tree Maker shows you possible matches based on the letters you have typed up to that point.

GEDCOM GEnealogical Data COMmunication. A standard designed by the Family History Department of The Church of Jesus Christ of Latter-day Saints for transferring data between different genealogy software packages.

genealogy report A narrative-style report that details a family through one or more generations and includes basic facts about each member in addition to biographical information that was entered through Family Tree Maker.

generation The period of time between the birth of one group of individuals and the next—usually twenty-five to thirty-three years.

GIF Graphic Interchange Format. A graphic file format that is widely used in Web pages.

given name The first name (and middle name) given to a child at birth or at his or her baptism. Also known as a Christian name.

GPS Global Positioning System. A navigational system using satellites that lets you pinpoint your location.

home person The main individual in your tree.

homepage The main page of a website.

HTML HyperText Markup Language. The standard language for creating and formatting Web pages.

icon A small graphic picture or symbol that represents a program, file, or folder on your computer. Clicking an icon with a mouse generally causes the program to run, the folder to open, or the file to be displayed. Sometimes you have to double-click an icon instead of just clicking once (see "Click" in this glossary).

import To bring a file into a program that was created using another program.

kinship In genealogy, this refers to the relationship between one individual and any or all of his or her relatives. This can be displayed through the Kinship Report in Family Tree Maker.

JPEG Joint Photographic Expert Group. Graphics that use the .jpg extension include a compression technique that reduces the size of the graphics file.

maternal ancestor An ancestor on the mother's side of the family.

media item Photographs, scanned documents, audio files, or videos that you can add to a tree.

MyCanvas A Web-based publishing and printing tool.

paternal ancestor An ancestor on the father's side of the family.

PDF Portable Document Format. A file format (.PDF) that retains printer formatting so that when it is opened it looks as it would on the printed page. It requires Adobe Acrobat Reader to view.

pedigree chart A chart that shows the direct ancestors of an individual. Known in Family Tree Maker as an ancestor tree.

pedigree view The pedigree tree on the People workspace that lets you see multiple generations of a family and navigate to other members of your family tree.

preferred A term Family Tree Maker uses in reference to parents, spouses, or duplicate events indicating that you want to see the preferred selection first or have it displayed in trees and reports.

Register Refers to the descending genealogy format used by the New England Historic Genealogical Society. This also refers to their periodical by the same name.

report A detailed list of individuals and facts in your tree that are grouped together based on specific criteria.

research journal A record used by genealogists to keep track of their research findings and tasks to be accomplished.

resolution The measurement of an image's quality or sharpness.

root or primary person The individual who is currently the focus of the workspace or charts or reports.

RTF   Rich Text Format. A cross-platform, cross-application text document format. It retains some of the formatting information that is supported by many word processors.

siblings   Children of the same parents.

Soundex   A system that assigns a code to a surname based on how it sounds rather than how it is spelled.

source   The record, such as a book, an e-mail message, or an interview, from which specific information was obtained.

spouse   The person to whom another person is married.

surname   The family name or last name of an individual.

timeline   A visual representation of events over time.

tree   The Family Tree Maker name for the database that contains the information about your lineage, e.g., you could create a tree for the Smith family or Jones family.

URL   Uniform Resource Locator. The address used by a Web browser to locate a page on the Web.

WAV   Windows Audio Visual. The sound files that work with *Media Player* and *Sound Recorder*.

Web browser   The software that lets you access pages on the Web. The browser reads the HTML code and converts it to the pictures, colors, menu options, and overall design that you view on your monitor.

Web clipping   The ability to "clip" text or images from a Web page and merge it into a Family Tree Maker file.

Web Dashboard   A feature on the Plan workspace that lets you view your Ancestry.com account information.

Web Merge   The ability in Family Tree Maker to take search results you've found online and merge them into your tree.

Web Search A Family Tree Maker function that automatically searches Ancestry.com for records containing information about your ancestors.

Web page or website A location on the Web maintained by a single individual, company, or entity that provides information, graphics, and other items.

World Wide Web A graphical interface that is composed of Internet sites that provide researchers with access to documents and other files.

workspace A major grouping of Family Tree Maker features. Each workspace can be accessed from the main toolbar.

Index

Index

About
the Author

Tana L. Pedersen

Tana has been writing and editing in the technology industry for more than ten years. In that time, she has earned several awards for her writing including the Distinguished Technical Communication award from the Society for Technical Communication. She is currently Publishing Manager for Ancestry.com Inc., a contributing editor to *Ancestry* magazine, author of *The Official Guide to Family Tree Maker 2008, The Official Guide to Family Tree Maker 2009*, *The Family Tree Maker 2009 Little Book of Answers*, and co-author of *The Official Guide to RootsWeb.com*.

Photo by Braden Lord